Mass Starvation

Mass Starvation

The History and Future of Famine

Alex de Waal

Polity

First published in 2018 by Polity Press

Polity Press
65 Bridge Street
Cambridge CB2 1UR, UK

Polity Press
101 Station Landing
Suite 300,
Medford, MA 02155
USA

ISBN-13: 978-1-5095-2466-2
ISBN-13: 978-1-5095-2467-9(pb)

A catalogue record for this book is available from the British Library.

Library of Congress Cataloging-in-Publication Data

Names: De Waal, Alex, author.
Title: Mass starvation : the history and future of famine / Alex de Waal.
Description: Malden, MA : Polity, 2018. | Includes bibliographical references and index.
Identifiers: LCCN 2017016793 (print) | LCCN 2017040886 (ebook) |
    ISBN 9781509524693 (Mobi) | ISBN 9781509524709 (Epub) |
    ISBN 9781509524662 (hardback) | ISBN 9781509524679 (paperback)
Subjects: LCSH: Famines–History. | Food supply–History. | Social policy. |
    BISAC: POLITICAL SCIENCE / Globalization.
Classification: LCC HC79.F3 (ebook) | LCC HC79.F3 .D4 2018 (print) |
    DDC 363.809–dc23
LC record available at https://lccn.loc.gov/2017016793

Typeset in 10.5 on 12 pt Sabon
by Toppan Best-set Premedia Limited
Printed and bound in Great Britain by Clays Ltd, St. Ives PLC.

For further information on Polity, visit our website:
politybooks.com

Contents

Tables and Figures

Tables

Figures

Preface

Almost all writing on famine seeks to explain why famines happen – exercises in the most dismal science – or how humanitarian responses succeed or fail. I began writing this book in 2016 by turning these questions around, asking why calamitous famines had become so rare in the contemporary world, and what could be done to abolish them entirely. These are still relevant questions, but over the course of writing this book my optimism faded. In 2017, famines came back. The head of the United Nations Office for the Coordination of Humanitarian Affairs, Stephen O'Brien, said in May, 'famine is knocking on the doors of millions tonight'.[1] As this book goes to press, we are left to consider whether the starvation in Nigeria, Somalia, South Sudan, Syria and Yemen represents a temporary setback or heralds a new era of famines and how we can best respond in either case.

Famine is a shapeshifter. Whether or not there are calamitous famines in the coming century, and where and how such famines will manifest themselves, depends on the forces that shape our global political economy. Let me highlight two elements and how they may interact to shape famine.

One is climate change and the societal transformations needed for humanity to live within the capacity of the planet. There is absolutely no good reason why global warming, and its adverse impacts on the natural environment and on food production, need cause famine.

The second element is the rise of transactional politics. Elsewhere I have called this the 'political marketplace'[2] – a governance system characterized by the exchange of political services and loyalties for material resources in a competitive manner, overwhelming any institutional forms of government. In such a system, private interest prevails over public goods and human lives are valued only in so far as they contribute to political gain. Humanitarian action is subordinate to political bargaining. It is no coincidence that each of the sites of mass starvation in 2017 qualifies as a political marketplace.

The logic of political power – ultimately, power over who is entitled to live and who doesn't enjoy that right – is often seen most clearly from the global margins. That is the case for Somalia, South Sudan and Yemen today. The mass starvation in these countries is both a scandal and a tragedy in its own right and also a lens for understanding global political trends. Security bosses and political entrepreneurs in these countries are candid that they are operators in a market in which political power is traded, and where people are commodities or bargaining chips. The same political logic is now recognizable in Washington, DC, and American political operators are using a political vernacular that is familiar to their counterparts in Khartoum or Kabul. President Donald J. Trump's security and economic advisors have written, 'The president embarked on his first foreign trip with a clear-eyed outlook that the world is not a "global community" but an arena where nations, nongovernmental actors and businesses engage and compete for advantage. ... Rather than deny this elemental nature of international affairs, we embrace it.'[3]

Transactional politics provides fertile soil for 'counter-humanitarianism' – the rolling back of the hard-won humane norms of the last seventy years. Among the counter-humanitarians are political-business elites, who use humanitarian actions only as part of power games, and ideologues, such as religious absolutists, who reject the norms altogether.

In so far as the Trump Administration can be said to have a humanitarian agenda or doctrine, it is tactical and instrumental. Consider the situations in Syria and Yemen in 2017. In both countries, military campaigns have inflicted starvation and destroyed the infrastructure necessary for sustaining life. In a remarkably candid address to the Security Council, O'Brien said:

> The people of Yemen are being subjected to deprivation, disease and death as the world watches. This is not an unforeseen or coincidental result of forces beyond our control. It is a direct consequence of actions of the parties and supporters of the conflict, and is also, sadly, a result of inaction – whether due to inability or indifference – by the international community.[4]

Most of the USAID staff working on these countries are responding with the same commitment and professionalism as they did under previous administrations. Some are compromised by clandestine second jobs in intelligence or logistics for special operations.[5] The bigger story is that their new political masters are whittling humanitarian action down to a matter of bargaining. This is evident from the statements of the US Ambassador to the UN, Nikki Haley, on Syria and Yemen. Haley has repeatedly condemned the Syrian government for starvation as a method of war, even comparing it to the use of chemical weapons, different in so far as it is 'a quieter, slower kind of death'.[6] On another occasion, she said 'the Assad regime – with help from Russia, Iran, and Hezbollah – has attacked and destroyed medical facilities in a relentless campaign of destruction.' But a few sentences later, her tone changed, 'Turning to Yemen,' she said, 'the fighting has led to the rapid deterioration of the country's healthcare infrastructure.'[7] It was rare for her to make any reference to a destructive and faminogenic campaign fought by US allies, using US weapons, and she did not acknowledge responsibility, express any readiness to curtail the infliction of starvation or concede that a universal principle was at stake.

Because it is funded by charitable appeals, the humanitarian business is particularly likely to succumb to such a transactional ethos. Apparently oblivious to relatively unsophisticated financial instruments such as insurance, international disaster relief is still financed by a mechanism akin to beggars sitting in a row pleading for alms, hoping that the benefactors' coins or pity don't run out halfway down the line.[8]

In only one of today's famine crises – Somalia – has climate played a major role. The trend away from drought famines to political famines is not set to change: we are not going to return to subsistence agrarian societies in which people starve when the rain fails. Without doubt, climate change will cause food production fluctuations and shortfalls and will cause great stress to societies, and especially the poorest. But there is no reason why global warming should increase the risk of famine anywhere in the world. The key links in the chain that leads to famine are *always* political.

Unfortunately, transactional politics amid traumatic ecological change spells very serious danger. The Trump Administration is treating climate change negotiations in a political marketplace spirit, as if there were no such thing as a global commons. The similar transactional habitus for managing planetary resources and the survival of human beings is, I suspect, the main thread linking climate change and famine. As I repeatedly stress in this book, the knowledge, capacities and resources for preventing famine are sufficiently well advanced that it requires a combination of different adversities and political malfeasance to perpetrate mass starvation. Unfortunately, such combinations may be in prospect. The probable route to climate-related famine is not through extreme droughts reducing farmers in poor countries to starvation, or through drying wells causing pastoralists to fight over water for their camels. It lies through tactical bargaining over getting a better deal than one's rival, in pursuit of power, at the expense of human welfare. In the pursuit of transactional political gain, all other causes give way. Public goods, science and its policy prescriptions, and the survival of human communities other than one's own, become expendable. Until now, the major international efforts of confronting climate change have been in science and public policy. An equally important and difficult task is defeating transactional politics.

The most uncomfortable part of the book to write was the challenge to colleagues who work on climate change and the natural environment to scale back alarmism on the faminogenic properties of global warming. The evidence for climate change is irrefutable, but the evidence that it will cause conflict and starvation is less robust. I also worry that the study of the ecology of human populations has proven susceptible to Malthusian logic, which has in the past contributed to ecological justifications for inhumane policies, and could do so again.

Meanwhile, there are three major reasons for remaining optimistic that calamitous famines will not return. One is that today's reversal represents – so far – a deviation from a strong baseline. In the thirty-five years since I began studying famine, there has been a spectacular decline in famines and famine mortality. Today's deterioration is real, but it is from a level without historical precedent, in which people have been better fed, less poor and longer-lived than ever before.

A related reason for optimism is that we have learned much more about the famines of the last century, and in doing so we can sharpen our analysis of their political causes. As Andrea Graziosi[9] points out, much famine theory – notably including Amartya Sen's seminal 'entitlement theory'[10] – was developed at a time when the greatest political famines of the age were still largely unknown. The historical exercise of re-assessing those military starvations and political famines not only helps explain why calamitous famines have declined but also sharpens the challenge of putting today's famines in today's global political-economic context.

A third reason is that the response to the 2017 crises has been prompt and (unevenly) effective. There has been a chorus of condemnation of the use of starvation as a weapon in South Sudan and Syria. Humanitarian efforts have been expanded. In June, the UN was able to withdraw its designation of 'famine' from the worst-hit districts of South Sudan, because humanitarian assistance had pulled people back from the brink – even though the overall number of people suffering hunger had increased.[11] Humanitarians are better at appealing for as-yet-unmet needs than at providing a robust empirical defence of their record. And it is a remarkable record, worthy of protection.

The best form of defending a beleaguered commitment to global public action against famine is to take the political initiative and argue for what can be achieved and for what must be stopped. I propose that at the top of the agenda should be a campaign to criminalize starvation. This book is written in the confident hope that well-informed and targeted activism can make a difference. There are many injustices and failings that contribute to famine, and for every famine there are numerous culprits to share responsibility. But, as the debate on resurgent famine has unfolded in 2017, one course of action stands out above all others: branding mass starvation as a crime and expressly prohibiting it. Let the legal scholars debate on how best to find a legal mechanism: the most effective route, and also the quickest, is well-directed public outrage. An international convention (or, more likely, an addendum to an existing protocol or statute) might be useful as a focal point for mobilization. The fundamental task is to summon sufficient universal revulsion to make it unthinkable to perpetrate famine.

Acknowledgements

This book draws upon research and experience stretching back thirty years, and to give full credit to those who shaped my thinking across the span of my career would be an impossible task. Among those who most influenced my approach to famine were Alula Pankhurst, Ken Wilson, Meghan Vaughan, Wendy James, Amartya Sen, Jeremy Swift, Ahmed Karadawi, Hassan Abdel Ati, Dessalegn Rahmato, Angela Raven-Roberts, John Seaman, Tony Vaux, Mark Duffield, David Keen, Stephen Devereux, Barbara Hendrie, Susanne Jaspars, Helen Young, Michael Medley, Luka Biong, Meles Zenawi, Abadi Zemo and Tekleweyne Assefa.

The immediate stimulus for this book was an invitation to contribute a chapter on hunger and armed conflict to the *Global Hunger Index 2015*. In particular I want to thank Olive Towey, Connell Foley, Sandra Lin, Georges Hounga, Andrea Sonntag and Klaus von Grebmer for their contributions during the writing, editing and launch of the GHI and thereafter. A complementary stimulus was an ongoing conversation with Bridget Conley, Programme Director at the World Peace Foundation, about famine as mass atrocity, and in particular how the insights from her project on 'how mass atrocities end' could be applied to mass starvation: Bridget's influence is evident in many places in this book. My research assistant Aditya Sarkar has been indispensable on all aspects of the research, especially assembling and maintaining the dataset of historic famines. Others who have provided essential contributions include Stefan Dercon, Andrew Dusek, Charles Fogelman, Mulugeta Gebrehiwot, Rachel Ibreck, Mary Kaldor, Dan Maxwell, Dyan Mazurana, Charlotte Morris, Sarah Nouwen, Jens

Pedersen, Henry Radice and James Tyner. It was a delight to work with Louise Knight, Nekane Tanaka Galdos, Neil de Cort and Gail Ferguson and the team at Polity Press. The functioning of the World Peace Foundation – and my ability to take the time to write a book such as this – are wholly reliant on the dedication of our Associate Director Lisa Avery. Finally, this book could not have been written without the support and love of my family: Hannah, Adan and Nimco.

This book is dedicated to the memory of my beloved son, Hiroe.

They crowd my memory with their faceless presences, and if I could enclose all the evil of our time in one image, I would choose this image which is familiar to me: an emaciated man, with head dropped and shoulders curved, on whose face and in whose eyes not a trace of a thought is to be seen.

Primo Levi 1996 (1958), p. 90.

Part I

Perspectives on Famine and Starvation

1

An Unacknowledged Achievement

The Biggest Picture

Something remarkable happened over the last thirty years. The risk of dying in famine has become much, much smaller than at any time in history. Calamitous famines – episodes of mass starvation that kill a million people or more – have vanished. Great famines that kill 100,000 people still occur, but they are rarer and less lethal. At least one hundred million people died in great and calamitous famines in the 140 years from 1870 to 2010, and *almost all of them* died before 1980 (see Figure 1.1).

The main purpose of this book is to explain why this happened. It is written in a spirit of sceptical optimism: today is the best time to be alive, but we also have reason to be fearful. I hope to explain the huge and under-celebrated success of nearly eliminating mass starvation from the world, with the aim of encouraging us not to casually abandon that achievement, but rather to appreciate and consolidate it – and take forward the eminently achievable goal of definitively ending famines.

This is a story of disastrous and exceptional episodes of famine and mass starvation. It is not about overall world hunger and undernutrition, although the two stories will occasionally intersect. Nor is it a story of global food supplies, though food markets play an important part. These problems are complex and persistent, but over the last century have become less relevant to the question of famine. Rather, this book is the story of how massive outbreaks of starvation used to be a persistent feature of our world, how they became less

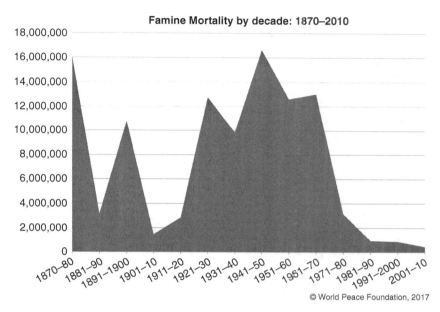

Figure 1.1 Mortality in great and calamitous famines by decade, 1870–2010
Source: World Peace Foundation

so over the last generation, and why we should be worried that they could yet recur.

Great famines resulted from the actions of imperial conquistadors and ideological fanatics. Starving people to death was hard work. The near-eclipse of famine in the last three decades is the result partly of the positive efforts of humanitarians and others concerned with human welfare and development, but much more so of the decline of megalomania and of political attitudes that regard people as dispensable. To overcome famine in the modern era, our main adversary has been political leaders, not the weather or the poor state of the roads. In other words, we must include *forced mass starvation* in definitions of famine and regard it as a variant of mass atrocities. The word 'starvation' is not intended to imply that everyone who dies in a famine dies directly of hunger – the biggest killers are in fact communicable diseases. But the verb 'to starve' should be understood primarily in its transitive sense to indicate that some (powerful) people have starved other (powerless) people, leaving them to die – from hunger, disease, exhaustion or violence. Mass starvation ranges from the outcome of recklessness (pursuing actions regardless of the known dangers) through persecution to murder and genocide.

This book concludes with a warning that in so far as we see a resurgence of ideologies and practices that reduce people to instruments or impediments to other political ends, or exclude them from our political communities, we need to be deeply worried that mass starvation will return: we will not see a demise but an eclipse of famines. To explain this concern, and the career-long research on which my argument is based, I turn to my own encounter with famine.

Encounters with Famines

I travelled to Darfur, the westernmost region of Sudan, to begin my field research in September 1985. It was a traumatic time for the people of Darfur, in the depths of the most lethal episode of acute hunger for seventy years. But there were some blessings that I didn't appreciate at the time. At that time, Darfur was peaceful, and over the next two years I travelled the length and breadth of the region in complete safety, welcomed with whatever gracious hospitality that people could muster in every village or nomadic encampment.

I had originally intended to study refugees, drawing on the pioneering Sudanese researchers in that field. More than thirty years on, it is salutary to recall that the flow of intellectual capital was *from* the University of Khartoum *to* the University of Oxford (where I was registered for my doctorate), not the other way around. Ahmed Karadawi, my host and guide at the Commissioner of Refugees, advised me to go to study the Chadians in Darfur, as almost no one had done any research on them. He then changed his advice: the Chadian refugees were submerged within the wider problem of mass displacement due to the famine, so I should study the famine.

My first day of fieldwork was spent in a camp for displaced people on the fringes of the regional capital al-Fashir. Desperately hungry people had sought food in the city and had congregated in the abandoned camel market, making makeshift shelters out of branches and plastic sheets. People who were utterly destitute chose the place because it was close to the airport, where sacks of American sorghum were unloaded from aircraft onto waiting lorries. Every now and then, a sack would spill or burst, and the labourers would scoop up grain to give to the hungry sitting next to the perimeter fence. One of the drawbacks of the place, which had been a thriving camel market until just a few months earlier, was that big, ravenous camel fleas still infested the ground. During one interview, with a woman who said she was forty years old but looked much, much older, my translator and I were continually slapping our calves and thighs whenever we felt their bites. 'How can you live in this place?' I asked her, 'Don't they eat you?' She replied, 'No, *we* eat *them*.'

The people who suffer and survive famine have a sense of humour, and more importantly, their own agency. I learned more from the people of Darfur than I could have learned from all the textbooks on famine. There was no theory or framework in the academic literature, which I had scoured so thoroughly in fourteen different libraries in Oxford, which explained the reality I found. Almost everything I had assumed about famine turned out to be wrong.

To begin with, I discovered that predictions of mortality were enormously exaggerated. Journalists who got news of the catastrophic harvest failure wrote that two million of the three million people who lived in Darfur at that time would soon be dead. That didn't happen: although food aid arrived only late, my estimate of famine mortality was 105,000.[1] Death rates peaked at 40 per 1,000 in 1985, with the great majority of those who died being children. This was bad, but far, far fewer than the predicted millions. In my first book, I tried to explain why. Part of the reason was 'disaster tourism' and the selective exposure of outsiders to the worst, which led to exaggerated forecasts. The other part was people's own impressive resilience and capacity to cope.

I chose a short poem by Bertolt Brecht as the literary frontispiece for my book on that famine:

> I have seen people
> Who were remarkable –
> Highly deserving of your admiration
> For the fact that they
> Were alive at all.

What I missed was the extent to which the famine caused a huge loss of social and economic capital in Darfur, helping set in motion the disaster of twenty years later. The short-term resilience shown by Darfurians came at a high price.

I completed my fieldwork in Darfur in early 1987. A year later, in the summer of 1988, reports came through of starvation on the southern borderlands of Darfur and the neighbouring region of Kordofan. The figures we heard showed death rates that were at their peak *one hundred times greater* than in Darfur during the worst of the drought-famine in 1985. The victims were displaced southern Sudanese, driven from their homes by war – specifically by raiding and pillaging by militiamen known as *Murahaliin* (forerunners of the notorious *Jan-jawiid* of the Darfur war), and crowded into displaced camps in the territory of their tormentors. Had the camp populations not been replenished by new arrivals from the war zones, they would simply have become graveyards within a few months. The Sudanese government was bankrupt and it ran its counter-insurgency on the cheap, declaring southern Sudan and its inhabitants an ethics-free zone in which the irregular militiamen and army officers could loot, burn and kill at will, and didn't need to report back.[2] The southern Sudanese were first robbed of all their possessions and then, when they trekked northwards to find food or work, the militiamen confined them to camps where they prevented them from gathering wild foods or working for money. The militia and army also blocked relief aid: railway wagons filled with food aid stood untouched in sidings just a few miles away.[3] Deborah Scoggins, the first foreign journalist to visit those camps, wrote, 'These are places so sad the mind goes queasy trying to understand them.'[4]

In trying to theorize these two famines, so close to one another but so different, I borrowed the metaphor of a thermometer, first used by John Rivers and colleagues. Famine isn't just extreme poverty; it is different in the same way that ice is different from freezing water.[5] I adapted it to distinguish between different severities of famine: the Darfurian villagers and the displaced southern Sudanese were both suffering famines, but of radically different kinds. The Darfurians in 1984–5 had suffered a famine that killed, but Darfurian society had survived. The war-stricken southern Sudanese in 1988 hadn't just starved, they had *been starved*. Within the broader landscape of famine, there were horrendous pockets of outright, frank starvation, with death rates that were far, far higher. Starvation wasn't something that just happened; it was something that people did to one another.

In the 1980s and 1990s, I wrote two books and a number of reports and articles that tried to advance understanding of famines. There were four ways in which I helped move the debate, each time refracting what I had learned from poor and vulnerable people in places such as Sudan and Ethiopia into something accessible for students, aid workers and government officials.

One way in which I identified and described the agency of the afflicted was by their skills and capacities. They, I argued, were the true experts in surviving famines. My biggest shortcoming here was that I should have been more attuned to the gendered experience of famine and expertise in surviving it. Second, I reminded academics and practitioners that famines were public health crises as well as nutritional crises, and that reducing infectious diseases was a route to decreasing deaths. On this topic, I overstated the case and exaggerated the relative importance of the changed health environment compared to rampant malnutrition, but the point was valid. My third contribution was arguing that foreign humanitarians may possess distorted perceptions of what is going on and their actions may have negative unintended consequences. This contribution elicited most attention and controversy, but I think that is more because the humanitarians love to examine themselves, and journalists and the western public like a controversy over charities and their workers, than because what I had to say was particularly new or interesting.

My fourth and last contribution was that I coined the term 'famine crime' as part of an exploration of how human rights violations, including war crimes, censorship and repression, caused famines. I was one of a small vanguard of scholars and relief workers working in Sudan and Ethiopia on these issues.[6] I spent three years at Africa Watch, and inserted famine into the agenda of its parent organization Human Rights Watch. For some years, of course, historians and geographers had recognized that famines were not natural disasters, like earthquakes or hurricanes, but were the product of politics – 'silent violence' in Michael Watts's apt phrase.[7] Moving beyond the point that famines are man-made to detailing exactly how and why men make famine was the next stage in our intellectual and political project.

This book revisits some of the central arguments and evidence of *Famine Crimes*, twenty years after its publication. It is a good time to reflect. I wrote that book, and the various human rights reports on which it drew,[8] as part of an effort to bring human rights attention to famines. I considered famines as both political crimes and a particular kind of war crime. But moving the study of famine into the arena of genocide and mass atrocity, a field defined by lawyers and their quest for prosecutions, was more problematic than I anticipated.[9] For sure, humanitarians had much to learn from human rights advocates, but the learning needed to be reciprocal.

The topic of famine has the misfortune to be a political issue, but many specific famines are best relieved by treating them as if they were not. Aid workers are often obliged to maintain a disagreeable performance of neutrality, doing business with murderers in order to do their jobs.[10] 'I would sup with the devil to get food to Abyei,' said a humanitarian worker struggling to feed a displaced camp in 1988. The 'devil' with whom he had to sup was an army brigadier named Omar al-Bashir, who the following year led a coup d'état and has ruled Sudan ever since. The question of whether to turn a blind eye to human rights violations – including those that cause starvation – and even to lend legitimacy to those who perpetrate such crimes is a perennial, with no good answer. But at least the terms of the debate can be refined. The scholarly critique of humanitarianism has focused on the ways in which emergency relief fails to address the political causes of famine and even consolidates those retrograde politics, in part by depoliticizing famines. The best scholarly defence of humanitarianism is, on the other hand, that assistance can massively reduce the human suffering caused by bad politics – and that transforming political systems is beyond the remit of emergency relief. This book provides evidence for both sides of the argument. My central thesis is that famine is a kind of atrocity, and that political and legal action is needed to complete the job of eliminating mass starvation. But the evidence also shows that the massive decline in famine deaths has been caused by reductions in not just the incidence of famines, but also their lethality. The fact that famines, when they do (still) occur, kill many fewer people is a laudable achievement of public health professionals and the humanitarian industry.

Organization of This Book

Chapter 2 provides the scaffolding for thinking of famines and mass atrocities together. I ask why these two terrible phenomena have been dealt with so separately, and what it would mean to treat them together. One means I use to tackle this question is by introducing the Nazi Hunger Plan of 1941 – the project of starving to death 30 million people in the western Soviet Union – as a canonical case of forced mass starvation.

Chapter 3 addresses the idea that famines are an inevitable outcome of an imbalance between population and food resources which results in a sufficient number of people starving in order to bring the two back into balance. This is the legacy of the Reverend Thomas Robert Malthus and his 1798 *Essay on the Principle of Population*. I call it a 'zombie concept' because it is so comprehensively refuted, yet tirelessly comes back to haunt us. There's a sound case that our species needs to live within our planetary means or face global disaster. But there's no solid case that *actual* historical famines occur because there are too many people for a limited food supply. Malthus's zombie conflates and confuses the two, to malign effect.

The remainder of the book examines what actually has caused famines and caused them to end. One way of conceptualizing the overall argument is with reference to Richard Tawney's apt description of the plight of the peasant in history as a man standing up to his neck in water, so that even a ripple threatens to drown him.[11] We can expand upon this metaphor. Our man can drown because of a ripple, or because the water level as a whole rises, or because he has to stoop to carry a heavy burden on his back, or because someone knocks him off his feet. These would be the proximate causes of his drowning. Correspondingly, our man can have a better chance of surviving because the water recedes, or the waves lessen, or because no one pushes him over. These are the longer-term reasons he won't drown. The metaphor is usefully borne in mind when we address the proximate and structural causes of famines and why they have decreased. The fundamental point is that, as the water recedes, it requires more and more exceptional combinations of factors – bigger and more freakish waves – to cause famine.

Chapter 4 provides a brief history of 'great' and 'calamitous' modern famines and episodes of forced mass starvation from 1870 to 2010 (more recent famines, and newer operational definitions, come later). The fifty-eight episodes that meet the threshold of 100,000 deaths (according to the lowest credible estimate) constitute a play in four main acts: colonialism; total war and totalitarianism; Asian communism; and the period since approximately 1980 during which famines have been much smaller and associated largely with civil wars in Africa.

Chapter 5 examines one set of explanations for why famines have become less of a threat. These structural factors, which include demographic, economic and public health, are contributors to the success. In particular, they explain why famines are less murderous than before, but in themselves they are an insufficient explanation.

Chapter 6 turns to the political explanations for famines. These are proximate factors: political and military. This is the analytical heart of the book, where I develop the account of famine as a variant of mass atrocity.

Chapter 7 examines the humanitarian international: the international relief system and legal apparatus for relieving famine and ending mass atrocities. I discuss the enormous growth of the famine relief business and the legal regimes for criminalizing starvation, arguing that these are both the cause and the product of a worldwide norm that refuses to tolerate mass starvation.

Chapter 8 takes the case study of Ethiopia, applying these hypotheses to a country that has in modern times been identified as the land of famine. If famine can be conquered in Ethiopia, as appears to be the case, then this has encouraging lessons for the world as a whole.

The final chapters turn to the situation today, in the second decade of the twenty-first century, and the immediate future. Will great and calamitous famines return? Chapter 9 examines some of the most widely feared reasons why we may face famine in the coming century, including economic volatility and the impacts of climate change.

I argue that populations are becoming less vulnerable to famine, but that the convergence of different shocks – economic, climatic, political – may create new risks.

Chapter 10 turns to what I see as the major threat of new famines: wars without end, fought without regard to the value of human life, especially at the nexus of realpolitik and the 'long war' on terror. I suggest that there is a 'counter-humanitarian' backlash. These reasons, I fear, are why the conquest of famine is stalling and may yet be reversed. The concluding chapter pulls the threads together and suggests some directions of thinking and policy, whereby the historic near-victory over famine could be consolidated.

2

Famines as Atrocities

Lemkin's Path Not Taken

Rafaël Lemkin is chiefly famous for having coined the term 'genocide' and advocated for its perpetrators to be prosecuted, and for all nations to be alert to its potential to recur. It is less well known that he was especially attentive to starvation as an instrument of genocide.

Lemkin defined genocide as a coordinated plan to destroy the 'essential foundations of the life of national groups'. In his seminal book, *Axis Rule in Occupied Europe*, he enumerated eight 'techniques of genocide': political; social; cultural; economic; biological (reducing the birthrate); physical; religious; and moral. It is notable that just one was the physical debilitation or annihilation of groups. In turn, under this technique Lemkin listed three separate mechanisms. The first was 'racial discrimination in feeding', under which he detailed the Nazi occupation guidelines specifying the percentages of required basic nutrients allocated to different groups, ranging (in the case of carbohydrates) from 100 per cent to Germans through to 76–77 per cent for Poles, 38 per cent for Greeks and 27 per cent for Jews. The second mechanism was endangering health, through overcrowding in ghettos, withholding medicine and heating fuel during winter, and transportation in cattle trucks and freight cars. The third was mass killings. Genocide came to be most associated with mass killing, which Lemkin tersely describes in a single paragraph addressing Nazi policies directed against Poles, Russians and Jews.[1]

In a 1951 lecture on Ukraine, Lemkin characterized Stalin's policy in the 1932–33 Soviet famine, which came to be known as the

Holodomor, as genocide by starvation. Lemkin was strikingly explicit in naming hunger as a weapon. Additionally, he identified not only how it destroyed people's physical bodies but a nation's soul and brain: 'The Soviet plan was aimed at the farmers, the large mass of independent peasants who are the tradition, folklore and music, the national language and literature, the national spirit of Ukraine. The weapon used against this body [the independent peasants] is perhaps the most terrible of all – starvation.'[2]

The now-conventional story is that Lemkin coined the word 'genocide' in response to Prime Minister Winston Churchill's radio broadcast of 24 August 1941, which is famous for these words: 'We are in the presence of a crime without a name.' However, Churchill's phrase should be put in the context of his immediately preceding sentences, which tell how, invading Russia, the German army had for the first time met military resistance, so that, '[f]or the first time Nazi blood has flowed in a fearful flood':

> The aggressor is surprised, startled, staggered. For the first time in his experience mass murder has become unprofitable. He retaliates by the most frightful cruelties. As his armies advance, whole districts are being exterminated. Scores of thousands, literally scores of thousands of executions in cold blood are being perpetrated by the German police troops upon the Russian patriots who defend their native soil. Since the Mongol invasions of Europe in the sixteenth century there has never been methodical, merciless butchery on such a scale or approaching such a scale. And this is but the beginning. Famine and pestilence have yet to follow in the bloody ruts of Hitler's tanks. We are in the presence of a crime without a name.[3]

Churchill spoke four months *before* the Wannsee Conference at which the Final Solution was adopted. During those months, the biggest crime committed by the Third Reich, in terms of numbers killed, was the famine and pestilence inflicted as part of the 'Hunger Plan'.

The Hunger Plan is the worst famine crime in the historical record. It was the project of reducing the population of the western Soviet Union by 30 million people in the winter of 1941 by means of starvation, thereby supposedly freeing up their food and farmland to support the Wehrmacht.[4] It began by starving 1.25 million Soviet prisoners of war in a matter of months (a death toll that more than doubled during the course of the war). As the historian Timothy Snyder writes: 'As of the end of 1941, by which time the Germans, with local help, had already murdered about 1 million Jews, the starvation of Soviet prisoners was still the greatest German crime.'[5] In her sweeping account of food in the Second World War, Lizzie Collingham takes the forced starvation–genocide link a stage further. She describes how one of the reasons for killing the Jews was the elimination of 'useless eaters' so as to make more food available for the German occupiers, and how the inefficiency of starvation as a method of killing large numbers of people contributed to the Nazi decision to use gas chambers as a more expedited means.[6] In fact, the exterminatory aims of the Hunger Plan exceeded the capacity of the Wehrmacht actually to carry out the project as intended. In exploring what actually transpired, which was horrendous enough, we also learn much about the realities of man-made famine and mass atrocity. The implementation of the Hunger Plan mutated into a number of different forms of forced starvation, pursued (or suspended) opportunistically for specific political, ideological, economic or military goals, or because in the chaos of the Eastern Front, the means of feeding captive populations such as prisoners of war was simply beyond the means of generals and commissars.

It was against this background that Lemkin documented the systematic nutritional deprivation of the populations of Nazi-occupied Europe and the use of starvation as a weapon of subjugation and extermination. Despite the scale of the atrocity and Lemkin's own concern, the Hunger Plan remains little known beyond a small corpus of scholars who are concerned with the economics of the Third Reich. Had it been elevated to a paradigmatic status alongside the Holocaust of European Jewry, the horrific imaginary of the twentieth century would have been shaped differently, and mass starvation would be positioned at the centre of our ethical and intellectual projects. Let me explore what it would mean for the Hunger Plan to serve as a canonical case of mass starvation, alongside our imaginaries of famine and mass atrocity.

What Is a Famine?

We may not know exactly how an economist, social scientist or demographer defines famine, but we know the phenomenon when we see it. Or, to be precise, we instantly recognize it in its extreme form. Similarly with mass atrocities and genocide: our starting point is human revulsion at evil, not legal or academic definition. So it's tempting to skip a discussion of definitions and theory and jump straight to the facts, numbers and explanations. But that would be wrong: in this chapter, let me try to build mental scaffolding that allows us to think of famines and atrocities together as a single family of phenomena.

Famine, genocide, mass atrocity, and starvation are powerful words that evoke compelling images. This makes them troublesome words: they seem inexorably drawn towards particular meanings as if by magnetic pull. Canonical cases are burned into our thinking. 'Famine' evokes a horde of skeletal people (typically Africans), a parched landscape, and no food.[7] With characteristic acuity, Amartya Sen pointed out that most definitions of famine are 'more interesting in providing a pithy description of what happens in situations clearly diagnosed as one of famine than in helping us to do the diagnosis'.[8] 'Genocide' evokes gas chambers, death camps, or mass graves, and for many years a diagnosis of genocide depended on how closely it resembled the Holocaust. (A philosopher might prefer to call it an 'ideal type', but that term is more than a little incongruous in this context – let me stick with 'canonical case'). Just as 'famine' is drawn to one set of image and 'genocide' to another, they are also forced apart from one another as if by magnetic repulsion. What is needed is an exercise in historical re-imagination that wrenches 'famine' and 'mass atrocity' from their misleading canonical cases, and welds them together. The Nazi Hunger Plan is the canonical case that can do just this.

Starting with a formal definitional exercise is, I suggest, not only arid but mistaken because concepts of famine and mass atrocity are defined by historical imagination, and therefore change over time and circumstance. But some clarifications are needed nonetheless. The necessary elements of famine are hunger, crisis and increased mortality. Overall, I find that a rudimentary definition serves us best: a crisis of mass hunger that causes many people to die over a specific period of time.

We should distinguish famine from (chronic) hunger and malnutrition, in so far as it is an exceptional increase in hunger over a particular time period. Famine is also different from starvation in that it has a numerical threshold: it must affect a large number of people. Famines imply starvation, but starvation need not imply famine. Famine is a social, economic and political phenomenon as well as a nutritional one. Yet our conceptualization of famine is dominated by the idea that it is a force of nature. For example, in writing accounts of a famine, it is easy to fall into the trap of giving it an animus, as though it were a living being that possessed a particular kind of behaviour, like a storm or a fire, and even attributing to it intent, as if it were a predator. That is a clear fallacy but it is remarkable how often writers on the subject allow the metaphor to determine the logic of the argument. It is perhaps particularly true for a phenomenon that is far outside the personal experience of most authors and their readers, which is at once elusive in its essence and so compellingly real in its effects, which is hard to define but often very easy to recognize when it occurs.

The most important positivist definition was the 'gigantic inevitable Famine' imagined by the Reverend Thomas Robert Malthus in his 1798 *Essay on Population*. Such 'Famine' is caused by overpopulation relative to food availability, and it consists of mass death through starvation until the balance between populace and food is restored. This is a canonical case that has never occurred, yet exerts an inexorable grip on our conceptualization of famine. This story is the topic of chapter 3. Even while trying to rebut Malthus's own arguments, economists and geographers tend still to see famine as an impersonal phenomenon, driven by the laws of nature, population and economics, albeit modulated by politics and society.

In reality, famines are a diverse set of phenomena with family resemblance. They involve hunger and starvation, disruption and disease, and social breakdown. They are crises: sharp deviations from what is normal. Famines have changed their shape over modern history: driven and shaped successively by colonialism, total war, totalitarianism, counter-insurgency and civil war, and political-economic globalization.

Those who study individual famines in depth – such as historians and social anthropologists – are often led into more subjective and situational definitions that bring into sharp focus the particular ills visited on the society in question. From the viewpoint of those who have suffered it, a particular famine may be experienced primarily as the loss of a way of life or a societal crisis that ruptures the moral fabric. But we need to be wary of generalizing from these conceptions, however much they capture the specifics of a particular society's historic experience. Famines can occur without a food shortage, for example when people starve because they can't get enough food in a land of plenty. Famines can occur without mass outright starvation unto death: people may suffer epidemic malnutrition that leads to increased susceptibility from infectious diseases.

Defining famine is inescapably bound up with measuring it. There have been two important efforts to do this. The first was initiated by Stephen Devereux and Paul Howe.[9] They distinguish between the *magnitude* of famine and its *severity*. Magnitude is best defined as the numbers who die. Devereux created a simple logarithmic scale for the magnitude of famines, and in this book I have used his categories of 'great' and 'calamitous' famines – that kill 100,000 people or more and one million people or more respectively – as my main point of reference. Measuring famine mortality is an exceptionally fraught business, requiring workable estimates of population size, normal or baseline mortality, causes of increased deaths, and the point at which death rates can be considered to have returned to normal. These issues are so complicated and the data and methodological problems are so vast that most scholars have been deterred from even trying the kind of overview I attempt in this book. It will not be difficult for critics to poke holes in the numbers: I invite them to produce better figures.

The magnitude of a famine can only be estimated afterwards, which is not very useful for those trying to stop it. The other dimension in the Howe and Devereux famine scale is severity: how badly it is affecting, or threatening, a certain population. This is the central metric used by the second important measurement initiative, the Integrated Food Security Phase Classification (IPC scale). Estimating the severity of an imminent food crisis has enormous practical value, and the IPC scale does this in a manner that is as technically robust as possible, given the constraints of good information in situations of conflict and crisis. However, it neglects the magnitude dimension: 'famine' can be declared for small populations, where the total numbers at risk may be small. The IPC scale has been formally adopted and used by the United Nations and many governments, and it is the basis on which 'famine' was declared in South Sudan in 2017. We should also note that the IPC scale was developed to provide a metric for the systematic measurement of populations suffering a spectrum of different kinds of food insecurity, with a definition of 'famine' as a by-product. The term 'food security' – encompassing the three pillars of food availability, access, and utilization – has been developed since the 1980s as a framework for understanding the nexus between food production, livelihoods and nutrition.[10]

As part of the growing science of emergency nutrition, nutritionists and epidemiologists have gained a much finer-grained understanding of who dies and why in food crises. Helen Young and Susanne Jaspars explain how the relationship between worsening malnutrition and increasing mortality is not linear but logarithmic:

As food insecurity evolves and deepens the underlying causes of malnutrition (food, health and care) change and interact with each other. In the non-emergency phases of the IPC, the three groups of underlying causes are on a par; food, health and care are each necessary but on their own insufficient for good nutrition. When food insecurity worsens, it influences the social and care environment (care-giving behaviours, family and wider social networks), and also access to health care and the health environment. During a humanitarian emergency food security is heavily influenced by the severe social changes – particularly where forced migration (or conversely restricted mobility and access as a result of conflict) affect the integrity of the household and their food security. At the final stage of humanitarian catastrophe all underlying causes of malnutrition are extremely elevated, as a result of the combined (multiplicative) effects of a complete failure in all three underlying causes. At each progressive stage of the IPC [scale] there is likely to be an exponential increase in malnutrition and mortality rates, because of the synergistic relationship between underlying causes.[11]

The evidence reviewed in detail by Young and Jaspars provides the details behind the older insight that famine is to poverty as ice is to freezing water. Famine is a process of desperate impoverishment and social collapse that reaches a vortex of starvation and vastly heightened mortality. This insight also sharpens the nutritionist's focus on preventing the descent into that vortex. The professional humanitarian's first duty is to prevent famines from becoming monstrously fatal, and only secondarily on preventing the crises themselves.

Part of the story of this book is also how the definition of famine has been shaped by history, politics and philosophy. Famines have been defined by the political authorities and publics of the time, and these definitions have changed. As the book progresses, I indicate different elements for how we should understand famines, depending on historical context and purpose.

What Is Mass Atrocity?

Lemkin's initial definition of 'genocide' was sociological: an analysis of how the Axis powers subjugated conquered populations and imposed new sociopolitical structures upon them.[12] However, in its subsequent use, 'genocide' has become focused on the first, destructive component, to the exclusion of the second component of being a transformative political project. Also, genocide has become a legal term first and a sociological one second, straitjacketed by the somewhat peculiar, politically negotiated and anachronistic language of the 1948 Genocide Convention. Genocide is a crime defined by *intent*: the perpetrator must intend the destruction, in whole or (large) part, of a target group. The protected groups are ethnic, national, racial or religious – excluding political groups, a significant weakness. Debates over whether a mass atrocity qualifies as genocide can readily become ensnared in definitional and legal niceties. Genocide is also popularly imagined as the 'crime of crimes', and there is a widespread misconception that identifying an event as 'genocide' entails an international responsibility to intervene. Together, these elements imply 'evil in the mindset of the perpetrator' which obscures understanding of what is really going on, and how it may be stopped.[13]

Genocide studies have long been conducted in the shadow of the paradigm of the Holocaust and, within that, with the Auschwitz camp as its ultimate exemplar. The current generation of genocide scholars has questioned this, and moved on from a focus on the Nazi Final Solution as an event defined by its uniqueness. Scholars of genocide now pay attention to imperial and colonial episodes of destroying indigenous peoples, counter-population warfare, state terror and deportation, and some episodes of famine, such as the Ukrainian Holodomor. Meanwhile, scholars of the most archetypical cases of genocide, including Rwanda[14] and the Final Solution itself,[15] have also increasingly paid more attention to the specific political circumstances of escalating mass killing. Scholars of genocide have increasingly become interested in its *rarity* – and the unusual concatenations of events, and how forces of escalation overcome pressures for restraint.[16] This is a frame usefully shared by the study of famine.

The terms 'mass atrocity' and 'atrocity crimes', while legally imprecise, have the utility of overcoming the arcane limitations of the term 'genocide' that make the latter ill-fitted for political purpose. Mass atrocities can be defined as 'widespread and systematic violence against civilians, largely characterized by killing'.[17]

What Is Starvation?

Outright starvation is exceptionally rare and is documented almost only in prisons and detention camps. It takes about two months for a healthy adult to die of outright starvation, a reality grimly demonstrated by the ten Republican Irish hunger strikers who starved to death in British prisons in 1981. One of them, Bobby Sands, was elected a Member of Parliament, 40 days into his hunger strike: he died 26 days later. The degree of self-will required for such deprivation is quite extraordinary. Starvation to death has also occasionally been used as a punishment. In Auschwitz-Birkenau in 1941, whenever there was an attempted escape, prisoners were randomly selected during the daily roll call, and held as hostages in a dark cell without food until the escapee was caught or – as in all known cases – the selected prisoners starved to death.[18]

Of much greater concern to this book is *semi-starvation*: a diet insufficient to maintain a human being in a healthy state. Ancel Keys's famous 'Minnesota experiment' in 1944–5 investigated the biology of semi-starvation, namely what happened to 36 young, fit male volunteers who were put on a reduced diet for six months.[19] They indeed suffered from many of the symptoms described for people undergoing famine or forced mass starvation, in particular an obsession with food and how to obtain it.

In my earlier writings on famine, I was reluctant to use the word 'starvation' because it implied a one-dimensional perspective on famine, focused too tightly on food and nutrition, and therefore overlooking the wider socio-economic and political pathology that is famine. In particular, I argued that outright or 'frank' starvation was rare in most famines, which were characterized principally by the widespread destruction of a way of life, with increased mortality driven primarily by infectious disease rather than by starvation per se. In this book, I reconsider this position. The uni-dimensional implication of 'starvation' remains a shortcoming. But the term has two particular assets.

First, starvation can refer to an individual, or a specific category of people within a population, as well as to a wider collectivity. 'Famine' has an implicit numerical threshold: a small group cannot suffer 'famine' and certainly not an individual. But individuals or selected categories of people can be starved. Thus an episode of extreme hunger and deprivation affecting, for example, prisoners of war or the residents of a besieged town would qualify as starvation while we might hesitate to call it 'famine'.

Second and even more important, the verb 'to starve' can be used in *both transitive and intransitive senses*. People can starve, and they can be starved by other people. While it remains common in popular usage, the transitive sense has been overlooked in the study of famine. Sen represents the economists' mainstream in explicitly disavowing this: 'In distinguishing between starvation and famine, it is not my intention to attribute a sense of deliberate harming to the first absent in the second.'[20] I reverse this, and reintroduce the transitive sense of starvation as the primary one.[21] My concern in this book is *mass* starvation, and I have a particular focus on *forced mass starvation*. In the same way that victims of persecution can suffer and die from many proximate causes, so too victims of starvation can suffer and die from disease, exhaustion or violence, as well as the effects of malnutrition. All these kinds of mortality should count.

Taking a lead from the way in which our imagination of genocide is gripped by the canonical instance of the Holocaust and our notion of famine is coloured by Malthus's imagined 'Famine', I put forward the canonical case of forced mass starvation epitomized by the Nazi Hunger Plan. I do this well aware of the perils.

The main danger of elevating a canonical case to take on a defining role in a scholarly paradigm is that its singularity squeezes out the necessary empirics of understanding actual human events. For example, the words of Primo Levi quoted at the opening of this book, in which he condenses 'all the evil of our time' into the image of a starving man, serves the purpose of symbolizing such a case.[22] But the words that follow, 'on whose face and in whose eyes not a trace of a thought is to be seen', while they may be accurate for the specific case of the starving concentration camp inmate, do not ring true in respect to the general case of people suffering famine, who continue to show a spectrum of human emotions and capacities, including being resourceful and humane.

But the canonical case is valuable in two other respects. The first is a 'what-if' rethinking of intellectual history. Had the Hunger Plan been the paradigmatic case of twentieth-century mass murder, how might our vocabulary for mass atrocity, or our laws prohibiting genocide and war crimes, be different today? The second is that it compels us to bring together two canonical types – 'Famine' and the Holocaust – that are rarely if ever considered together. Adding the Hunger Plan as the third point of a triangle creates a conceptual arena, defined by the three canonical cases, in which we can map the associations between mass starvation and mass atrocity. For example, it obliges us to consider starvation as a *method* of mass killing, alongside the food–population equation as a *rationale* for genocide. It brings into focus the parallel with the forced starvation-genocide of the Herero in Namibia in 1904 and other colonial-settler famines and genocides.

The Hunger Plan compels us to think about famine and mass atrocity in a seamless way – as Lemkin himself appears to have done. What forced starvation and genocide have in common is that those in authority just didn't care whether those in their care lived or died. Human lives – or, to be precise, *some* human lives – became expendable in pursuit of other goals, or simply disregarded as worthless. This is the core point at which the scholarship on famine and mass atrocity can converge.

But if we take the idea that starvation is (or should be) a crime, exactly what kind of crime is it? Is it a crime of murder (of individuals) or extermination (of collectivities)? If so, we encounter an evidentiary problem. When there's a murder, there is a body with evidence of foul play; when there's extermination, there are a lot of bodies. But deaths from starvation typically have a complex aetiology with different causes including malnutrition, infection and exhaustion combining to kill individuals. Famines are multi-causal events. So while it is, in principle, straightforward and conclusive to show that a particular accused person killed a particular victim with a gunshot or a poison, it is far more difficult to prove that a perpetrator has killed a victim by starvation. The exceptional cases are prisoners, and those are rare.

Is starvation an inhumane act? It can be the outcome of seeking to degrade or humiliate a person or persons with the aim of demonstrating mastery or forcing them to do something such as abandon their homes. It can be tantamount to an act of torture. Is starvation a variant of persecution or a tool used to persecute people? Hunger can be inflicted on people as punishment because of their identity or because they have refused to surrender. Is starvation the by-product of other crimes and blunders, such as disproportionate violence against civilians during wartime or mistaken economic policies in peacetime? Like manslaughter, is it a crime of recklessness – actions pursued with wilful disregard to likely consequence?

I suggest that famine crimes are all of the above. This poses enormous difficulties for the jurists who draft international laws and the prosecutors who frame charges against war criminals. For example, despite Lemkin's emphasis on famine, the Allied lawyers who wrote the Nuremberg indictment of Nazi war criminals included starvation only as a subsidiary component of other crimes, not as a crime in its own right.[23]

Silences and Singularities

There are huge social, political, legal and scholarly silences around starvation. We fear that starvation involves a kind of biological reductionism that is not only painful but so shameful that it is beyond social and political analysis. Certainly, it is difficult, but not impossible.

Official memory is often remarkably silent about mass suffering. This is infamously true of epidemics, from the medieval Black Death to influenza and HIV/AIDS. The 1919 influenza epidemic killed far more people than the First World War, but there are no memorials to its scores of millions of victims and just one book-length treatment of it.[24]

Official memorials to the victims of famine are also remarkably rare. In her book, *Trauma and the Memory of Politics*, Jenny Edkins makes repeated passing mention of famine alongside genocide and war as a national trauma demanding memorialization, but the only example actually explored is the Irish famine of the 1840s.[25] Marking the 150-year anniversary, memorial sculptures were erected across Ireland and in North America, making that famine and the associated mass emigration to the New World the most memorialized famine. (It is also no coincidence that the Republican prisoners who starved themselves to death in British prisons in 1980 and 1981 evoked this

memory.) Memorials to the Ukrainian Holodomor of the 1930s have
been built in Kiev and in Washington, DC. I know of just two cases
in which mass starvation was memorialized in its immediate aftermath.
The Soviet authorities erected a memorial to those who died in the
siege of Leningrad, which includes figures representing victims of
starvation (though after the war they were keen to obscure the true
numbers that had died). The Martyrs' Memorial in Tigray, northern
Ethiopia, remembers the fighters who died in the 1976–91 war, and
the civilians who died in massacres and in the famine of 1983–5.
What these cases have in common is that a famine is remembered as
an element of national narrative. Much more common around the
world is official silence, along with local efforts to remember.

Famines live on in the vernacular, even when suppressed or forgotten by those in power. The Syrian famine of the First World War is
recounted in memoirs and novels; the Russian famine of the early
1920s in literature. A particularly striking case is Mao Zedong's 'Great
Leap Forward' famine of 1958–62, which was denied for decades and
is still only grudgingly acknowledged. The Chinese film-maker Wu
Wenguang has set up the 'Memory Project' to document life in rural
China during the mid-twentieth century, which includes numerous
efforts by local people to record and remember those who died in the
famine. Another informative case is the Bengal famine of 1943, which
was politically highly salient at the time and massively discredited the
British Raj. It has subsequently played only a minor role in the national
narrative, though it is remembered vividly among families in Bengal.

Edkins posits an explanation for the paucity of famine memorials,
which is that, 'There is no possibility afterwards of survivors claiming
that those who died sacrificed themselves for some greater cause.'[26]
We can elaborate on this. Unlike war, hunger seems to constrict the
reach of our social concerns and solidarities. The acts of selflessness
in famine are typically inconspicuous, such as parents going hungry
for the sake of their children. Families and individuals often experience their hunger in an isolated way, and feel shameful rather than
heroic. The idea of famine as a natural calamity or starvation as a
personal misfortune remains powerful, and it is only in those cases
in which there is an obvious perpetrator that a famine is remembered
as a crime demanding recognition and reparation.

By contrast, the *perpetrators* of famine have often been memorialized and celebrated. A conspicuous example is the memorial to the
twenty-six German soldiers who died in the 1904 battle of Waterberg,
the encounter that heralded the genocide of the Herero. Colonial
capitals and settler cities have long been decorated by statues of men
who starved, pillaged and dispossessed faraway peoples who had done

them no wrong. But of course their remembrance is silent on these
atrocities. Over time, as the descendants of the victims have found
political voice, conquistadors' monuments are being challenged.

Those who write the history of famines have rarely themselves
starved. The exceptions are worth examining: cases in which socially
and politically significant people have suffered starvation. One famous
case is the conductor Karl Eliasberg and the musicians who performed
Dmitri Shostakovich's Seventh Symphony in Leningrad, while themselves starving, in the depths of that city's suffering on 9 August
1942.[27] The performance, broadcast not only through the city but to
the German trenches outside, was an act of heroic defiance.

The best-known case is Primo Levi, whose extraordinary intimate
and frank account of death and life in Auschwitz is threaded through
with the experience of hunger, and the attendant obsession with food,
with possessing a spoon, and with the manner of eating – *fressen* like
animals, not *essen* like people. Levi writes, 'A fortnight after my
arrival I already had the prescribed hunger, that chronic hunger
unknown to free men, which makes one dream at night, and settles
in all the limbs of one's body.' Deprivation reaches the point at which
'how could one imagine not being hungry? The Lager *is* hunger: we
ourselves are hunger, living hunger.'[28] Levi describes those prisoners
who had given up the struggle and who were passively following the
camp routines. Known as 'musselmans', a term of uncertain origin
that may echo colonial or Orientalist stereotypes, 'Their life is short,
but their number is endless'. Levi writes, 'All the musselmans who
finished in the gas chambers have the same story, or more exactly,
have no story; they followed the slope down to the bottom, like
streams that run down to the sea.'[29]

It is tempting to suppose a singularity here: that human beings are
reduced to animals, and that extreme hunger displaces all other emotion
or thought. This is in line with Theodor Adorno's famous statement
– provocative but wrong – that after Auschwitz, poetry could no
longer be written.

The idea that lack of food removes the distinguishing elements of
humanity is one that recurs in accounts of famine. It is a theme of
Cormac Ó Gráda's book, *Eating People is Wrong* – a title which
could well be followed by the qualifier, 'but does indeed occur for
reasons we understand but find hard to accept'.[30] The Russian sociologist Pitrim Sorokin, who lived through his country's post-
revolutionary famines, researched a book, *Hunger as a Factor in
Human Affairs*, during that time.[31] Half of the pages are given over
to human physiology and behaviour during starvation. In his preface,
he pre-emptively responds to his social scientific critics:

'Too much biology', I expect to hear from some 'ardent sociologists'. 'True,' I reply calmly, 'but there is very little unfounded fantasy.' 'Too much attention is given to man's behavior, and too little to the sociological processes,' others will remark. 'Without studying the former, it is impossible to know anything about the latter, because social life is ultimately created by the actions of the people,' I answer.[32]

Sorokin argues that as starvation progresses, human beings become focused more and more exclusively on food and on doing anything necessary to obtain food. He writes, 'to hunger, nothing is sacred,' and recounts cases in which people deceive and steal from even their closest family members, and of cannibalism. Describing how religious duties are abandoned, the dead are buried without funeral rites and forbidden foods are eaten, he writes: 'In this case, hunger makes a norm of abnormality and the sacrilege becomes a tolerable and admissible act. Since this "sacrilege" would prevent satisfaction of hunger, starvation mercilessly rips off the "social" garments from man and shows him as a naked animal, on the naked earth.'[33]

The point at which human beings are reduced to simply biological beings could be called a singularity. In chapter 3, I use the term 'alimentary economics' to describe theories of population and food – seminally, Malthus's – that reduce society *in extremis* to this condition. I argue that we must treat claims about such singularities with extreme care. There are biological constants but I can find no case in which a human society has reached the point at which they are the determining factor. Let me give two very different examples.

In my fieldwork in Darfur in 1985, I came across a phenomenon that appeared to be an economic version of this singularity: the reduction of human beings to simply biological beings. One of the features of famine is that the price of food rises. To be precise, the prices of staple foods, such as wheat, maize, rice or sorghum, rise. The prices of assets fall as people sell them to buy food. This includes herders and farmers selling their animals, at lower and lower prices as they flood the market, and as a consequence the price of meat also falls. In famines, meat is cheap – but it is almost always still more expensive, calorie for calorie, than staple food grains. There is still a premium for protein and taste, and richer people who are ready to pay. Meanwhile, edible items that aren't normally sold in the market – 'famine foods' – acquire a price. Leaves, berries, nuts and grasses that are normally despised and don't taste good, which can be collected for free or at very low prices, suddenly appear in the marketplace and, as famine worsens, their prices rise.

What I found at the very depths of the famine in Darfur in early 1985, in the worst-hit areas, was that the price differential per calorie between different foodstuffs dwindled to zero. The price of the staples, sorghum and millet, rose to historic highs. The price of meat fell to historic lows. A market in famine foods opened up in the towns, where the women who knew which grains and berries to gather and how to prepare them sold pitiful little piles for pennies. Remarkably, calorie for calorie, there was, for a short period, no difference in price between any of the above. The market had adjusted to people's overwhelming need just for energy to keep their metabolism working, to stay alive.

The convergence of calorie prices for different foods appears to be a singularity in the famine market data: the point at which human beings are reduced to sheer survival, in line with Sorokin's observation that 'starvation mercilessly rips off the "social" garments from man'.[34] At that point, there was no economy beyond the market in food. People's consumption was what they ate that day.

Now, consider what is required to get to this point. Taste preferences are put aside. Anything other than food, than translating resources into energy to keep the body alive, is put aside. Considerations about the future are put aside. People, it appears, were thinking as biological beings: the value of food was solely its energy content. But reflect also on how rare and how brief this episode was, just a few places for just a few weeks. The singularity was also a *market* phenomenon and a transient one. It passed: the market responded: traders moved food in, and hungry people moved elsewhere. It requires a sociologist and an economist to explain how people reached that point and came back from it.

My second example returns us to Primo Levi. My reading of his book *Survival in Auschwitz* is less as an account of dehumanization and more of the story of how, even at the utmost extreme of deprivation, human beings remain complex social and moral beings. Levi puts this in a somewhat light-hearted way, describing his journey to the camp: 'Sooner or later in life everyone discovers that perfect happiness is unrealizable, but there are few who pause to consider the antithesis: that perfect unhappiness is equally unattainable.'[35] His account of the previous day, when the assembled Jews were told to be ready for transportation, makes the point poignantly:

> All took leave from life in the manner which most suited them. Some praying, some deliberately drunk, others lustfully intoxicated for the last time. But the mothers stayed up to prepare the food for the journey with tender care, and washed their children and packed the luggage; and at dawn the barbed wire was full of children's washing hung out in the wind to dry. Nor did they forget the diapers, the toys, the cushions and the hundred other small things which mothers remember and

which children always need. Would you not do the same? If you and
your child were going to be killed tomorrow, would you not give him
to eat today?[36]

They were not, at that point, starving. The reach of their concerns,
the ambit of their reciprocity, had not yet constricted, as it does with
extreme hunger. Social anthropologists have detailed this contraction
in the web of obligations in diverse societies, calling it the 'accordion
effect',[37] but also showing that social behaviours never vanish. The
anthropologist Raymond Firth, having documented how the Tikopian
islanders responded to famine by, among other things, eating in secret,
stealing food and breaking food taboos, commented: 'morals degener-
ated...[but] manners remained.'[38] They were not only victims but
were resisting hunger, and sometimes selectively inflicting it on one
another. Similarly, Levi recounted how, as the deprivations of the
camp were enforced, the prisoners' horizons of concern narrowed.
But while some of those who were starving abandoned hope and
passively drifted into submission and death – a similar phenomenon
of 'starvation suicides' has been observed in many famines – others
kept alive hope and functioned in a much reduced but nonetheless
recognizably social manner. They too were victims, collaborators,
resisters and even perpetrators. There is never a point at which humanity disappears. The extremities of human deprivation may be difficult
to describe and still more difficult to explain, but they are not inher-
ently inexplicable or reducible to animal behaviour.

The Scholarly Gap between Famine and Atrocity

Those who study famine tend to have a blind spot regarding political
and military criminality.[39] Those who study genocide and mass atrocity tend to have the counterpart blind spot on famine and starvation.
Given Lemkin's own writings, this is unfortunate. Ironically, Lemkin's
rapid success in obtaining an international legal instrument had the
effect of constraining the scholarly imagination of genocide within a
rather peculiar legal definition. Academics, like lawyers, have focused
on the destructive component of genocide and almost exclusively on
the element of mass killing (and, more recently, sexual violence). They
have neglected other means of destruction and have wholly overlooked
those parts of the genocidal political project that entailed building
something in its place. The prosecutor seeks to identify the culprit,
specify the crime and win a conviction in court, which is most straightforward where there is a body with evidence of a violent death. Many

scholars follow a comparable path, and in doing so they channel their efforts away from the complicated and shifting politics, culture and economics of mass atrocity. In this reorientation of effort, the role of starvation, food and livelihoods was neglected.

The current generation of genocide scholars has broadened its field of study and has begun to grapple with the history of famine crimes, but the field remains fragmented without a paradigm that brings them together. The distinct literatures of colonialism and indigenous studies have done much to document and present argument as to why policies that targeted these groups should be understood as intentional, but even then only a few scholars overtly draw on the discourse of genocide to present their arguments.[40] Important studies of colonial logic, indigenous experiences and specific case studies have addressed state policies that resulted in mass death through starvation, but only in a case-by-case way.

There is no shortage of empirical material, in the form of historical accounts, concerning the role of starvation in genocide and mass atrocity. Scholars have just not yet developed a taxonomy or a theory. My colleague Bridget Conley, reflecting on a catalogue of mass atrocities she had compiled, began to explore this. She identified five ways in which hunger was used by perpetrators. The first is as a method of killing as such, for example in the genocide of the Herero and against the Armenians. A second was as a method of weakening a group already under the control of perpetrators in preparation for other policies, such as the Jewish ghettos in the early 1940s, and the siege of Srebrenica in 1995. A third, perhaps the commonest, is as a means to force people to move or surrender, as in East Timor, Guatemala or Sudan. A fourth is forced hunger as punishment, as occurred when the Serbian besiegers tightened the blockade of Sarajevo as retribution for other actions happening elsewhere. A final way is as the predictable but not specifically intended outcome of other policies, such as counter-insurgency or land-grab. We can also add scorched earth and ecocide as faminogenic actions during wartime, genocide or imperial conquest. This is a preliminary taxonomy – it is striking that two generations of research into genocide and mass atrocity has scarcely begun to tread this ground.

One symptom of this scholarly vacuum around famine crimes is that, when it comes to counting deaths, historians and genocide scholars tend to use aggregate figures that include both those killed violently and those who died of starvation, exhaustion and disease. There is, however, an implicit hierarchy among victims of atrocity, with those who died of direct violence qualifying without question, while those who died from hunger, cold, or disease added only hesitantly to the rolls. In his study of how the Armenian genocide has been portrayed by scholars and political commentators, my brother Thomas de Waal notes the evidentiary, methodological and political problems surrounding estimates for the numbers of deaths in the genocide, noting that the official Armenian figure of 1.5 million 'seems to be a high number, unless one includes all Armenian deaths from all causes, such as disease and malnutrition' during the whole period 1915–23. Among these dead are up to 200,000 who died from a famine in 1919.[41] Similarly, in his otherwise superb history, Ronald Suny writes, 'The Genocide of the Armenians can be said to have ended by late January 1917. Mass starvation continued...'[42] A more recent case is that of the Cambodians who died under Pol Pot. Most writers simply cite the aggregate figure of 1.75 million dead. Ben Kiernan has undertaken the extraordinarily difficult tasks of both estimating these numbers and disentangling those who died directly through violent execution (31 per cent) from those who succumbed to starvation, exposure, exhaustion and disease (69 per cent).[43]

There are counterpart lapses on the side of food security studies. It is only recently that scholars in the field have begun to grapple with the issue of culpability. Paul Howe developed a taxonomy of how famine could be an outcome of peacetime policy decision.[44] Governments could aim to create famine, could regard famine as the tolerable or welcome outcome of other goals, or could have conflicting demands that relegate famine prevention to a lower priority. A related question is which deaths count towards the tally of famine mortality. Those interested in measuring famine mortality tend not to include those who died on account of the wider social crisis, but not of a cause directly associated with hunger. To give a pertinent recent example, by the summer of 2016 the South Sudanese civil war had caused a humanitarian crisis with an overall civilian death rate that potentially qualified it for 'famine' status according to the IPC scale. However, some international officials successfully argued that those who died from drowning (escaping massacre and seeking refuge and sustenance) should be excluded from the numbers – which brought the death rate below the threshold for declaring famine.[45] In January 2017, this assessment was revised and the UN declared famine.

Another weakness is the lack of a systematic study of famine perpetrators. Twenty years ago, David Keen challenged academics to focus on the beneficiaries of famine.[46] That challenge is still largely unmet in contrast to the growing literature on the perpetrators of massacre and genocide. There is a growing experience of negotiations over humanitarian access to besieged and suffering populations, documented by relief agencies and diplomats,[47] which could form the material for a substantive analysis of the beliefs and behaviours of famine perpetrators and how they respond to changing political, military and humanitarian circumstances. Some historians have documented the political decision making involved in, for example, the Holodomor, the Nazi Hunger Plan and the 1958–62 famine in China. But there's no comparative political scholarship on those who create famine and why. We can begin to chart an agenda. Could it be that most famine crimes have the character of being committed remotely and anonymously, rather than face to face and in the heat of the moment? Is it that starvation may be inflicted by the routine workings of bureaucracy following standard patterns of organizational behaviour, rather than by bold political diktat? Is there an element of uncertainty at the time of commission about how many victims there are or will be? These are all possible factors in an explanation, but we have no solid evidence for whether they will survive rigorous inquiry.

Moralities and Practicalities

The study of how famines and mass atrocities end is dominated by the study of what 'we' – outsiders, humanitarians, intervenors – do to bring them to an end. International action to stop famines and mass atrocities is important. But if we make it the main focus of our inquiry, we are en route to a distorted understanding. When a problem is framed by its purported solution, we are unlikely to analyse it rigorously. This is the intellectual starting point for my quarrel with dominance of the agenda by humanitarian intervention (and latterly the responsibility to protect) in approaching famine and genocide. For this reason, I disliked the simplistic paternalism of Band Aid in 1984, I opposed the despatch of the US Marine Corps to Somalia as Operation Restore Hope in 1992, and I criticized Samantha Power's narrative in *A Problem from Hell* that portrayed the central challenge to ending genocide as ensuring that America was ready to intervene to stop it.[48] Power's book analysed the origins and course of mass atrocity with insight and rigour, but then turned normative when it began to deal with endings. Instead of documenting what *actually* happens at the end of a genocide, she instead concerned herself with how genocide *ought* to end – and set an agenda of military intervention to halt the killing and international trials to bring the perpetrators to justice. This was an analytical shortcoming, which she then doubled because she didn't subject such purported endings through international action to the same critical acuity as the analysis of the events themselves. Too often, advocacy descends into a fairytale of salvation.

The entire intellectual agenda for studying famine and mass atrocity has been corralled into two quite separate fields, partly because of the different institutions for policy and practice. Notably, there is a gap between humanitarians who are concerned with saving victims' lives, and human rights' advocates concerned with calling perpetrators to account. These two kinds of practitioners tend to think very differently about the same events. The separation is both problematic and valuable.

Consider a crisis that involves both lethal violence, in the form of massacres, and also starvation and disease. Though they arise from the same cause, the two dimensions of the crisis look quite different. Different kinds of people suffer and die in different ways and at different times. Consider Figure 2.1, representing the numbers of people who died in Darfur in 2003–5 from violence and from hunger and disease.

The line representing violent deaths is jagged, following the timeline of the military offensives. The deaths from hunger and disease lagged,

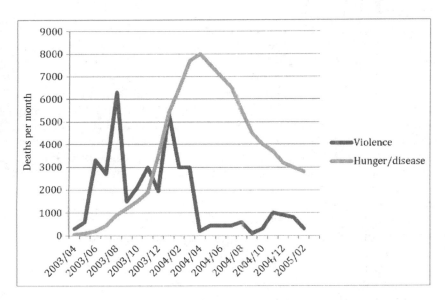

Figure 2.1 Causes of death in Darfur per month, 2003–5
Sources: Violent deaths: ICC, scaled by a factor of three to be commensurate with the CRED estimate; hunger/disease: CRED, smoothed. See de Waal 2016.

peaking slightly later and somewhat higher, and falling away more slowly. Geographically, the massacres were focused in the small towns and villages close to where the battles raged, while mortality due to hunger and disease was spread more widely.

The contrasts are sharper if we focus on the kinds of people who die in massacres and in famines. The Sudanese soldiers and militiamen chiefly targeted adult men, though there were many cases in which they shot and burned indiscriminately, killing women, old people and children. Deaths from hunger and disease were concentrated among children under five. We didn't witness starvation camps for prisoners of war.

A practical and non-political response, such as flooding markets with (cheap) food and providing primary health care through humanitarian agencies, can be effective at blunting mortality in famine atrocities, while there is no comparable humanitarian-economic action for ending mass murder. Meanwhile, the kind of actions specifically targeted at ending mass atrocity – such as calling the perpetrator to account – may be ineffective or even counterproductive for the humanitarian response. In the case of Darfur, when the International Criminal Court (ICC) issued an arrest warrant for Sudanese President Omar al-Bashir, the Sudanese government responded by expelling thirteen international humanitarian agencies.

The differences between aid practitioners and prosecutors echo the polarity defined by the extreme canonical cases of 'famine' and genocide. Introduce the third canonical case, in the form of a mass starvation crime, and the complexities of addressing these events come into focus. There were cases of outright deliberate starvation to death in Darfur, but they were mercifully rare. Also, only one side was using hunger as a weapon. In other instances, such as southern Sudan in the late 1980s – the case that prompted my initial reflections on starvation as a deliberate act – both government and rebels were using hunger, and the famine crime against the population was general in scope. In southern Sudan, neither the provision of non-political relief assistance nor the condemnation of the perpetrators for their outrages would have been a sufficient response. We need a deeper understanding of the dynamics of how such compound atrocities come to an end.

A Common Agenda for Understanding Famine and Mass Atrocity

What binds the problems of famine and mass atrocity together is the question of how rulers make a political decision, and publics tolerate it, that significant portions of a population will suffer terribly and die. The decisions themselves and the instruments for implementing them can be organized in very diverse ways, concealing the underlying commonalities. Mass lethal violence and famine appear at times as fundamentally different phenomena. What they share is an assumption that *the lives of the victims don't matter*. This consensus can be held narrowly within an elite circle or can be accepted among a much wider population. It is typically inflicted on an outsider group – foreigners or a stigmatized minority. The means of implementing this indifference to human life can be organized by military or bureaucratic means, or can take the form of licensing anyone, with any motive, to treat the target group as they wish without repercussion. The lives of the targeted people may be irrelevant because leaders wish to destroy the group, or they may simply be an obstacle in pursuit of another goal. But once people are designated in this way, their lives are transported into a zone of exclusion in which their continued living or imminent death loses any political significance for those whose decisions will determine their fate.

It is at this point that the common features between famine and mass atrocity come into focus. *Both are primarily political projects that consider (some) human lives expendable or worthless.* They both arise from reprehensible, inhuman political projects. This book does not provide a rigorous theoretical framing of how famine is a mass atrocity, but rather an untheorized common ground on which scholars of the phenomena might find a set of cases and questions in common on which they might speak to one another. And, just as attempts to understand society undergoing the extreme stress of starvation run up against limits to theorization, so too it may be extremely hard to find cogent theory for the perpetration of starvation. Writing about the Hunger Plan, the historian Adam Tooze finds a 'sense of a vacuum' at the heart of Nazi German planning.[49] We should perhaps not expect our explanations for famine crimes to be too coherent.

3

Malthus's Zombie

More People, Fewer Famine Deaths

Over the last century and a half, world population has expanded at a rate without precedent, from about 1.3 billion in 1870 to 7 billion today. Over the same time period, the number and lethality of famines have fallen. This is no minor reduction: *mortality in great and calamitous famines has all but disappeared*. The death toll from these famines used to average more than 10 million people each decade, up to the 1970s. Then the numbers declined, and in the last twenty-five years the decadal mortality has been just 500,000. As world population has expanded, deaths famines have declined.

Let me repeat this simple, easily verified and common-sense fact because it is, for strange reasons, the exact opposite of what is often claimed. The correlation between population and famine is *inverse*: more people are associated with lower mass starvation (see Figure 3.1). This is not spurious. There are plausible explanations for why there are more people in the world and fewer people dying in famines.

The decline would be even more pronounced if the mortality levels were indexed to global population to show the risk of dying in a great or calamitous famine. The risk of dying of famine in the decade 1901–10 was higher than in the 1971–80 decade.

This story stands on its head the famous prophecy by Thomas Robert Malthus, which was that *population growth inevitably ends in gigantic famine*, which reduces population to a level commensurate with food availability. Although it has been disproved many times,

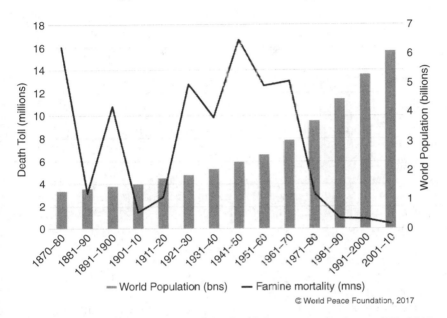

Figure 3.1 World population and death toll from great famines, 1870–2010
Sources: for world population: US Census Bureau; for great famines and episodes of deliberate mass starvation: World Peace Foundation

Malthus's fallacy has a remarkable capacity for resisting refutation. Malthus's famous insight was that a human population can grow until it consumes more resources than a territory, or the entire planet, can sustain, and any such imbalance must be corrected either by curtailing that population's size or consumption habits, or else by calamity. This is indisputable: Malthus's genius was to formulate this in a compelling and precise manner. Unfortunately, however, the particular manner in which he chose to formulate it – the relationship between human population and food, with famine as the limiter – is historically wrong. It has been refuted by experience and by logic. The concept of gigantic inevitable famine reducing a human population to the available food is what Ulrich Beck has called a 'zombie concept': an idea that cannot be killed by normal means, and with limitless endurance keeps coming back to torment and infect the living.[1]

I open this chapter by elucidating Malthus's core ideas about famine and their contemporary recitation. I then repeat a summary version of the refutation, and examine the subsequent intellectual history of famine. I then turn to the questions: How does 'Malthus's zombie' manifest itself? Why is it so resistant to being killed off?

Malthus's Two Concepts of 'Famine'

Malthus's writings elicit strong reactions two centuries on. For our purposes, I must clarify my objection. I am *not* arguing that the human population of a country, or of the world, can increase without limit, or that our collective resource consumption can increase indefinitely, without ending in disaster. Nor do I argue that population dynamics are not a cause for political and economic concern. My argument is specifically that Malthus's *concept of famine* is erroneous, empirically and analytically, and that this leads us astray in both scholarship and policy.

I begin this argument by elucidating what Malthus means by 'famine'. In fact, his writings contain two distinct concepts which we need to disentangle.

People have experienced famines for millennia. All cultures recall them, all languages have words for them, sometimes quite complex and subtle, distinguishing between the many manifestations of acute and widespread hunger. It took a clergyman living in a country that hadn't seen famine in his lifetime to create a single unifying theory of famine. Malthus's famous tract was first published in 1798 under the title *An Essay on the Principle of Population as It Affects the Future Improvement of Society, with Remarks on the Speculations of Mr. Godwin, M. Condorcet, and Other Writers.*[2] This *Essay* is remarkable for two things: first, its pessimistic view of human nature and society – a deliberate rebuttal of the utopianism of those who lauded the French Revolution and a challenge to the Christian premise of natural abundance – and second, its author's attempt to ground this pessimism in a law of nature. Malthus's purported natural law was that population increased geometrically (in sequence 1, 2, 4, 8, 16, etc.) whereas the food production could increase only arithmetically (in sequence 1, 2, 3, 4, 5, etc.). With Newtonian simplicity, this meant that unless population growth were limited by virtuous means (in particular delayed marriage to reduce fertility), it would necessarily be checked by vicious ones, notably war, epidemic disease, or famine. Malthus concluded chapter 7 of his *Essay* with the following passage:

> Famine seems to be the last, the most dreadful resource of nature. The power of population is so superior to the power in the earth to produce subsistence for man, that premature death must in some shape or other

visit the human race. The vices of mankind are active and able ministers of depopulation. They are the precursors in the great army of destruction; and often finish the dreadful work themselves. But should they fail in this war of extermination, sickly seasons, epidemics, pestilence, and plague, advance in terrific array, and sweep off their thousands and ten thousands. Should success be still incomplete, gigantic inevitable Famine stalks in the rear, and with one mighty blow levels the population with the food of the world. (Malthus 1798: 44)

This simple, 'ideal' or canonical concept I will capitalize as 'Famine'. This is Malthus's zombie concept: mass starvation, inevitable, gigantic, that reduces population to a level commensurate with food. It must be understood not only in the context of Malthus's own (changing) writings but in those of his contemporaries as well.

Malthus's *Essay* provoked a storm,[3] achieving wider readership and fiercer debate than its author – initially anonymous – could ever have expected. Many were outraged, others impressed. Still others made the point that Malthus's ideas weren't all new, and Malthus graciously acknowledged his forerunners in his revised editions.

In terms of theory, the most significant precursor was Joseph Townsend, who also innovated in applying universal asocial laws to population and the market.[4] In a book published in 1786, Townsend encapsulated rather precisely the theory of population that later came to bear Malthus's name. Townsend tells a parable of the goats and dogs on a desert island, their numbers increasing and diminishing in line with their food.[5] For example, after visiting sailors' hunting expeditions had reduced the goats' numbers, 'all had abundance…what might have been considered as misfortunes, proved a source of comfort; and, to them at least, partial evil was universal good.'[6] We can call this *alimentary economics*: the principle whereby food availability determines population size, transferred from grazing animals and their predators to human beings. Townsend himself made the jump: 'It is the quantity of food which regulates the numbers of the human species.'[7]

In terms of political impact, the most influential of Malthus's contemporaries was the farmer, traveller and polemicist Arthur Young. Drawing on his travel diaries, Young in 1792 chronicled what he described as the excessive 'populousness' of France and the country's resulting self-destruction through an excess of misery.[8] Young described how the French urban poor responded to hikes in the price of bread by rioting and recounted the fearfulness of the landed gentry as they anticipated food price rises spreading across the country and bringing unrest. Two years after publishing his diary, Young wrote a counter-revolutionary polemic, in which he attributed the 'anarchy…revolt[,] massacre and famine' in France to the rights of man, liberty and equality in political representation.[9] He sarcastically proposed that Britain should recall its convicts transported to Australia, empty its gaols and prison hulks, and choose from the poor and property-less who could advance themselves only through crime and anarchy, in order to create a convention on the model of the French Republic.[10]

England's Poor Laws had been designed two centuries earlier to provide charity so as to keep at bay the disorderly potential of the hungry and unemployed. Parish relief provided a guaranteed safety net that meant that the poor would be fed whether they laboured or were idle. Both Townsend and Young drew the moral that the Poor Laws were self-defeating: they encouraged the poor to go forth and multiply, without needing to work for their living. Meanwhile, the cost of relief was borne by wealthier parishioners who paid local property taxes. Under the influence of Young and Malthus, among others, the Poor Laws were finally reformed in 1834. In the following decades, the controversy on English parish welfare was reprised by a debate on famine relief in Ireland and India, with similar arguments put forward to the effect that it was wise, moral and ultimately in the interests of the populace to limit or even abolish relief for the starving.

The response to Malthus's *Essay* spurred its author to research systematically the evidence for what he had so boldly asserted. Having travelled to Scandinavia, France and Switzerland, and read avidly, in 1803 Malthus published a revised version of his *Essay*.[11] He kept the same title but said that 'it may be considered as a new work.'[12] Much was added, and some passages – including that quoted above – were conspicuously cut out entirely.

Malthus's contemporaries noted – usually with scorn – his readiness to abandon ideas he had formerly championed. His more sympathetic biographers applaud his readiness to change his mind when the facts changed (or became better known). In fact, from the second edition of the *Essay* onwards, Malthus displayed a different intellectual persona. His recent biographer Robert Mayhew describes the 'Trondheim moment' when Malthus realized how the determinants of the food consumption of that Norwegian town were much too complicated to be reduced to local supply.[13] In the new version of the *Essay*, there is no reference to 'gigantic inevitable Famine', but rather to specific famines, with detailed observations on their specific and varied causes. Throughout the second to the sixth and final editions of the *Essay*, Malthus presented a different concept of famine, one grounded in the particularities of history. Or, to be more exact, the singular concept of Famine faded so far into the background as to become invisible. Never again did Malthus write about 'gigantic inevitable Famine'.

Even in the first *Essay*, the tension between the two concepts can be found. Malthus observes, for example. 'The traces of the most destructive famines in China and Indostan are by all accounts soon obliterated [by population regeneration].'[14] If famine is only a temporary setback to population growth, it logically follows that it cannot serve as the fundamental limiter. As Susan Cotts Watkins and Jane Menken confirmed almost two centuries later, historic famines have never actually served as a check on population growth in complex societies.[15] But the facts came too late: the Malthusian zombie was abroad.

Malthus's subsequent career ranged more widely in political economy. He coined two concepts that have particular significance: legitimate supply and effective demand.[16] By the former, he meant the supply of productive land that could be acquired without forcibly dispossessing its existing inhabitants. It's an important political and moral slant on the purported natural law of population and resources. The latter refers not to the hypothetical demand of an aggregation of people, but what they can actually procure for what they bring to market. Effective demand came not only to be one of the fundamental analytical tools of economics, but also a concept that explained why famines occurred in the absence of an overall food deficit. It also prefigures Karl Marx's critique that the determinant of a population's welfare is employment, not subsistence, and it provides the underpinning for Amartya Sen's 'entitlement theory' of famine.[17]

Early Incarnations of Malthus's Zombie in India and Ireland

There is no indication that Malthus himself intended his theory to serve as a pretext for withholding food relief from the starving. Indeed, his second, empirical-historical, concept of famines would provide no such justification, and his concepts of legitimate supply and effective demand would indicate that complex policies, designed with specific social and economic conditions in mind, are required. But the overall thesis of the first *Essay*, interpreted by contemporaries in the context of the day, invited political leaders to conflate the two kinds of famine and to see *actual* famines as manifestations of the purely *theoretical* 'gigantic inevitable Famine'.

In 1805, the East India Company appointed Malthus to the newly created post of professor of history and political economy at its college in Haileybury, Hertfordshire. He was the first person to hold a professorship with 'political economy' in its title. He remained there until his death. There are layers of irony to this, as the East India Company had presided over disastrous famines in Bengal in the immediately prior decades. Indeed, its own reports detailed how the calamitous collapse of the local cotton industry – a direct result of colonial economic policy – was pauperizing the populace and creating starvation.[18] British rule in India in the eighteenth and nineteenth centuries caused one of the most dramatic de-industrializations and pauperizations in history. The logic of Malthus's law – or perhaps more accurately, of Townsend's alimentary economics combined with Young's reactionary politics – was to blame the victim. The Malthusian zombie stalked colonial India, with British administrators repeatedly considering that famines posed a necessary natural corrective on overpopulation, and that famine relief was, like the English Poor Law, an encouragement to idleness and a drag on industriousness. The British supposed that the freedom from war and disease that colonial rule supposedly brought, along with policies to eliminate infanticide, removed the pre-colonial checks on population growth with the result that rapid demographic growth outstripped food supply. Possibly the Indian population did indeed grow. But there is no reason to suppose that the famines that occurred were caused by that growth.

Malthus never travelled beyond Europe, and the eminent demographer John Caldwell notes that he 'wrote little about India'.[19] Mayhew observes:

> [W]hat we know of the political-economic teaching of 'Old Pop' (as Malthus was affectionately known by his pupils' at Haileybury suggests that he mainly instructed his pupils in the ideas of Adam Smith's *Wealth of Nations*, not in his ideas about population-resource issues from the *Essay*. As such, we should not imagine regiments of Malthus's disciples filing into colonial India thanks to his direct indoctrination. If Malthus's ideas did impact upon the English colonial understanding of Indian population and resource questions, this should be seen to emanate from the general cultural circumstances of Victorian intellectual life...not the specific efforts of Malthus himself.[20]

Reviewing the wider nineteenth-century debates on Malthus's ideas, Kenneth Smith found that some influential exponents of Malthus admitted to not actually having read his *Essay* at all.[21] It is in the nature of a hegemonic idea that it captures the public imagination, without people understanding its content – or despite them appreciating that it is wrong. However, the clergyman-turned-economist owed his disciples and contemporaries the duty of at least trying to slay the zombie he had brought forth. This he did not do. Malthus taught at a time when the greatest imperial power of the day was subjugating the Indian subcontinent and inflicting famine on its inhabitants, invoking his precepts.

The East India Company appears in the history of famine as villain: directly responsible for an appalling drumbeat of famines in India, which continued even after it formally handed over the government of India to the Crown. In the 1790s, the self-enrichment of the Company's officers, at the price of the immiseration of the subcontinent, was becoming a public scandal at home. As many as 10 million reportedly died of starvation in Bengal in the 1770s, and comparable numbers in the Chalisa and northern India famines of 1782–83 and again in the Madras presidency during 1788–94. The trial of the governor-general of India, Warren Hastings, conducted by the House of Commons from 1788 to 1795, was the first and only effort to use judicial process to examine the criminal acts of a British colonial prelate. After a seven-year trial, Hastings was acquitted and the East India Company immediately began the task of rehabilitating its reputation in the court of public opinion. Malthus's 1798 *Essay* nicely shifted responsibility for these terrible episodes of starvation from the company, its officers and practices, to the Indian people themselves on account of their purported and uncivilized insult against an inexorable law of nature. Ideas have impacts. The doctrinaire application of Malthusian precepts meant that British rule in India, until the 1880s at least, was dedicated to doing the absolute minimum to prevent famine, and even thereafter famine relief was dispensed with reluctance.[22] *In extremis*, famines were welcomed as a corrective to supposed overpopulation, like the culling of Townsend's island goats.

Malthusian dogma as applied in Ireland was even more notorious. Caldwell observes that '[t]he Irish famine of 1846–7 was rarely treated as a test of Malthus's ideas' because his thesis 'was so taken for granted by the 1840s'.[23] The historian Cecil Woodham-Smith writes:

> Officially, it was declared that no deaths from starvation must be allowed to occur in Ireland, but in private the attitude was different. 'I have always felt a certain horror of political economists', said Benjamin Jowett, the celebrated Master of Balliol, 'since I heard one of them say that he feared the famine of 1848 in Ireland would not kill more than a million people, and that would scarcely be enough to do any good.' The political economist in question was Nassau Senior, one of the Government's advisors on economic affairs.[24]

Fear of a Malthusian 'gigantic inevitable Famine' turned the meeting point of demography and political economy into a justification for laissez-faire policies of allowing the free market – to be precise, market forces imposed on societies subject to imperial domination – to cause millions of famine deaths in nineteenth-century Ireland and India. It was only when the inhumanity of these policies became politically untenable, causing deep hatred and incipient rebellion abroad and disgust at home, that Her Majesty's Government began to revise its policies and institute famine relief at scale.

Subsequent Incarnations of Malthus's Zombie

Malthus's zombie is undead, routinely brought back from the grave to terrify the living. There is a straight intellectual lineage from the English clergyman to some of the most abhorrent episodes of the modern era.[25] Hitler read and invoked Malthus in support of his ideology and programme of removing the 'useless eaters' of eastern Europe. Churchill's policies that led to the 1943 Bengal famine were influenced by Malthusian alimentary economics and a racist view of Indians.

Nothing comparable has occurred since the Second World War, but we need to be alert to political crimes perpetrated using the alibi of a natural law of population. Examples include the rationalization of land grabbing and governmental protection of agro-industries based on the purported need to grow sufficient food for national populations. Anti-immigrant arguments often descend into the employment version of alimentary economics, as though there were a fixed number of jobs in an economy.

The updated variant of radical pessimism and the limits of human consumption is the fear of scarcity, both through overconsumption of non-renewable resources, and through the despoliation of the planet and anthropogenic climate change. I do not wish to challenge these. I wish to challenge the role played by the idea of 'gigantic inevitable Famine', which misdirects our attention.

A slew of influential public intellectuals, including Robert Kaplan, Jared Diamond and David Attenborough, have interpreted African crises as vindications of Malthusian precepts – in each case in opposition to the more nuanced and carefully informed views of experts on the countries concerned. Most of the crises in question – in Liberia, Rwanda and Darfur (Sudan) – are notable in that the purportedly 'Malthusian' check on population is not famine as such but rather anarchy, genocide and war. Only in the Ethiopian case is famine itself invoked, and in that case wrongly. This points us to the way in which 'Famine' has moved quietly into the background of population-resource arguments as the number of famines has declined since the 1980s:

it will be interesting to see if the recent resurgence of mass starvation re-energizes the Malthusian narrative.

While the economic theories of Malthus and his contemporaries are still dominated by the alimentary imperative,[26] today we recognize that food production is but a small part of the sustainability of human life and a small component of the impact of a society on the environment. Paul Erlich and John Holdren's 'IPAT' equation states that the impact (I) of a society on the environment is the product of population (P), affluence or consumption (A), and technology (T).[27] Affluence and consumption are concentrated in rich countries, while the frontiers of land exploitation are more often concentrated in poor ones. Nonetheless, the spectre of population growth *as such* repeatedly rises, as in Paul Erlich's 'population bomb' and Julian Cribb's 'coming famine'.[28] Increasing population – and demographic changes such as youthful populations in some nations and ageing ones in others – pose serious threats. They just don't pose a threat of famine (or 'Famine'), and invoking this spectre is both wrong and dangerous.

Fears about climate change, the natural environment and the sustainability of current patterns of resource use are entirely justified. What is not justified is to make Townsend's leap from the food supplies that constrain populations of goats and dogs on a desert island to the threat of human famine. Greedy and short-sighted mismanagement of our planetary resources may bring about catastrophe, but it won't bring gigantic and inevitable Famine.

An influential example of fine and humane reasoning that goes awry at a critical juncture is the renowned environmentalist Sir David Attenborough, in his President's Lecture at the Royal Society of Arts in 2011.[29] As Attenborough himself emphasized, he is not an economist, sociologist or politician, but an expert on animals and ecology, who approaches the question of human population growth and famine through this lens. He said:

> I am a naturalist. Being one, I do know something of the factors that keep different species of animals within bounds, and what happens when they don't. Thanks to our intelligence and our ever-increasing skills and sophisticated technologies, we can avoid such brutalities. We have medicines that prevent our children dying of disease. We have developed ways of growing increasing amounts of food. But we have removed the limiters that keep animal populations in check.

Without such natural limiters, he said, we must either control our population consensually or face famine, disease or predation, like other creatures. 'There is, alas, no third alternative of indefinite growth.' Attenborough emphasized 'the fundamental truth that Malthus proclaimed remains the truth: there cannot be more people on this earth than can be fed.'

This is Townsend's alimentary fallacy revisited. Food production is *not* the constraining factor on humanity today nor in any foreseeable scenario in which we have political economies. Managing the planet's resources in a sustainable way is vitally important – and managing agriculture and fishing are part of that global project. But if we are focused on the population–food equation, we are missing the bigger point about total human-resource use, and we risk misdirecting our concern and our energy. My concern is the way in which Attenborough invokes Malthus's prophecy and how the Malthusian notion of Famine haunts his presentation. He made the same point in a later television programme on human ecology, in which he argued that the world was 'heading for disaster unless we do something' about population.[30] 'What are all these famines in Ethiopia?' he continued. *This* is the point that I want to refute: 'these famines' happen to have disappeared in Ethiopia even while that country's population has quadrupled in size.

Why? For the simple reason that food is but a small part of the natural resource consumption of any human population. Alimentary economics holds only for animals. Food production and consumption is rarely more than 40 per cent of GDP of any country. Even the poorest people rarely devote more than 70 per cent of their effort or income to food. Traders import food; governments borrow to buy emergency stocks; people change production and consumption patterns to avoid scarcity turning into calamity. Historically, isolated agrarian communities (paradigmatically on Easter Island in the Pacific, as described by Jared Diamond[31]) may have been required at times to devote all their resources to feeding themselves, and ultimately failed to do so. It just doesn't happen in modern societies.

Important Slayings of Malthus's Zombie

One of the disturbing things about Malthus's zombie is that even those who have refuted the argument find themselves still fighting the undead idea. The key point is not whether Malthus was right or wrong – few political economists could claim to be 'right' two centuries on – but that he defined the terms of a debate that has raged ever since. In the dark centre of that debate, rarely analysed, is his concept of Famine as food shortage leading to mass starvation until enough people die to level the population with the food available. As repeatedly shown by fact and theory, famines can occur without food shortage and indeed without causing population loss at all.

The practical policy science of responding to famines was, by the second half of the nineteenth century, well ahead of the theory. The Indian Famine Codes, belatedly adopted by the British Raj in the 1880s and revised twenty years later to become more thorough and effective, contained in them an implicit theory of famine which was at odds with Malthus. The writer Lovat Fraser, in his adulatory account of the British Raj in India, cited a colonial officer's self-congratulation on abolishing 'extreme and general scarcity of food' and 'widespread death from starvation', concluding that '"Famine" now means a prolonged period of unemployment, accompanied by dear food.'[32] An exaggeration for sure, this nonetheless indicated that administrators recognized famine as an economic phenomenon not a natural-ecological one.

On the political left, anti-colonial activists and theorists repeatedly pointed to the political-economic origins of hunger and challenged those who sought to exonerate imperial and post-colonial powers. Of these, Josué de Castro was particularly influential: his book *The Geography of Hunger* could more accurately be entitled 'hunger and politics'.[33] De Castro assailed what he called the 'Malthusian scarecrow' and wrote that '[Malthus's] theory, long buried in the ruins of his frightening predictions, has lately been dug up and used to project new and still more terrifying forecasts, culminating in the prophecy of a world depopulated by famine.'[34] But, concerned to shift the focus of hunger from mass starvation to chronic under-nutrition, de Castro did not theorize famine itself.

It took Amartya Sen to bring a sensible definition of famine to the academy. As a child, he lived through the Bengal famine of 1943, and it had a formative impact on his intellectual trajectory and social conscience. Sen saw that the fisherpeople and labourers of Calcutta were starving even while food was available for the better off. The simple observation that famine is not a shortage of food per se, but the inability of some people – invariably the poorest – to obtain food was the foundation of his re-theorization of famine. Sen's critique began with clarifying a category mistake: he opened his book with the statement, 'Starvation is the characteristic of some people not *having* enough food to eat. It is not the characteristic of there *being* not enough food to eat.'[35] This was substantiated by the 'entitlement approach' to famine, which is that the ability to obtain food is the key factor in famines, rather than the availability of food as such. Sen did not, of course, claim that food shortage could never be a contributory cause of famine, but rather that the immediate cause of starvation was a 'failure of entitlements': the ability of people to exchange their labour, assets or products for sufficient food to keep them alive. Famines occurred when the 'exchange entitlement' of labour for food collapsed, which did not necessarily correspond to any food shortage, as indeed happened in Bengal in 1943.

Let me make three important asides before continuing. First, the word 'entitlement' has misled some students to think that Sen is talking about legal or moral claims to food. He is not: he did develop a political theory of the causes of famine and the mechanisms for preventing famine, but that was separate from entitlement theory. Second, following on from this, Sen's work on famine falls into two distinct parts. As well as entitlement theory, he argued (a decade later) that the driving force behind the conquest of famine in India has to be seen as the growth of political freedoms. And, third, I must resist the temptation of resorting to argument from authority and prefacing his name with 'Nobel Prize-winning'. The Nobel citation was for Sen's broader work on the multi-dimensional nature of poverty and development, not his work on famine. In fact, entitlement theory is an anomaly in Sen's overall corpus of work in so far as it is a conventionally economistic framework, ignoring other dimensions of famine. And of course winning a prize doesn't make one's arguments correct.

Those who hoped that Sen had slain Malthus's zombie were mistaken. Sen's most relentless critic, Peter Bowbrick, tirelessly and tiresomely attempted to rebut the 'failure of exchange entitlements' approach to famine, trying to show that food shortages, or at least food availability declines and disruptions, caused famines.[36] In his book *Poverty and Famines*, Sen showed empirically in three cases that famine had occurred without a decline in national-level food availability (Bengal 1943, Ethiopia 1973 and Bangladesh 1974) and that in one (Sahel 1973) there had been a food crisis as such. Many other cases confirm this point. Famines can occur during times of recession, as incomes collapse, or boom times, when food prices rise due to increasing demand, but leave poor people without the means to procure enough to feed themselves. Sen's framework has undergone revisions and sharpenings, but his fundamental reconceptualization of the nature of famine stands.[37]

Another insight long known to practitioners took an unconscionably long time to penetrate the academy: famine mortality is not equivalent to mass death by starvation. In almost all famines, and notably so in the well-documented South Asian famines of the nineteenth and twentieth centuries, the major causes of excess death were epidemics of communicable diseases, including malaria, smallpox, measles, and water-borne infections.[38] This pattern was also the case for African famines in the late twentieth century.[39] In cold-climate famines such as Russia and the Ethiopian highlands, typhus was a common famine disease. Outright starvation was relatively rare. Famine victims' *exposure* to disease was increased by migration, the collapse of public health infrastructure and, above all, the congregation of distress migrants in overcrowded and unsanitary camps and settlements. These exposure factors are primarily driven by social disruption and migration and are second-order impacts of food crisis. Famine victims' *susceptibility* to disease was heightened by malnutrition and the stresses of migration, a first-order impact of food deprivation.

There is no universal pattern of communicable disease in famines. The 'Great Leap Forward' famine in China from 1958 to 1962 was notable for the prevalence of frank starvation as a cause of death.[40]

Controversially, famines may occur without any measurable increase in mortality at all. This appears to have been the case for the Sahelian famine of 1969–73, which in almost every location passed with major impoverishment and disruption, but no rise in death rates.[41] Vernacular definitions of famine in Bangladesh also include episodes without elevated mortality,[42] and some South Asian political economists have insisted that famine is a process that is well underway even before there are any deaths from hunger.[43] These cases must be taken seriously, even if we ultimately want to exclude them from the catalogue of what we call famines. The people who experienced them defined them as events involving most of the elements that constitute famine: hunger, widespread immiseration and destruction of communities, and fear that death by starvation will follow. They are perhaps borderline or mild cases of famine, but they nonetheless point to the essential components of famine.

All of the above points us to the importance of famine as a societal phenomenon rather than only a demographic and nutritional one. Another feature of famine is that people – commonly thought of as 'victims' – still make choices. Some of those choices may seem irrational, such as a farmer feeding his cattle even while his own children are in danger, or continuing to make contributions to religious festivals even at the cost of further famishing his own family members. These choices illuminate the social complexity of famine. Even in the worst famines, only a small minority of adults die. Most will survive, and even in the worst times, they must think about their future and their needs for a livelihood and for dignity within a community. The choices that the starving are compelled to make are painful. In communities that have a history of experiencing extreme hardship, there is a cultural archive on which they can draw to validate their decisions and make them less painful.

Writers on famine document some deeply distressing social behaviours, breaking fundamental taboos. Probably the worst is cannibalism.[44] We are attracted and repulsed by these, wanting to cover our eyes but also to peep between our fingers. These things happen. There are also acts of generosity and selflessness. Most common is a sustained effort to maintain a pretence of normalcy.

Even the basic metrics of famine, such as deaths, must be seen in this societal context. What people expect of a famine and how they respond determines its gravity. In this respect, Sen's assumption that famine is defined by mass starvation must be revised to include destitution (loss of an acceptable livelihood) and social disruption (including migration, family dispersal and abandoning homes), as well as hunger and death.[45] The meanings ascribed to famine by the affected people, and the actions that they take accordingly, are part of what constitutes famine.

Famines and Feminism

At the launch of the 2015 Global Hunger Index[46] in Milan, I presented the argument that famine is man-made, adding as an aside that the gendered wording was deliberate – 'and not woman-made, as I have yet to find a single case that was created, purposely or otherwise, by a woman'. This remark generated a lot of tweets. It is true. Famines are made by adult males. This is an important insight. But after that, the story grows a little more complicated.

Generally, disasters disadvantage women relative to men. This seems to be the outcome of outright gender discrimination, the amplification of this discrimination in times of distress (and the greater the distress, the greater the increase), and the fact that women are usually poorer and less educated than men so that the socio-economic differential in victimhood maps onto gender.[47] But the story is complicated. One of the more unexpected findings from the demographic study of famine is that in many cases there is a female mortality advantage – that is, women and girls die less often than men and boys. This was noted when mortality statistics were compiled in colonial India and is reported in more recent peacetime famines in Asia and Africa.[48] In almost every population, women have longer life expectancy than men, and this differential is often exaggerated rather than reduced during famine.

The explanations for this paradox are complicated. On one hand there's biology, which favours females, and on the other hand there's socio-economic factors, which usually favour males. Evolutionary logic is on women's side: the survival of a group depends on the survival of females far more than on males because female fertility is the constraining factor in the reproduction of small populations, such as hunter-gatherers. But the fact that female-advantage gender-differentiated mortality persists in complex societies, is more of a puzzle. It is especially so because in those few populations that have a male mortality advantage in normal times, such as northern India, that advantage sometimes disappears during famine. There is a plausible biological reason for this: women are more physically resilient, resisting hunger and disease better than men. Given exactly the same nutritional and disease environment, females will consistently survive better than males. Where epidemics of infectious diseases are the major killers, women also have better chances. Adult women are most vulnerable when they are pregnant or nursing and during times of food stress, fertility rates fall, reducing this vulnerability.

Socio-economic factors work against women and girls most of the time. But there are also plausible reasons why gender divisions of knowledge and labour may sometimes advantage them during famines. For example, women typically know which wild foods to collect and how to prepare them, a skill handed down from grandmothers to granddaughters. In many agrarian societies, women are traditionally paid for their domestic or farm labour in food, and men in cash. This advantages men in good years and women in lean ones. Lastly, men's response to the stress of famine is often to migrate, either to look for work or (in pastoralist societies) to keep animals alive. Separated from their wives, sisters and mothers, these men may struggle to feed themselves. In the famine I studied in Darfur in the 1980s, by far the greatest male mortality disadvantage was found among young men and older boys who travelled long distances with sheep and camels.[49]

All the non-biological elements will vary with circumstance: in other cases, more than women and girls, men and boys may have better incomes, more salubrious surroundings and access to foodstuffs such as milk. In numerous crises, including famines, there is a clear female mortality *disadvantage*, for example with intensified discrimination against feeding infant girls when food is scarce.[50] Moreover, while most instances of forced mass starvation are targeted at men – most notably, prisoners of war – the wider impacts of armed conflict are at least as devastating to females as they are to males. The *indirect* impacts of civil wars on women and girls, measured by life expectancy across the entire population, regularly exceed those on men.[51]

Risk of dying is not the only measure of suffering in famine: impoverishment and the severing of community relations may prove to be even more significant in the longer term. In this regard, women and men experience famine differently. This was explored by Meghan

Vaughan in her insightful book on a little-known famine in colonial Nyasaland (today's Malawi) in the 1940s.[52] She writes: 'When asked about famine, women tell about family, marriage, divorce and children. In their pounding songs [sung when pounding maize] they sing about the role of husbands in the famine – either praising them for their exemplary behaviour or (much more frequently) berating them for their neglect.'[53]

The central women's experience of the famine was abandonment by their menfolk, leaving them to care for children, and the uncertain mercies of government feeding schemes. We would of course expect that, in famines in different countries at different times, the impact and experience would be different, in each case mediated by the power relations, structures and norms of that society. The stresses of famine can also bring out, with sometimes disturbing clarity, the bare bones of how a society's power relations operate, stripped of the flattering wardrobe of normality.

Over the last twenty years, there has been a growing literature on women's experience of war,[54] augmenting the better-established fields of women in development and gender and development. These analyses speak to the question of the gendered experience of famine, and to the fact that famines – like wars – are created by highly gendered power structures. Commensurately, the overall contribution of feminist scholarship and the gender lens should be to demand that the human experience of famine, in all its social complexity, be placed at the heart of what we mean by 'famine'. It is the antithesis of the depersonalized, reductionist political economic tradition that has dominated thinking about famine for far too long. It is also an integral part of the agenda of *not* blaming the victim.

In fact, the central story of the intellectual history of 'famine' over two centuries has been an effort at unpicking the poisonous legacy of Malthus's fallacy. In many respects, we have come full circle, back to where we were before the invention of 'Famine', in which we understand famines as desperate societal crises, including hunger and other forms of distress, that threaten a way of life, created by the powerful, resisted by the affected and mediated by human skills and societal structures.

4

A Short History of Modern Famines

A Tragedy in Five Acts

In this chapter, I recount the tragedy of famines over the last two centuries in a prelude and five acts, beginning with Europe's last great agrarian food crisis which struck in 1816. Then I turn to the overall data for famines from 1870 to 2010, before elaborating on the main acts of the historical drama.

- Act One is European colonialism, and its direct and indirect repercussions, in terms of famine, on every continent but most lethal in terms of sheer numbers in Asia. These were conquest famines, a part of the process whereby colonialism 'made the third world', in Mike Davis's apt phrase.[1]
- Act Two is the extended world war from 1914 to 1950 and the deliberate mass starvation it unleashed. During these terrible decades, the worst famines were in Europe and East Asia, ravaging the world's bread baskets. All warring parties used hunger as a weapon, but the most ambitious was Nazi Germany.
- Act Three is post-colonial totalitarianism and its famines, including the most terrible on record, the famine caused by Mao Zedong's Great Leap Forward – a famine that warrants its own 'catastrophic' category. This era saw fewer and more singular famines.
- Act Four is the enormous diminution in famine deaths since the 1980s, but a continuing rumble of famines and humanitarian crises in sub-Saharan Africa.

There is no single story to tell but rather several parallel stories in two clusters. The first cluster is a pattern of shape-changing famines over the century, shifting in their locations and causes. Famines ended in Europe after the Second World War and in Asia after the 1970s (excepting North Korea). In Africa they continued and in the Middle East they are returning after almost a century of absence. The underlying story is that famines caused by natural disaster and economic crisis have become rarer, so that all today's famines are caused by political decision. A second cluster of stories is the massive rise and decline in famine deaths during the extended world war and post-colonial totalitarian period. Throughout, it is important to bear in mind that the causes of *famines* and the causes of *very large-scale famine mortality* may be different, sometimes subtly, sometimes distinctly.

I will turn to the possibility of a Fifth Act in which famines return in new forms in the final chapters.

Prelude: the Year Without a Summer

In 1816, the volcano of Tomboro on the Indonesian island of Sumbawa erupted, pumping a cloud of ash into the atmosphere and causing the coldest and wettest summer on record. Residents in Massachusetts woke to frosty mornings in July and August, and European farmers complained that the rain continued without ceasing. The harvest failure was compounded by economic recession in Europe following the end of the Napoleonic wars. Hunger was widespread. Death rates increased by 9 per cent across Europe, driven in large part by epidemics of typhus and bubonic plague.

The historian John Post has described it as 'the last great subsistence crisis in the western world'.[2] Measured by mortality, it was far less severe than the famines of the early eighteenth century, let alone the catastrophes of the 'little ice age' of the mid-1600s and the devastation caused by the continent's wars, or the drumbeat of failed harvests and hunger of the Middle Ages. Its significance is that it was an exemplar of an age-old pattern of widespread crop failure causing widespread hunger in an overwhelmingly agrarian society. Europe has seen adverse weather and economic recession since then. It has also experienced mass starvation. But 1816 was the last occasion on which natural calamity impacting on food supply caused a food crisis that killed large numbers of people.

The Tomboro ash cloud reminds us of the possibility of an unforeseen calamity that massively disrupts global food supplies. Short-term global cooling driven by a volcanic ash cloud can happen again. So could a nuclear winter. Or crop diseases, human pandemics that so disrupt global trade that it becomes hard to move goods from one part of the world to another, or indeed the many possible climatic anomalies caused by global warming. But the world has been transformed over the last two centuries. Two hundred years ago, exceptional governmental action would have been needed to stop a natural calamity causing a famine. As state capacity grows, acts of omission – failures to intervene in markets or provide relief – could allow food crises to threaten famine. Today, acts of commission – political decisions – are needed to turn a disaster into mass starvation.

Numbers

The systematic and comparative study of historical famines is complicated by many definitional and methodological difficulties. These problems loom so large that the kind of quantitative rigour beloved of political science faculties in American universities is simply not possible. There is no consistent method for estimating famine deaths across different time periods. This has deterred scholars from attempting the exercise. But it is worth trying because the exercise reveals a compelling story. Certainly, historians and demographers will question every figure, and the precision of some of the estimates should not be taken for an illusory accuracy. The point of the exercise is not statistical rigour but rather narrative trajectory.

In this section, I present the results of an exercise in tabulating every major famine and mass starvation from 1870 to 2010. It is not a definitive catalogue but it is good enough for our purposes. The choice of 1870 as the start date was inevitably arbitrary but was aimed at a point in time at which the evidence basis for famines was improving, but sufficiently far back into the nineteenth century that the dataset will include a significant number of famines from the imperial era.

For comparative purposes, I chose to use a common-sense English definition whereby a famine is defined as a crisis of mass hunger that causes elevated mortality over a specific period of time. In this definition, 'elevated mortality' includes anyone who died, of any causes, above the baseline: it includes deaths from communicable diseases (often the single biggest cause of death), exposure and exhaustion, and in some instances, violence as well. Including all these deaths can be justified because famine is not just an aggregate of individual cases of starvation: it is a far-reaching social disruption that involves epidemics of infectious diseases, movements of desperate people, crime and an array of other social disorders. Including all causes of death is also sometimes a practical necessity because there is rarely a list of those who died from hunger, separate from those who died from disease, exposure or exhaustion. Indeed, when a malnourished child dies from diarrhoea, it is impossible to say whether that child's death should be attributed to hunger or the waterborne pathogen that made him fatally sick. But this doesn't mean that the list should include episodes of elevated mortality in which hunger was not a major causal factor. So, the influenza pandemic of 1919 was not in any sense a famine, though people may have gone hungry as a result. There are some borderline cases, which I will revisit later.

The list includes both instances conventionally regarded as 'famine' and cases of forced mass starvation. I use Stephen Devereux's classification of 'great famines' (100,000 or more excess deaths) and 'calamitous famines' (one million or more excess deaths),[3] and extend it to episodes of forcible mass starvation. I exclude famines that killed fewer than 100,000 people because of the difficulties of reliably identifying these episodes from earlier decades. The list is defined by magnitude not severity, meaning that terrible but localized instances of starvation are excluded. Among these missing cases are internment camps in South Africa and Libya, the genocide of the Herero and many famines among pastoralist populations – far-flung but small in number.

There are enormous methodological issues with the estimation of excess mortality (the number of deaths above the normal for that population). Generally speaking, better demographic calculations lead to lower estimations of excess deaths than those provided by journalists, aid workers and other contemporary observers. Examples of the inflation of mortality figures abound, especially in the media and policy arena. A schematic example is that an aid worker estimates that between 255,000 and 505,000 people will go hungry. This becomes a prediction that 'more than 500,000' will starve, and soon a figure of 'over half a million dead' becomes the standard. No one wants to be that person who minimizes the suffering, and it seems indecent to cite anything lower than the most recently cited number. Aid agencies are desperate to generate funds. Also, foreign visitors to famine zones are taken to see the camps for the displaced and to the therapeutic feeding centres where the most severely malnourished children are found. These 'disaster tourists' are told by their aid worker guides that 'these are the lucky ones' and come away with an exaggerated sense of the gravity of the crisis – and an inflated sense of the importance of foreign aid.[4]

Closer demographic study of famines usually leads to lower estimates for deaths. A recent and controversial example is the reduced numbers for famine mortality in North Korea in the 1990s. Initial estimates were approximately three million, and they were subsequently reduced to somewhere between 240,000 and 600,000.[5] We might therefore reasonably expect a large upward bias in the figures widely used for earlier famines on the record. For this study, we have used the lowest credible figure in the record. But there are also major gaps: famines without any figures at all. This is particularly a problem for the earlier decades and during the Second World War. In the absence of any well-sourced figures for starvation among the civilian populations of Poland and Burma, these cases are simply left out. For many famines, there are neither population records nor survey estimates, and we have to use the numbers produced by contemporary observers. Our catalogue of famines includes many in Africa and the Middle East in which the death toll is in the low hundreds of thousands, but none in China with a toll lower than a million. It is very likely that famines of this lower magnitude occurred frequently in China in the late nineteenth and early twentieth centuries but simply have not been sufficiently recorded or studied to make the archive. For this reason, before the 1950s, the number of famine incidents recorded must be regarded with special caution.

Other methodological challenges arise with episodes of mass intentional starvation, such as the Armenian genocide and the Nazi mass starvation of prisoners of war. In so far as starvation is an action perpetrated by some people on others, like persecution, it does not require that the victim die of hunger to be counted. Also, as a simple evidentiary matter, deaths from exposure due to the intolerable living conditions of prisoner-of-war camps, or from exhaustion due to overwork, cannot be separated from deaths due to hunger and disease, so they are automatically included in an overall toll. Some of these deaths were also mass executions, or were associated with physical brutality including torture: it is a moot question as to whether these should also be included. In practice, the impossibility of ascertaining numbers of deaths attributable to different causes means that they are included, but the theoretical issue remains.

Another issue of the comparability of historic and modern-day famines arises because contemporary definitions of famine provide thresholds for nutrition and mortality that correspond with normal or near-normal conditions in many historic societies. In line with this, Cormac Ó Gráda makes the point that nutritional and mortality levels that were commonplace in Europe two centuries ago would be defined as humanitarian emergencies today.[6]

A related problem is the difficulty of estimating baseline mortality. Figures for normal mortality levels are simply unavailable for most famine-stricken societies, so that estimates of excess deaths are derived from reports of depopulation and starvation, sometimes extrapolated on a questionable basis, rather than analysis of population data. There's also the problem of how to separate out famines – distinct and time-limited events – from cases of longer-term deterioration in the health of a population, and consequently higher death rates. For example, there is good reason to suppose that when civil wars began in Ethiopia in the mid-1970s and southern Sudan in the early 1980s, there were decades-long increases in general death rates, distinct from severe outbreaks of famine. If all the deaths above the pre-war baseline were measured, the excess mortality would quickly add up to millions, mounting higher with every passing year. There is only one case in which such an exercise has been attempted, which is the Democratic Republic of Congo after 1998, where Les Roberts and colleagues from the International Rescue Committee (IRC) undertook repeated surveys with this in mind.[7] The IRC surveys resulted in extraordinarily high estimates of increased mortality since the outbreak of the war, amounting to more than five million deaths by 2007. These figures have been challenged[8] and there is no consensus as to what a credible figure would be. Additionally, for our purposes here, it is difficult to know how to use these numbers in a study of famine and starvation. What we really need is a more detailed account of the numerous local food crises and episodes of forced starvation that occurred.[9]

Figures for reduced births are not included in measures of the severity of famines. Famines typically cause as many delayed or cancelled births as excess deaths – an issue of interest to demographers, though not of much concern to humanitarians. Neither is migration included, although the single biggest demographic and social impact of famine is usually irreversible mass migration,[10] including accelerated urbanization.

The Big Picture

On this basis, I combined a catalogue of great and calamitous famines, including episodes of forcible mass starvation, since 1870 containing 58 entries (with the Hunger Plan subdivided into four episodes, making an overall total of 61). These famines killed at least 104 million people (see Tables 4.1–4.5 below and the World Peace Foundation website[11]). Here, I will summarize the main trends over time, the geography and the causes, to derive a schematic history. The big picture is presented in Figures 4.1 and 4.2. There are two clear trends. The main trend in numbers who die is downwards. Famines killed between three million

Table 4.1   Distribution of great, calamitous and catastrophic famines

	1870–1914	1915–50	1951–85	1986–2010	
	Total deaths	Total deaths	Total deaths	Total deaths	Total deaths
Catastrophic			25.0		25.0
Calamitous	29.50	38.13	2.71	0	70.34
Great	2.00	3.82	1.87	1.42	9.11
Total	31.50	41.95	29.58	1.42	103.45

Death totals in millions. The 'Hunger Plan' episodes are treated as a single calamitous famine in this table.
Source: World Peace Foundation

and 25 million each decade from the 1870s to the 1970s, at an average of just over one million per year. The last calamitous famine (over one million dead) was Cambodia in 1975–79. Since 1980, the annual death toll in great famines has averaged 53,000, about 5 per cent of the historic level. The downward trend is uneven: it is very jagged indeed. It might be more accurate to say that there is a historic shift in about 1980 between regular famines, which kill millions, and no such famines. Were it not for the catastrophic famine of 1958–62 in China, the downward trend would have been evident fifteen years earlier.

But the number of episodes of famine has not declined in the same way. To be precise, there was a one-off decline following the end of the Second World War, since when the number of famines has fluctuated between two and five per decade. If we combine these two trends, we see how calamitous famines have been eliminated, and great famines have nonetheless continued.

The geography of modern famine is overwhelmingly a story of Asia and eastern Europe, which account for 87 per cent of famine deaths in the period (see Figure 4.3). Approximately half of these (56.5 million) were in East and South-East Asia: mostly China but also Vietnam, Indonesia and Cambodia. South Asia accounted for a further 16.6 million. Europe, including the USSR, accounted for 18 million.

African famine deaths during the entire period are estimated at 9 per cent of the total, 9.5 million, most of them in the late nineteenth century, in Congo and north-east Africa.[12] Latin America counted about 1.5 million famine deaths, all of them in Brazil in the nineteenth century. The Middle East has an estimated two million deaths, most associated with the First World War and the Armenian genocide.

Table 4.2 Catalogue of great and calamitous famines and forced mass starvation, 1870–1914

Date	Place	Cause	Deaths	Source
1870–1	Persia	Economic crisis, drought	500,000–1.5 m	Foran 1989; Okazaki 1986.
1876–1879	China (Shanxi, Henan, Shandong, Zhili, and Shaanxi)	Drought, lack of state capacity due to rebellion and colonialism	9 m	Edgerton-Tarpley 2008; Fuller 2015; Davis 2002; Li 2007.
1876–9	India	Drought, colonialism	6 m	Davis 2002
1876–9	Brazil	Drought, economic crisis	500,000	Cunniff 1970
1885–99	Congo	Colonialism, forced labor	3 m	Hochschild 1998; Acherson 1999 (1963).
1888–9	India (Ganjam)	Drought, colonialism	150,000	Dyson 1989
1888–92	Ethiopia	Drought, war, rinderpest	1 m	Pankhurst 1968
1888–92	Sudan	Drought, war	2 m	De Waal 1989
1891–2	Russia	Drought, economic crisis	275,000	Robbins 1970
1896–7	India	Drought, colonialism	5.5 m	Dyson 1989
1897–1901	China	Drought, economic crisis, colonial warfare, internal rebellion	1 m	Li 2007; Esherick 1987; Cohen 1997
1896–1900	Brazil	Drought, economic crisis	1 m	Smith 1946
1899–1901	India	Drought, colonialism	1 m	Dyson 1989
1905–7	Tanganyika	Repression of rebellion	200,000	Iliffe 1979
1906–7	India	Drought, colonialism	250,000	Dyson 1989
1913–14	Sahel	Drought, colonial conquest	125,000	Schove 1977

Note: I note that a famine (caused by drought, floods and economic crisis) in Anhui and Jiangsu provinces of China is reported to have resulted in the deaths of 24 million people in 1907 (Kte'pi 2011) but was unable to find any other sources to corroborate this. Consequently, I have not included this in the famine data.

Table 4.3 Catalogue of great and calamitous famines and forced mass starvation, 1915–50

Date	Place	Cause	Deaths	Source
1914–16	East Africa	War	300,000	Paice 2007
1915–18	Greater Syria (including Lebanon)	War, blockade, locusts	350,000	Schilcher 1992: 229; Antonius 1946: 241; Fawaz 2014
1915–16	Turkey (Armenians)	Genocide, forced deportation	400,000	Morgenthau 1918; Gilbert 1994; Suny 2015; Kévorkian 2011
1917–19	Germany	Blockade	763,000	Vincent 1985
1917–19	Persia	War, drought	455,200	Afkhami 2003
1919	Armenia	Post-conflict	200,000	Hovannisian 1971: 130
1920–1	China (Henan, Shaanxi, Shandong, Shanxi, Zhili (Hebei))	Drought, economic crisis	500,000	Mallory 1926, Fuller 2013; Edwards 1922; Li 2007
1921–2	Russia	Civil war	1 m–10 m (5 m official)	Lowe 2002; Patenaude 2002: 196–8
1928–30	China (NW – Gansu, Shaanxi, Shanxi, Henan, Shandong and Zhili (Hebei))	Drought, war between Chiang Kai Shek and warlords	5.5 m–10 m	Li 2007: 304; Fuller 2015
1929–30	China (Hunan)	Drought, war	2 m	Devereux 2000; Becker 1996; Ó Gráda 2009
1932–4	USSR (Ukraine)	Collectivization, collective punishment	3.3 m	Snyder 2012; Graziosi 2009

continued

Table 4.3 Catalogue of great and calamitous famines and forced mass starvation, 1915–50—cont'd

Date	Place	Cause	Deaths	Source
1932–3	USSR (Russia, Kazakhstan)	Collectivization	1.5 m	Snyder 2012
1934, 1936–7	China (Sichuan)	War, economic crisis	5 m	Ó Gráda 2008; Wright 2000
1941–4	Hunger Plan*			
	Germany/USSR	Starvation of Russian POWs by the Wehrmacht	2.6 m	Snyder 2012
	Germany/USSR	Siege of Leningrad	1 m	Snyder 2012; Collingham 2012
	Germany/USSR	Deaths of Soviet Citizens due to starvation in the USSR, including those killed in the occupation of Kiev and Kharkiv	1 m	Snyder 2012
	Poland	Death of residents of the Warsaw Ghetto from starvation	83,000	United States Holocaust Memorial Museum nd.

1941–50	Germany/USSR	Death of German POWs in Soviet captivity	1.1 m	Collingham 2012
1941–2	Greece	Blockade	300,000	Mazower 1993
1942–3	China (Henan)	War	1.5 m	Muscolino 2015; Garnaut 2013
1941–5	East Asia (various locations)	Japanese soldiers who died of malnutrition and starvation	1.044 m	Collingham 2012
1942–5	Indonesia	Japanese occupation	2.4 m	Van der Eng 2008
1943	India (Bengal)	Government wartime policy	2.1 m	Dyson and Maharatna 1991
1943–4	Rwanda	Drought	300,000	Devereux 2000
1944–5	Vietnam	Japanese occupation	2 m	Dung 1995; Gunn 2011
1945–7	Eastern Europe	Reprisals against Germans	250,000	Lowe 2012
1947	USSR (Moldova and other areas)	Food shortage and policy	600,000–1.5 m	Ganson 2009; Ó Gráda 2015: 12–13

* The 'Hunger Plan' includes all episodes of mass starvation associated with the Eastern Front 1941–45, including the starvation of Jews. The total numbers who died of starvation on account of the Hunger Plan and the Final Solution is undoubtedly well in excess of the total in these lines. Starvation deaths in the Warsaw Ghetto are included because it is classified within the Hunger Plan

Table 4.4 Catalogue of great, calamitous and catastrophic famines and forced mass starvation, 1950–85

Date	Place	Cause	Deaths	Source
1958	Ethiopia	Drought	100,000	Wolde Mariam 1986
1958–62	China	Government policies	18.5–32 m	Ashton et al. 1984; Peng 1987; Ó Gráda 2015: 159
1969–70	Nigeria	War/blockade	500,000	Leitenberg 2006
1972–3	India (Maharashtra)	Drought	130,000	Dyson 1991a
1973	Ethiopia	Drought	200,000	Wolde Mariam 1986
1974	Bangladesh	Flood, cyclones, economic crisis	1.5 m	Alamgir 1980
1975–8	East Timor	Conflict	104,000	Van Klinken 2012
1975–9	Cambodia	Year Zero	1.21 m	Kiernan 2008; DeFalco 2014
1983–5	Ethiopia	War, drought	600,000	Africa Watch 1991
1984–5	Sudan (Darfur, Kordofan, Red Sea)	Drought, economic crisis	240,000	de Waal 1989

Table 4.5 Catalogue of great famines and forced mass starvation, 1986–2011

Date	Place	Cause	Deaths	Source
1988	Sudan (South)	War	100,000	Burr 1998
1992–3	Somalia	War	220,000	Hansch et al. 1994
1991–9	Iraq	Sanctions, war and dictatorship	166,000–300,000	Garfield 1999a; Ali and Shah 2000
1995–7	North Korea	Food shortage and government policy	240,000–600,000	Goodkind et al. 2011; Spoorenberg and Schwekendiek 2012
1998–2002	Democratic Republic of Congo	War	290,300–5.4 million	Roberts et al. 2001, 2003; Coghlan et al. 2006, 2007
1998–9	Sudan (South)	War	100,000	Medley 2010; Burr. 1998
2003–5	Sudan (Darfur)	War	200,000	Government Accountability Office 2006
2003–6	Uganda	War	100,000	Mazurana et al. 2014
2010–11	Somalia	War, drought and policy	244,000	Checchi and Robinson 2013

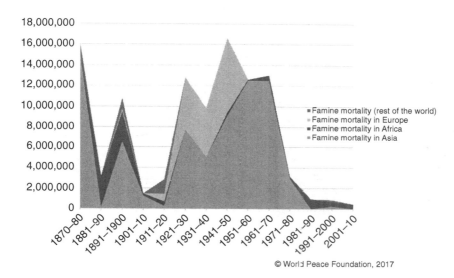

Figure 4.1 Mortality in great and calamitous famines by continent and decade, 1870–2010
Source: World Peace Foundation

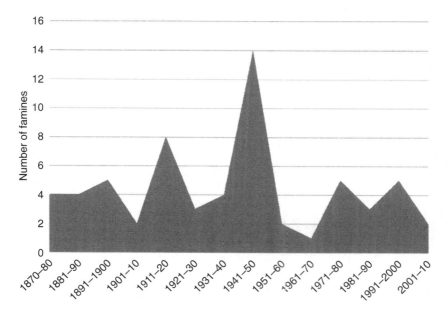

Figure 4.2 Numbers of famines per decade, 1870–2010
Source: World Peace Foundation. Note that each famine incident is attributed to the decade in which it began, and the pre-1950 figures are believed to be underestimates

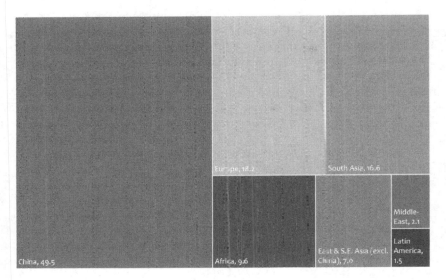

Figure 4.3 Geographical distribution of famine mortality, 1870–2010
Source: World Peace Foundation

The vast majority of famine deaths were associated with conflict or political repression: 35 million occurred in wartime, with a further 1.7 million in countries emerging from armed conflict; 42 million deaths occurred in famines under active political repression, such as repressive colonial rule or dictatorship. A smaller number, 25 million deaths, was associated with neither.

Act One: Imperial Holocausts to 1914

The Age of Empire was the age of famine. Our famine database begins in 1870 for inescapable methodological reasons – there simply aren't good enough data for famine deaths before then. But imperial conquests have created starvation throughout history,[13] and the famines of the 1870–1914 period were a continuation of what had gone before.

Colonial-settler genocide famines in North America and Australia deserve a special place in the history of atrocities. The use of hunger to subjugate the indigenous peoples of the Americas is rarely included in catalogues of famine. One reason why these episodes are missing is that those genocidal acts are themselves obscured, hidden by justificatory narratives that attribute too much of the catastrophic destruction of these peoples to purportedly 'natural causes' like disease and ecological crisis, and overlook the policies and practices of colonial governments and settlers. The total impact was astonishing. Four centuries of colonial conquest and settlement reduced many Native American populations by more than 90 per cent.[14]

The causes of this hemispheric calamity varied from deliberate annihilation to the by-products of disease transmission and destruction of the environment. In many cases, policies that destroyed populations were continued even when their outcomes were known. Genocide was perpetrated through killing (during wars or massacres), slave labour, internment, deportation, destruction of livelihoods, spread of disease (often with intent) and forcible assimilation, including taking children away from families. Of these, intentional withholding or restricting access to food occurred during slave labour, deportation and internment. Seizing land caused famines. Native populations were often worked to death, unlike people brought from Africa as slaves, who were valued for their work. The native population was often treated as disposable, cheaper to kill or let die off than to care for. During deportations, as, for instance the 'trail of tears' (Cherokee, 1835–40) or 'the long walk' (Dine or Navajo, 1864), starvation was cited as a cause of death. Food was also withheld in some internments until Native American communities relented to signing away land rights. In 1877, the Lakota were starved until they agreed to transfer ownership of the Black Hills to the United States.

The Australian experience was, if anything, even worse. The indigenous population of Tasmania was eradicated entirely.[15] In New Zealand, the imperial adventurer Commandant George Hamilton-Browne wrote of the Maoris' celebration of their honourable warrior traditions, adding sardonically that, 'Civilised white men, however, use hunger and thirst as two of their most formidable weapons.'[16] The sheer comprehensiveness of the policies of conquest and subjugation, over such prolonged periods of time, creates a challenge to thinking of these episodes as famines. But once we integrate our study of famine and mass atrocity, it is straightforward to see atrocious man-made famines in North America and Australasia.

Europe's colonial encounter with Asia was a different kind of calamity. The imperialists' main goals weren't land or labour: they were looting the world's richest civilizations and forcibly dragging them into imperial markets. In 1700, on the eve of the European imperial assault, India and China between them produced almost 50 per cent of global GDP. Britain, France and Germany between them produced 12 per cent. By 1820, India's share had collapsed – 'the most rapid and cataclysmic deindustrialization ever'.[17] Fifty years later, China's share had collapsed too. In 1913, Britain, France and Germany's share was 22 per cent; India and China's was 16 per cent (see Figure 4.4). The long nineteenth century was an enormous wealth grab by well-armed Atlantic maritime powers at the expense of the historic centres of world civilization and prosperity. Empire is often no more than glorified robbery – as was the case for the Spanish in the Americas and the Portuguese in the Indian Ocean in the sixteenth century – but in the case of Anglo-Saxon imperialism, the proceeds of the crime were used, in part, as the fuel for the Industrial Revolution and its unprecedented economic growth. The belle époque was an era in which the concentration of wealth among the European elite had no precedent, and it followed what Sven Beckert calls the 'war capitalism' of the age of imperial globalization.[18] Today, Asia has become the world's industrial engine room, and the intercontinental distribution of global GDP is (more or less) returning to the relatively equitable pattern it had prior to the onset of Europe's spree of looting and piracy in the fifteenth century. But, in the nineteenth century, Asians rarely benefited and their continent was repeatedly ravaged by famines. This is illustrated in Figure 4.4.[19]

Some of the worst imperial famines struck India in the 1770s and 1780s, killing millions – possibly tens of millions – in Madras and

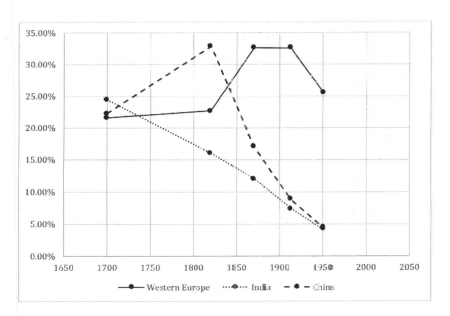

Figure 4.4 Economies of Western Europe, China and India as a proportion of world GDP, 1700–1950

Bengal. In the 1860s and 1870s, there was another series of calamitous famines, in part caused by the forcible incorporation of peasant economies into the imperial market. China became 'the land of famine'[20] from the mid-nineteenth century onward. Though not directly colonized, China felt the impact of the imperial powers' mercenary armies and trade policies. The dismantling of the economic infrastructure of the biggest Asian countries, and the reorientation of those economies, at the point of a gun, to serve the demands of manufacturers and traders half a world away, was the cause of tens of millions of deaths through hunger and disease.

Europe's most terrible famine of the Victorian era was the Irish potato famine of the 1840s. The cruel inequities of English rule and the callous indifference to the plight of the people, even in the depths of misery and helplessness, and the self-serving justifications for this systemic inhumanity, have rightly condemned the instigators of this famine. In its aftermath, Irish nationalists were quick to identify the aspects of their experience in common with other peoples subject to the British imperial yoke, notably in India, and to campaign to make famine a scandal that refuted any pretensions to a 'civilizing mission'. And they were right to do so: famine in India, as in Ireland, was the product of imperial conquest and rule, and a profound illustration of its illegitimacy.

Describing the devastation of the third quarter of the nineteenth century, Mike Davis coined the phrase 'late Victorian Holocausts'.[21] His book describes how the combination of the El Niño climatic anomaly, the economic turmoil built into the functioning of international commodity markets and violent conquest unleashed a series of famines in China and India.

Table 4.1 is a catalogue of famines and episodes of forced mass starvation during the height of the imperial era. It includes only 'great' and 'calamitous' famines, using the lowest credible mortality estimate, and therefore does not include important starvations such as the Herero genocide which did not reach that threshold.

The imperial-era holocausts in India and China started a century before the 1870s and ranged beyond those two countries. And the role of war – especially wars of conquest – in famine is surprisingly neglected in the literature. Much of the writing about famines takes them out of their political-economic and military context. An example is the northern Chinese famine of 1876–9. As part of the research for this book, I asked my research assistant Aditya Sarkar to document this episode.[22]

Imperial China had a long history of famines and disasters, but the north China famine of 1876–9 was its most lethal. Drought struck

China's five large northern provinces in 1376 and, by the time the rains returned, an estimated 9–13 million people had died of starvation or famine-related diseases.[23] A number of scholars have written about this, but they only seemed to refer to conflict in passing,[24] and it seemed, initially, that state incapacity was the primary reason hampering famine relief.[25]

When Sarkar presented the research in London, a member of the audience challenged his findings and argued that there was active armed conflict in China at that time. Returning to the library, Sarkar found that our initial research had not fully captured the political-military context of the famine. The famine had been preceded by periods of colonial conflict with Japan, Britain and Russia. Further, China's north-western frontier had suffered conflict: the region now known as the Xinjiang-Uighur Autonomous Region had been occupied by Russia in 1871 and then had been the centre of localized revolts. The perception of colonial threat and conflict led the Qing Court to allocate scarce resources to the construction of coastal defences rather than famine relief and, although this changed as the famine worsened, the damage was done. These added to the difficulties of coordinating famine relief and transporting the available grain.[26]

Davis's 'late Victorian Holocausts' also ranged beyond Asia. Davis describes the famines in Brazil. This is one of the few occasions in which Latin America figures in international accounts of famine. Scholars and activists from the region are more concerned with structural deprivation and chronic hunger than famine as such.[27] There were holocausts in Africa, too, both the direct outcome of the scramble for Africa and its repercussions into countries that successfully kept the conquistadors at bay, such as Ethiopia and (briefly) Sudan. Of these cataclysms, the most notorious was the Congo under King Leopold, which included many episodes of forced mass starvation and recurrent famine. Estimates for numbers of deaths during Leopold's rule are notoriously elusive, and writers on the topic, from Roger Casement and E. D. Morel to Neal Acherson and Adam Hochschild, provide figures that range from 3 million to 15 million. Causes of death are also difficult to disentangle. Acherson writes:

> I suggest that it is impossible to separate deaths caused by massacre and starvation from those due to the pandemic of sleeping sickness (trypanosomiasis) which decimated central Africa at the time. As Hochschild says, these causes are closely related. The gigantic disruption of African rural society brought about by forced labour, punitive raiding to enforce wild rubber quotas, the destruction of villages

and the abandonment of crops left a starving and often homeless population.[28]

A parallel story can be told for Sudan and its immediate neighbours, with the important differences that the mid-nineteenth century devastation was organized by Egyptians, in a hybrid version of colonialism, and that it provoked a nationalist-millenarian reaction in the form of Sudanese Mahdism. The revolutionary Mahdist army expelled the Egyptians and their multinational mercenaries (most famously the British General Charles Gordon) in 1885 and set up an Islamic state, which ruled Sudan for the following thirteen years. During this period, Sudan suffered a terrible famine, caused by (among other things) cattle disease, drought, war, forced relocation of people and onerous taxation. The ravages extended across central Africa as far as Nigeria, leaving huge areas underpopulated to this day. Ethiopia, still independent though threatened by colonial powers, also suffered its worst-recorded famine at this time, known in popular parlance as *kifu qen*: 'cruel days'. The rinderpest epidemic that destroyed the country's cattle (and went on to do the same in Kenya and other countries), drought and the requirements of fighting a war for national survival, contributed to famine. Just because the population was hungry and desperate, the affairs of state could not be put on hold. As the previous Emperor Tewodros pithily said, 'soldiers eat, peasants provide.'

This crescendo of calamity culminated with the Indian and Chinese famines of 1899–1901, each of which killed a million people. There was then a lull: relatively few famines between 1901 and the First World War. Asia had just the one: the 1906–7 famine in India that killed 250,000 – a small number compared to the routine tolls of millions of previous decades. Does this show that colonial rule by this time was consolidated and less oppressive? Or that the globalization of world trade and associated economic growth were bringing real benefits to the global poor? Or that the Indian Famine Codes, updated after the 1901 disasters, were finally achieving their stated goals? We should be cautious. Famine is by its nature episodic: each occurrence requires either a dedicated architect or a combination of adverse circumstances, and it is hard to draw conclusions from a decade and a half that escaped major ravages.

Several exceptions in Africa remind us to be cautious. During the Anglo-Boer war of 1900–2, British generals invented the concentration camp to house people forced off their land through scorched earth tactics. Of 115,000 Boer civilians in the camps, 28,000 perished of hunger and disease; of 100,000 black South Africans, between 14,000 and 20,000 died. The 1904 genocide of the Herero by the colonial governor of German South-West Africa is a paradigmatic case of an imperial genocide famine. In response to an uprising against colonial rule, the German army destroyed the crops, livestock and livelihoods of the Herero people and forced them into the wilderness to starve. At least 40,000 died, and a further 10,000 Nama subjected to a similar mass starvation. The suppression of the Maji Maji uprising in Tanganyika two years later killed larger numbers, albeit in a less graphic fashion. And the drought of 1913 across Sahelian Africa, from Senegal to Sudan, caused widespread famine. In Darfur seventy years later, it was still remembered as the point of historic reference for a 'famine that kills'.

The Herero case, when it is remembered at all, is usually told as a precursor to the Nazi atrocities four decades later. In the context of the era, however, it is better seen as a particularly rigorous execution of a general colonial policy. In his handbook for 'small wars', Colonel Sir Charles Callwell advised his fellow officers:

> But when there is no king to conquer, no capital to seize, no organized army to overthrow, and when there are no celebrated strongholds to capture, and no great centres of population to occupy, the objective is not so easy to select. It is then that the regular troops are forced to resort to cattle-lifting [stealing] and village burning and that the war assumes an aspect that may shock the humanitarian.[2*]

A minor theme in this period is the subsistence crises in Europe, brought on by bad weather and the localized despotisms associated with feudalism. Two notable cases in the historical record were in Finland in 1868 and Russia in 1891.

Act Two: the Extended World War, 1915–50

The world wars and the interwar period saw the worst famines and forced mass starvation of the modern era. In these decades, more people died from hunger than from direct violence.

The First World War did not begin with wars of starvation, but several followed. The historical records of famine are unreliable: the researcher frequently finds passing reference to a disaster costing tens of thousands of lives, and very often the causes of mass death are mentioned only vaguely. The war in the Levant and the destruction of the Ottoman Empire, compounded by Allied blockade and locust infestation, led to famine and forcible mass starvation. In Greater Syria, perhaps 350,000 died, and comparable numbers in

Persia. Starvation and associated diseases were major killers in the Armenian genocide of 1915–16: of the one million victims, at least 400,000 perished this way. The Armenians' suffering did not end there: the newly independent Armenian state was stricken by famine in 1919.

Victory in the war was, arguably, decided by the relative speed with which Britain and Germany could starve the other into submission. Germany's unrestricted submarine warfare against merchant shipping was intended to bring Britain to the point at which it could no longer continue the war effort, unable to sustain industrial production while also feeding its people. It nearly succeeded. The British blockade of Germany was less destructive in terms of ships sunk and sailors drowned (the Royal Navy impounded the ships and confiscated their cargoes instead of torpedoing them), but had the same ultimate intent, and succeeded. The winter of 1916–17 became known as the 'turnip winter' in Germany as people turned to eating crops normally used for livestock feed. As many as three-quarters of a million Germans died from the effects of malnutrition, many of them *after* the 1918 Armistice as the British maintained the blockade for a further six months to force Germany to sign the peace agreement. One lesson that the Nazi leadership later took from this was that Germany needed to be self-sufficient in food if it were to prevail in a future war: they attributed the 1918 defeat to hunger and resulting discontent, not the losses of battle.

During the following three decades, the history of famines is the story of exceptionally destructive civil wars (Russia and China especially), of wars of annihilation (notably the Eastern Front in the Second World War), and of totalitarianism (notably in the USSR). The geographic span of these famines was chiefly Eurasia and East and South-East Asia and they include the largest episodes by far of forcible mass starvation – famine as genocide.

The Russian civil war of 1921–2, along with communist attempts to collectivize agriculture, caused a wide-ranging famine. Mortality estimates ranged from one million to ten million; the officially recognized death toll was five million. It is now famous chiefly for the American relief efforts organized by President Herbert Hoover.

A decade later, Stalin's collectivization of peasant farming and repression caused a famine in Ukraine, adjoining parts of southern Russia, notably the Kuban region of the north Caucasus in the Russian Federation, where Ukrainians predominated, and Kazakhstan. A second and even more terrible phase of the famine was concentrated in Ukraine. The lowest credible estimates are 4.8 million fatalities, two-thirds of them in Ukraine.

During the Second World War, deaths from starvation and related causes almost certainly exceeded combat deaths: at least 20 million succumbed to hunger, exposure and related diseases.[30] The worst of the starvation was on the Eastern Front. The Nazi Hunger Plan aimed at eliminating 30 million people, as both an objective of the German occupation and an instrument of war and genocide. Impossible to implement as envisaged, the Hunger Plan nonetheless led to millions of deaths. During the siege of Leningrad, about a million people died of hunger. Starvation in the German-occupied cities of Kiev and Kharkov was comparably severe: hundreds of thousands perished in each. Millions of Soviet prisoners of war were deprived of food, shelter, warmth and sanitation, and nearly 60 per cent of them died; after the war, Stalin reciprocated and a million German prisoners of war were worked to death. Three million Poles perished during the war. The chaos of the German occupation of Greece, combined with an Allied blockade, contributed to a famine that cost 100,000 lives in 1941–2, and an estimated 250,000 during the course of the war which is remembered in Britain for being the foundational cause of the Oxford Committee for Famine Relief (Oxfam). Behind the Soviet lines, food rations were so low that there are numerous reports of people dying of starvation in unheated apartments, on shifts in factories, or in the streets.

One of the most striking things about the European famines of this era is that their epicentre was Ukraine and south-west Russia. This area has the most famously rich soils of Eurasia – the 'black earth' – and was perhaps the most productive agricultural area in the world. It was the source of riches. My own family, the Ephrussis, made their fortune shipping grain from Odessa on the Black Sea to feed Europe: the family emblem was intertwined ears of wheat. The surplus was the foundation of land empires. That was its curse: the wheat fields were coveted by rulers from both east and west. Russia imported most of its grain from Ukraine, and – in Snyder's words – the Nazis sought to transform it into 'an exterminatory agrarian colony' to feed their armies and their fatherland.[31]

East Asia was equally a theatre of famine. In 1920–1, drought and economic crisis in China (Henan, Shaanxi, Shanxi, Shandong and Zhili (Hebei)) caused a famine that killed half a million people. In 1928–30, in the same provinces, drought, economic crisis and war between Chiang Kai-Shek and warlords caused a larger famine that killed upwards of 5.5 million. Another contemporaneous famine in Hunan killed two million. Four years later, war, drought and economic crisis in Sichuan killed five million.

The Second World War in Asia caused mass starvation also, numerous episodes not conventionally regarded as famines which nonetheless meet our definition. Though the Japanese had no starvation operations comparable to the Nazi Hunger Plan, the chaos and brutality of their expansion and occupation, and the exactions of war, caused numerous famines. The Japanese occupation of Indonesia caused hunger with a death toll of 2.4 million, and in Vietnam a further two million. The Japanese also worked and starved hundreds of thousands of prisoners of war to death, while starvation was the single largest cause of death among Japanese troops themselves: more than one million died, along with uncounted numbers of local people in the areas where they fought. In China, a combination of natural calamity and the exactions of the Nationalist army killed 1.5 million in Henan; there were also famines in Guangdoing and elsewhere. The American blockade of Japan reduced the country to near-starvation, and Japanese settlers in Manchuria were starving to death at the end of the war. The lack of record keeping means also that numerous famines were unrecorded, for example in upper Burma and Malaya.

Though not the largest of the Second World War famines, the Bengal famine of 1943 warrants a special mention in this story. As mentioned earlier, this calamity shaped the thinking of a young Amartya Sen, contributing to rejection of the food shortage theory of famine. It is also now well established that the colonial government in London bears the greater responsibility for causing the famine by requisitioning food reserves and stopping all waterborne means of transport, including fishing boats, for fear that these might be useful to the Japanese army which was advancing through Burma, and for failing to enact standard relief measures when the famine was underway.[32] Prime Minister Churchill insisted that food supplies to Britain itself should in no way be jeopardized by providing famine relief to a British imperial possession. Churchill's offensive views of the Indian people undoubtedly played a role in this, the most lethal of British crimes during the war. Noting that the pressures of the war were certain to bring food crisis to some part of the British empire, Lizzie Collingham writes, '[i]t is difficult to reach any conclusion other than that racism was the guiding principle which determined where hunger struck.'[33] At least 2.1 million Bengalis perished.

Two other famines warrant mention during this period. One was the Italian fascist repression of opposition in Libya, including a policy of concentration camps, which killed 50,000 people, and the other a combination of drought and forced labour in central Africa, which caused 300,000 deaths in Belgian-ruled Rwanda during the Second World War.

The peak of famine and forcible mass starvation was these three decades of the extended world war, when all the belligerents fought total wars and either used starvation as a means of extermination, or were prepared to tolerate famines that killed millions upon millions, in pursuit of other political and military goals. This, the most dreadful period of famine in world history, ended with the end of total war. That end was not neat: the surrender of the German armies in May 1945 did not signal an end to killing, ethnic cleansing, and forced starvation.[34] The food crisis was compounded by drought. Famines continued to reverberate in the USSR, notably Moldova, causing a million deaths. The German homeland, relatively well fed during the war, felt the deprivations of the catastrophe in terms of hunger for the first time. Food rations were also cut in Austria and Hungary in 1945–6. The economies and systems of governance of those areas ravaged by the Eastern Front – the 'bloodlands' – were so shattered that vast populations were destitute, often homeless and on the brink of starvation. German prisoners of war in Soviet hands suffered death rates ninety times greater than those who surrendered to the British and Americans: the USSR continued to use them as slave labourers until 1950.

Act Three: Post-Colonial Totalitarianism: 1950–85

The legacy of the Second World War lived on with the numerous anti-colonial insurgencies, civil wars, and vicious end-of-empire counter-insurgencies that afflicted Africa and Asia for decades. It also lived on with the legitimacy of Soviet and Asian communism, its ideology and methods of rule legitimized because the communists had resisted fascism and imperialism. While there have been no famines in Europe since the immediate aftermath of the Second World War, the story in Asia and Africa is different.

The worst famine in recorded history, and almost certainly the most gigantic ever in terms of sheer loss of life, was Mao Zedong's 'Great Leap Forward' famine of 1958–62, which probably killed 25–30 million people.[35] The story of this famine is quite astonishing, testament to the extraordinary capacity and inhumanity of the Chinese communist state. It was caused by hubristic economic policies. It was made possible by a centralized control of all organs of power and information, such that no truth other than that ordained by the leadership could be heard by that leadership. It was intensified by a stubborn refusal to change those policies even when their failure was spectacularly evident. And, most astonishingly, a calamity of human death on a scale as large as the First World War remained a secret for twenty years.

An even more intense man-made famine was the work of Pol Pot in Cambodia, whose comprehensive 'Year Zero' attempt to remake not only the Cambodian state but also its entire society caused the death from hunger and related causes of 1.21 million people from 1975–9 (69 per cent of the 1.75 million who died overall), until the Khmer Rouge regime was overthrown by an invasion from Vietnam. Such was the dominance of realpolitik calculus at the time that the Vietnamese acknowledged no humanitarian motive in their intervention, and the western powers, led by the United States, continued to recognize the Khmer Rouge as the legitimate Cambodian government even when it had been defeated, driven from the country and the scale of its crimes made public.

The era of Asian communist famine faded with the death of Mao (1976) and the defeat of Pol Pot (1979). But there is a postscript to Act Three: the North Korean famine of the 1990s, which killed a minimum of 240,000 people (and probably many times more) due to a comparably self-destructive amalgam of central planning, state terror, incompetence and secrecy.

Two other Asian famines are worthy of note during this period. One was in Bangladesh in 1974 in the aftermath of the war of independence. This was a rare case of a famine in a country at peace that did not have a totalitarian government. But, newly emerged from civil war and desperately unstable, Bangladesh was chaotically unprepared for the repercussions of crop failures, economic crisis and an abrupt cut-off in American food aid. An estimated 1.5 million died. The second episode was the counter-insurgency famine in East Timor, conducted by the Indonesian army, which killed just over 100,000 people.

African famines during this era were considerably smaller, with some important exceptions. One case was Biafra, which became a cause célèbre among humanitarians, leading among other things to the creation of Médecins Sans Frontières (as a breakaway from the International Committee of the Red Cross). There are no reliable estimates for deaths, but one million is regularly cited.

Given the widespread identification of Africa with famine in recent decades, it is notable how few African famines register on the list. Indeed, one of the best-publicized famines, the crisis in the west African Sahel in 1969–73, appears to have caused very few excess deaths.[36] It is also notable how many of the killing famines occurred in just one country, Ethiopia. Under Emperor Haile Selassie, that country suffered famines in 1958, 1966 and 1973, each killing scores of thousands. The feudal system left peasants desperately poor and vulnerable in the case of crop failure from any cause. By far the worst famine in the country was in 1984–5, which killed 600,000. The cause was a communist military regime relentlessly pursuing titanic social engineering, and a counter-insurgency of extreme brutality, which turned crop failures into a major famine.

At the same time Sudan, a country that had just a few years earlier advertised itself as the 'bread basket' of the Arab world and had attracted vast investments in commercial agriculture, suffered a severe famine. A military authoritarian ruler, his regime collapsing under him, denied the reality of a nationwide food crisis, allowing it to develop into a famine that cost 240,000 lives.

Act Four: Small Wars, Small Famines: 1986 Onwards

The final era is the last thirty years, during which time there have been no calamitous famines. Great famines have continued and notably, for the first time, the main location of these famines is Africa. All Africa's famines have been associated with wars, in particular the kinds of war that involve multiple irregular forces, and the governments themselves using militia.

Sudan and Somalia have the unfortunate distinction of dominating Africa's great famines since 1986. One case is southern Sudan in 1988, when the militia war caused famine and forced displacement, compounded by obstructions on relief. Perhaps 100,000 died. A similar story unfolded in Darfur in 2003–5. The civil war that followed the collapse of the government in Somalia in 1992–3 killed an estimated 220,000 people. This famine struck Somalia's most agriculturally productive areas: its two river valleys and the rainlands in between. The farming peoples who lived in these areas were powerless in the face of an onslaught by political-military elites from elsewhere – yet another illustration of how the ruthless quest for resources can destroy the people who happen to live in the areas possessing them. Almost twenty years later, a combination of drought, economic crisis, war and associated depredations by armed groups, notably the extremist group Al-Shabaab, and a shockingly slow international relief response caused a famine that cost at least 244,000 lives.

The wars in the Democratic Republic of Congo (DRC) after 1996 caused an incalculable number of deaths, a substantial number of which were caused by food crises. This was a 'small war' on a vast scale. The first Congo war (1996–7) was the invasion by the Rwandese Patriotic Front which overthrew the regime of Mobutu Sese Seko. During their military campaign, the Rwandese forces massacred many Hutu refugees, and undoubtedly many more died of hunger, disease and exhaustion during their forced treks across the country. The second

Congo war (1998–2002) involved forces from nine African countries as well as a multiplying array of national armed groups. This caused an enormous spike in civilian deaths. Although that war was formally resolved in 2002, new armed conflicts erupted in eastern DRC with ongoing humanitarian crises and a continually mounting death toll. The death toll we attribute here is 290,500.[37]

There were two exceptional famines in this period. One was North Korea – an anomalous Asian totalitarian famine, more characteristic of Mao's China than the 1990s. This killed many hundreds of thousands of people. The other was the doubling of child mortality in Iraq in the 1990s, due to the havoc caused by the first Gulf War, the international sanctions regime and the policies of Saddam Hussein. There was a vigorous controversy about how many people had died as a result, with the Iraqi government claiming a (wildly inflated) figure of 1.5 million, and researchers producing a lower estimate of 500,000, later retracted on the basis of unsound method.[38] At the end of the 1990s, two careful studies indicated that child-death rates more than doubled after the Kuwait war, with an early peak in the immediate aftermath of the war and a second peak as sanctions hit hardest in 1994–6, impacting unevenly across the country. Malnutrition was a major contributing factor. Somewhere between 166,000 and 300,000 children died.[39] There was a definitional controversy over what to call the crisis. Sarah Graham-Brown argues that 'the cry of imminent famine in Iraq has been used too often', and that it 'conjures up images of an Ethiopian or Somali-type situation which are not substantiated', when the reality was increased deaths due to structural problems in the health, water and sanitation sectors.[40] Obviously, I disagree with this. Haris Gazdar argues the opposite point: that Iraq under sanctions met all of the definitional criteria for 'famine'. He frames the crisis as a 'postmodern famine', namely a sustained macro-economic shock working on a modernized economy and welfare infrastructure to result in a sustained mortality increase.[41]

Additionally, the civil war in Bosnia during 1992–5 witnessed starvation used as a weapon of war, in the camps, and to try to force besieged enclaves to submit. 'Decision Number Seven' by the Bosnian Serb forces tightened the sieges of the so-called 'safe havens': Sarajevo, Srebrenica, Gorazde, Zepa, and Bihac. The worst case was Srebrenica in 1993 and again, more dramatically, in 1995, as a prelude to the attack and massacres.[42] Dozens died of starvation – well below the thresholds I use in this book – but the tactic and the intent were there for the first time in Europe for almost half a century.

As our story moves into the last two decades, and humanitarians have become more sensitive, capable and knowledgeable, we know a great deal more about the smaller famines and can begin to compile reliable lists. Since the turn of the millennium, there have been several famines that killed ten thousand or more. They have struck Ethiopia, Angola, Malawi and Niger, cases that I examine later in this book. Whether the humanitarian crises in north-east Nigeria, South Sudan, Syria and Yemen point to a new pattern of famine is another question I will address in chapter 10.

Part II

How Famines Were Almost Eliminated

5

Demography, Economics, Public Health

Sifting the Hypotheses

In this chapter, I ask what caused the decline in the number and lethality of famines. My answer is that creating (or committing, or perpetrating) a famine requires a lot of hard work and determination, that economic development and modern technologies make it even more difficult to do effectively, and that inclusive democratic politics make it all but impossible.

The decline in famines correlates with many things: from increased population to global temperature rises, from telephone connectivity to women's suffrage. But of course correlation is not cause. The list of 58 great and calamitous famines is an imprecise dataset. Every number is questionable. This makes a weak basis for detailed statistical analysis. That wouldn't stop many of my political science colleagues from having a go, using the most sophisticated modelling methods to compensate for the weakness of the raw data. They would excel at finding equations to fill missing data points and would populate the tables with a constellation of these precise but entirely invented estimates, and then generate all manner of correlations. But it wouldn't be worth it. Much more useful is to consider the small number of observations in the list as its strength rather than its weakness, and apply a historian's lens. With just sixty or so items to examine, it is possible to construct a plausible story for each one in a manner that allows us to make some broad comparisons. Then we have some results that are worth talking about.

This chapter briefly examines the demographic, technological and economic reasons that we might plausibly attribute to having reduced famines or famine mortality. Public health and humanitarian action count among them. I will argue that each one has indeed been a contribution, but the causal story needs another factor: political action. Shifts in population dynamics, technologies and resources are the factors, which mean that a capable and willing government has the means to prevent famines and respond to them effectively. They don't in themselves explain why famines have been reduced.

In the following chapter, I turn to the other part of the story, which is the political dimension. First, I examine the democracy-prevents-famines hypothesis, associated with Amartya Sen. Is it true, as he asserts, that the real driver of famine prevention is political liberty? I argue that there is both truth and simplification in this claim. And, finally, I turn to the 'famine crimes' hypothesis. As war and mass atrocities have declined, so have famines.

The Demographic Transition

Malthus didn't foresee the demographic transition, though his more sympathetic commentators are confident that he would have welcomed it. In stage one (high birth rates and high death rates) population growth is slow, and population pyramids have a broad base, tapering rapidly because of high death rates at all ages. In stage two (when mortality has come down but fertility remains high), the pyramid still has a broad base, but tapers more slowly: this is the period of accelerated population growth. In stages one and two, as many as 15–20 per cent of the total population may be children aged five or less, and half of the population is aged 20 or younger. Finally, birth rates fall and the pyramid becomes a column: most people live to something approaching their natural lifespan. As developing countries pass through the demographic transition, the world population is expected to stabilize.

An interesting side effect of the demographic transition is its impact on famine mortality. One of the most straightforward explanations for the decline in famine deaths is that high-mortality famines occur only in populations in stages one and two of the demographic transition, but when birth rates fall, so too do deaths in famine. The argument behind this is beguilingly simple: famines selectively kill young children and, where there are fewer young children, there are fewer famine deaths.

Classic agrarian famines have a distinctive demographic impact. This can be seen in the famines for which we have the best data

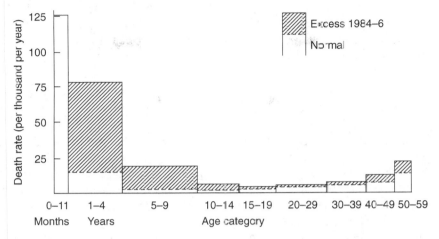

Figure 5.1 Famine mortality by age group in Darfur. The widths of the columns are proportionate to the size of the age cohort, the heights are the age-specific death rates, and the size of the shaded areas is equivalent to the share of overall famine mortality.
Source: De Waal 1989, p. 180. The size of the shaded areas is equivalent to the share of overall famine mortality

(India, and some recent African famines).[1] Most of the excess death is concentrated among young age groups, particularly children under five, and elderly people. My own study in Darfur in 1984–85 found that two-thirds of deaths occurred in children under ten and about half in children under five (see Figure 5.1).

A famine like that in Darfur or like those in South Asia in the nineteenth century killed so many in large part because they struck populations with large numbers of children in the most vulnerable category. As the demographic transition proceeds, the number of highly vulnerable children falls and, for that reason alone, famine mortality will fall.

The pattern of famines selectively killing young children is very consistent. The exceptions are rare cases of forced mass starvation of certain demographic subgroups, for example if the targeted population are prisoners of war who are adult males. The demographic transition and the associated challenges for defining and measuring excess mortality point to the way in which famines, their lethality and their causes must be analysed in their specific historical contexts.

In passing, we should also note that the most consistent finding of studies of famine demography is that the biggest impact is migration. Not only do famines cause short-term movements of people in search of food, work and charity, but also they contribute to long-term out-migration. Famine mortality and migration are linked in complicated ways. People leave famine zones to save their lives and, to that extent, emigration is an alternative to increased death rates. But the weakest rarely leave and migration brings its own risks.

Economic Growth, Agriculture, Markets

Throughout the nineteenth century and most of the twentieth, Tawney's description of the peasant as a man standing up to his neck in water fitted the Chinese peasant better than most. Almost half those who have died in famines since 1870 were Chinese. The astonishing economic growth in China over the last 40 years has meant that the Chinese villager today is, perhaps, up to his waist in water: it would take a big wave to knock him to his knees and leave him at risk of drowning.

As people's income grows, a decreasing proportion of it is spent on food. And as food purchase becomes a smaller element of a household budget, the amount of stress and adversity needed to plunge that household into hunger increases. This is the underlying theme of this section: economic growth, improvements in agriculture, markets and public health reduce the water level, bringing formerly vulnerable people out of the danger zone. These factors reduce the risks of famine, each in slightly different ways: they reduce the risk to entire populations; or they reduce the numbers of people at risk within a population; they reduce the lethality of famine; and they increase the public policy tools with which a government can prevent a famine or reduce its lethality.

But all these factors, even in combination, do not eliminate the risk of famines. Even rich populations with fine agriculture, public infrastructure, developed markets and public health systems can be devastated by famine crimes. For example, by the mid-twentieth century, the Netherlands was one of the most prosperous nations in the world. But a combination of war, blockade and economic crisis inflicted the 1944 'hunger winter' on the Dutch people. Economic development and growth is a powerful correlate of reduced famine, not an exclusive cause. A political leader needs to spend greater effort in creating a famine, but nonetheless he can succeed if he tries hard enough.

The Green Revolution

For people to be fed, there must be food supply. Although my focus on this book is almost entirely on effective demand for food, the supply element is not irrelevant. This is best examined by looking at the innovations in farming that increased food production in poor countries. The 'Green Revolution' in high-yielding food crops was introduced first to Mexico and then to Asia in the early 1960s and achieved rapid and remarkable successes.

High-yielding varieties of rice and wheat were developed first with research funding from the Rockefeller Foundation and the Ford Foundation, but this was followed by higher yielding varieties of other major food crops important to developing countries, including sorghum, millet, maize, cassava and beans. The use of these newly developed varieties, combined with the expanded use of fertilizers, pesticides and irrigation, led to dramatic yield increases in Asia and Latin America, beginning in the late 1960s. The result was record harvests in many of the countries that adopted the new technology – total food production in the developing world more than doubled between 1960 and 1985.[2] Given that small farmers have historically comprised a large segment of the poor, improving farm productivity made many farmers less poor and their children better nourished.[3] This is important in itself and it is also a contribution to reducing famine in so far as it moves poor agrarian populations further away from the threshold at which their chronic hunger dips into famine. On the other side of the balance sheet, critics of the Green Revolution have argued that it resulted in environmental degradation and increased inequality, and it did not address the plight of the very poorest – and in some cases made it worse.[4]

Green Revolution technology made a substantial contribution to improving food production, and therefore making large numbers of people in Asia less hungry and less vulnerable. But to credit the Green Revolution with abolishing famine itself is to miss the key point that an increase in food availability is not relevant to those who lack the land on which to grow crops or the income with which to buy them – they remained, for the most part, ill fed and with precarious livelihoods.[5] The mantra 'give a man a fish and he will have food for a day, teach a man to fish and he will have food for life' sounds very silly (to be polite) to the scores of thousands of skilled fishermen who died of starvation in Bengal in 1943 because the government impounded their boats.

Similarly, Green Revolution technology would not have been useful in Cambodia under the Khmer Rouge. Advocates of the argument that higher-yielding crops prevented famine will respond that this is an exceptional case. But the point about great and calamitous famines is precisely that they *are* exceptional. The fact that a land – Ukraine, Holland, Cambodia, South Sudan – is amazingly fertile and populated by skilful farmers and herders does not mean that there won't be a famine there.

Markets and infrastructure

Another argument is that better-functioning markets – more integrated and efficient, with improved transport infrastructure – have ended famines. Again, there is much truth to this, but it is incomplete. Studies of markets in famines find that dysfunctional or collapsed markets can contribute to famines – or, to be precise, different kinds of market failures can lead to different kinds of famines. Beyond this point, economists don't agree.

Since the days of Adam Smith, there has been a vigorous debate among economists about the role of markets in famines. Cormac Ó Gráda 2005 summarizes it pithily:

> How markets influence famines is a contentious issue. One tradition, dating back beyond Adam Smith to the French enlightenment, holds that free markets minimize the damage done by harvest failure. Another argues that, on the contrary, well-functioning markets may exacerbate famines, by removing food from locations with insufficient purchasing power to richer, less affected areas. A third tradition holds that markets may not function well during famines, for a variety of reasons.[6]

The second position is Amartya Sen's[7]: even a perfectly functioning market will not prevent famine if a certain group of people do not have enough effective demand to purchase food and, in so far as other people who are not facing hunger do have such a demand, food may flow out of a famine-affected area to meet that demand. Sen's case studies, for example Bengal in 1943 and Ethiopia in 1973, include instances of merchants transporting food out of famine-stricken districts to places (such as the Ethiopian capital city Addis Ababa) where people were not hungry but had money to buy. The global integration of food markets can therefore leave poor populations more vulnerable to price volatility originating on the other side of the globe or because of a speculative bubble in financial markets. When there was an unexpected hike in the global price of food in 2008, the price shocks were transmitted rapidly across the world.[8] The effects were felt across Africa – from Ethiopia to Liberia and Guinea – where higher food prices pushed people to resort to the kind of coping strategies we would normally expect to see in the hungry season, with measurable increases in malnutrition.[9] There was no famine but there were worrisome indications that this kind of market aberration could contribute to creating one. Three years later, the second round of the world food crisis reverberated in food markets in Somalia and, coming on top of other shocks, this generated famine.[10]

Elements in Ó Gráda's explanation number three include market segmentation (meaning that some markets are isolated from others), poor flows of information, intervention in the market by authorities and hoarding and profiteering by merchants. Ó Gráda reviewed famines in pre-industrial Europe and in modern Asia, including the French famines of 1693–4 and 1708–10 and nineteenth-century Ireland and Finland: markets appear to have functioned well – though not to provide affordable food to the poorest – until overwhelmed by catastrophic food availability declines.[11] His summary: 'Markets were not panaceas; even if they worked like clockwork, they could not have overridden mismatches between entitlements and market positions.'[12] In short, he comes out in support of Sen against Smith: if people's purchasing power collapses, it doesn't matter whether the market functions or not.

The malfunctioning of markets, meanwhile, can also turn crisis into famine. This can happen in several distinct ways. One way is panic buying and hoarding when people anticipate a food crisis. Another is market manipulation by cartels that see the chance of making windfall profits from famine prices. In Bengal in 1943, Sen observed that a relatively small reduction in food availability translated into a major decrease in food being brought to market.[13] Martin Ravallion's study of the Bangladesh famine of 1974 identified the problem in part as a speculative crisis, with traders hoarding food in anticipation of further price rises.[14] This has been observed in countries where a relatively small cartel of grain traders can control the markets, such as Sudan.[15] A third kind of market failure occurs when a remote, peripheral market is too poorly integrated for traders to serve it. For example, in rural Ethiopia market segmentation has historically been a major problem, with many people in remote villages in the highlands living far from roads and markets, places where traders simply don't go because the demand is too small and the transport costs too high.[16]

The implication is that an efficient free market alone is not enough. Ensuring that people's exchange entitlements (especially exchange of wages for food) do not collapse into the starvation zone requires public action in food markets. This means both improving basic market infrastructure and preventing malfunctions such as speculative price spirals through interventions to stabilize prices. Even with these measures, public policy to maintain basic incomes and livelihoods may also be needed.

Public Health

Public health systems can prevent epidemics. While they cannot prevent food crises, they can make famines much less lethal. And indeed the massive decline in famine mortality is correlated with improved global public health. Improvements in sanitation, the control of communicable diseases and the eradication of smallpox were critical in reducing famine deaths. Until the middle of the twentieth century in Asia, and somewhat later in Africa, famines routinely unleashed epidemics which were more deadly than the hunger itself. Drought famines were typically followed by malaria epidemics when the rains returned, and the story of famine mortality in colonial South Asia is to a substantial degree the story of infectious diseases and malaria.[17]

The medical profession was shockingly ill informed about how to treat starvation as recently as the 1940s. Notoriously, the Allied physicians who tended to the starving survivors of the Bergen Belsen concentration camp in 1945 killed many of their patients through inappropriate feeding methods. This was a salutary shock. As Josué de Castro wrote shortly afterwards, this story 'constitutes a tremendous accusation against our Western civilization. It was necessary for famine to return and ravish Europe before Western science took an interest in combating it.'[18] But nutrition and public health made enormous advances thereafter.

In the last thirty years, the expansion of humanitarian programmes in Africa and better emergency health and nutrition technologies have further reduced mortality in food crises. The speed at which population mortality levels returned to normal during the Darfur crisis in the mid-2000s compares favourably with the trajectory of death rates in refugee camps in Sudan in the mid-1980s.[19]

Recall that, irrespective of the increased susceptibility of the malnourished to disease, if there is increased exposure to disease, and especially several diseases at the same time, rates of illness will rise. Exposure to disease can be reduced by better sanitation, widespread immunization against childhood diseases and minimizing the concentration of people in camps. It is hard to recall now but in the 1970s and 1980s, famine camps were the standard response to food emergencies and refugee crises, not only from necessity but also by design. It is easier to feed people if they congregate in one place. In a camp, people can be counted and given ration cards. By the end of the 1980s, the standard policy had changed: avoid camps if possible. People themselves learned this lesson, too. For example, after experiencing the high death rates in famine camps during the 1984–5 famine, the people of Darfur and Kordofan avoided migrating to towns during the food crisis of 1990–1.

Meanwhile, emergency public health was transformed. Where they were unavoidable, camps were better designed, with far more attention to water supply and sanitation. For example, Oxfam became the specialist in clean water for emergencies. Vaccination against childhood infectious diseases became routine. Procedures for treating child malnutrition improved.

Public health advances undoubtedly cut the levels of mortality during famines, especially in Africa and South Asia. But, in the worst man-made famines, from the Hunger Plan to Year Zero, health services were withheld deliberately. In the Great Leap Forward, where frank starvation and not disease was the overwhelming killer, the public health advances of the previous decade were overwhelmed – though possibly the death toll would have been still higher had there been major epidemics.

Conclusion

Since we emerged from a world of subsistence economies, at the dawn of the age of imperial globalization, every major famine has arisen as a combination of the exceptional. In most cases, there's a production shock, a market shock and a political or military shock. Not every element needs to be present every time, but as agricultural systems have become more productive, markets have become stronger and people have become less poor, the political element has become more and more important. It is to that element that I now turn.

6

Politics, War, Genocide

Political Freedoms

The reduction in famines is strongly associated with improvements in political freedoms and the number of democracies worldwide. This is consistent with Amartya Sen's observation that the freedom of the press, the right to organize and the ability to call the government to account through the mechanisms of democratic governance are inextricably linked to the ability to secure basic economic rights. Sen first wrote this as something of a throwaway remark in an article in the *New York Review of Books*[1] and elaborated upon it in his later book *Development as Freedom*.[2]

Sen could have added that commissions of inquiry play an important role in public accountability in the aftermath of famine, and that institutionalized humanitarianism is also a feature of democracies. Compared to the thoroughness with which Sen developed 'entitlement theory' and his other economic work, his analysis of democracy and famine was an insightful sketch, not a fully fashioned work of art. More importantly, the interpretation of his observations by liberal scholars and human rights advocates was simplistic. As Sen himself emphasized, the success of the Indian media in exposing famines and thereby bringing about their ending in the subcontinent was not matched by comparable press activism on the issue of chronic hunger.[3] It is well documented that elected officials are much more incentivized to provide high profile relief, rather than low-profile but much more effective prevention and, conversely, that the best disaster response systems exist where professional civil servants are empowered to do their jobs.[4] Moreover, as Jean Drèze and Sen pointed out, 'It is important to note that despite the gigantic size of excess mortality in the Chinese famine, the extra mortality in India from regular deprivation in normal times vastly overshadows the former...every eight years or so more people die in India because of its regular death rate than died in China in the gigantic famine of 1958–61.'[5]

Drèze and Sen were also aware of some other anomalies, such as deaths due to hunger following droughts in the Indian states of Bihar in 1966 and Maharashtra in 1972–3 and the famine in Bangladesh at a time when that country was ostensibly democratic. To this we can add the starvation under the elected government in Sudan in the late 1980s and smaller famines in the early 2000s in liberalized African states including Malawi and Niger. There are two kinds of explanation for these failures of democratic polities, one focusing on who decides and what interests are served by the decision, and the other concerned with the substance of democratic political contestation. Both kinds of explanation are needed.

Eric Neumayer and Thomas Plümper developed an elegant model for why it can be rational for a democracy to permit famine.[6] It's a classic political science rational choice theory. In an autocratic system, the narrow selectorate need only reward the ruling elites and can disregard the population at large. So the choice of famine may be consistent with interests. In a large majoritarian democracy, most voters may also rationally decide to permit a famine that affects a minority. Olivier Rubin undertook a more ambitious empirical study (dealing with each of the episodes mentioned above) and rather grandly claimed to have 'refuted' Sen's hypothesis.[7] But Rubin was dealing with a narrow slice of famines, each of them a case in which the deficiencies of democratic systems were implicated in the political decisions that allowed famine to develop or impeded an expeditious response.

In *Famine Crimes*, I explored the question of why famine seemed to matter so much more than chronic hunger in Indian politics, and why there was no comparable sustained politicization of famine in Africa. I hypothesized that a 'political contract' to end a social ill was needed, and for that to occur the problem needed to be visible, politically salient and tractable (that is, amenable to readily accessible policy measures).[8] Historical circumstances had meant that the Indian nationalist movement had mobilized around famine in the late nineteenth century, and the issue had subsequently become sufficiently politicized that no government could afford to ignore it. In African countries, the post-colonial state was legitimized by a narrower remit of obligations, and indeed the 'democracy wave' of the 1990s had coincided with a retreat of the state from even those limited welfare obligations, with the result that democratization was associated with increased vulnerability to famine. I also argued – with the 1988 famine in southern Sudan as my prime exhibit – that a democratic system that was limited to one part of the country would not prevent famine in the other part and might even inflict it.

Famine and flawed democracies

The 'democracy prevents famine' explanation does not take us far as a monocausal theory – it is just as limited as any single-factor explanation for the causes of famine. Much more interesting are the frayed edges of the explanation. I will briefly examine several famines that have occurred in countries with parliamentary systems and a free press, occasions in which governments have been weak and communities divided or at war, and turn to the disturbing implication that, should the advance of democracy be halted or reversed and exclusionary politics be resurgent, famines may become more common.

The famine in Bangladesh in 1974 is a case in which many factors, none of them fatal in themselves, combined to create famine. The central story is the collapse in the capacity of the public food distribution system (PFDS), which was the government's central policy instrument for providing subsidized food to the population and also its mechanism for withstanding shocks to the national food supply. Bangladesh was chronically food insecure. In other years of food crisis, such as 1979 and 1984, not only was the PFDS able to balance supply and demand but grain merchants were confident that it would do so, and in 1998 the most severe deficit ever in the country's history did not lead to famine because of prompt government action to ensure that the market functioned effectively.[9] In 1974, however, market confidence evaporated. One reason for this was that, for geopolitical reasons, the United States imposed an aid embargo, encompassing both regular food aid and emergency assistance. In 1973–4, American food aid was just 17 per cent of what it had been the previous year.[10] The embargo also led to a rapid drain on the country's foreign exchange reserves.

With confidence in the government's capacity collapsing, the PFDS failed to contain a speculative price spiral. This is lucidly explained by S. R. Osmani, who concludes, 'The limitations of PFDS in 1974 and its vitality in the two later years [1979 and 1984] should therefore constitute the key explanation of why famine occurred in one case and not in the others.'[11] Ben Crow goes further, documenting how the government prioritized food allocations to those with political clout over those in greatest need: 'The Statutory Rationing and Priority Group rations (to major urban centres, industrial workers, police, army, state employees) were not curtailed. Instead the government cut back those food distributions targeted at poor rural populations...and [famine] relief.'[12] In short, a government facing a disastrous financial and food security crisis prioritized its own political survival over the lives of its poorest citizens. Child death rates spiked early and high.[13]

An even more graphic and egregious example is Sudan in 1988. This was a time when the country had a parliamentary system and a free press – in the north. But it was also at war: the government was fighting the Sudan People's Liberation Army (SPLA), adding a new layer of fear to pre-existing racist exclusionary politics. In the opening pages of this book, I mentioned the extraordinarily high death rates of displaced southern Sudanese that year, driven from their homes by militia raiding and confined to camps in small towns on the southern marchlands of Darfur and Kordofan. Thousands died there. A few managed to move out. One train arrived in Khartoum in April that year, bringing a remote, hitherto invisible famine to the streets of the capital city. But even that solicited only individual acts of charity, not any change in policy by the government. Khartoum railway station is opposite the city's main hospital, and its doctors and nurses rushed across the street to tend to the sick and dying. Residents of the city who were bringing food to their relatives in the hospital instead went to feed the starving. Six children died at the station, many others were fed and treated. But the only Sudanese newspaper that covered this shocking story was the *Sudan Times*, edited by a prominent southern Sudanese, Bona Malwal.[14]

At precisely the same time, one of the key issues in the Sudanese parliament was whether the government would scrap an expensive and inefficient bread subsidy. Removing this subsidy was key to Sudan becoming eligible for debt relief from the International Monetary Fund, which would in turn unlock other assistance from donors. The Khartoum residents who benefited from this weren't hungry, but they regarded cheap bread as an entitlement. Demonstrations in Khartoum forced the government to back down. A famine that devastated an excluded minority simply wasn't an issue in a political system that was dominated by political constituencies that had other priorities. The government's focus was on political survival in a highly contested and volatile environment – it was overthrown by a military coup the following year.

Neither Sen's formulation, nor my 'anti-famine political contract', addresses situations in which a stable democratic political order is in jeopardy. Modern famines are by definition exceptional and occur when the processes regarded as normal in a stable polity breakdown. A general trend or correlation can explain what makes famine rarer or harder to create but cannot explain how famines are eradicated entirely. The growth of democracy and political inclusion, a free press and respect for civil and political liberties is one of those trends that is indeed an effective inoculation against famine – except when it breaks down.

Famines strike selectively: it is the poor and politically excluded who are its first and principal victims, commonly its only ones. Starvation relentlessly hunts out outsiders and marginalized minorities – or, to phrase it more accurately, those in power administer famines so as to target these people. In a large number of the famines in our catalogue, including all the most recent cases, the victims have been constituencies identified as subversives or enemies of the state. Today's resurgence of xenophobia and resource nationalism across the world bodes ill for the politics of faminogenesis.

The link between famine and political breakdown is, however, complicated – the causal arrows point both ways. There are many historic cases in which famines or food crises have caused revolutions or popular uprisings (at least in part) or when a country weakened by famine has been vulnerable to invasion or destabilization. Even the national humiliation of being reduced to a spectator while foreign aid agencies feed one's own people is politically de-legitimizing.

These are some of the reasons why food security and famine prevention are often national security priorities, and why an 'anti-famine political contract' need not necessarily be a democratic contract. An authoritarian government with an astute sense of its political interests can sustain a robust anti-famine mechanism for national security reasons. Examples include the PFDS in Bangladesh,[15] the rationing system in Saddam Hussein's Iraq and the drought response mechanisms in Ethiopia over the last decade. However, a security-based political contract that depends solely on an elite pact is likely to be less robust than a democratic one that can be enforced by the populace.

War, Dictatorship and Atrocity

Explaining famines requires explaining events that are exceptional and becoming more so. In this section, I turn to those exceptional cases, and ask what specific political, military and criminal actions created famines. The argument moves in three steps. The first is the overall descriptive statistics: the basic correlation between war, dictatorship and famine. The second is an examination of some paradigmatic cases of famine and mass atrocity, in particular the Nazi Hunger Plan of 1941. The third step is placing the 58 individual famines in a common framework.

Correlating war, dictatorship and famine

As well as the correlations with economic, technological and governance factors described thus far, the decline in famines is also closely correlated with the decline in wars, the lethality of wars, and mass atrocities. The number of ongoing armed conflicts per year averaged more than fifty during the Cold War. It declined in the 1990s and remained steady, in the low thirties, until 2010, when it began to rise again.[16] Each twenty-first century conflict on average kills many fewer people than did those before 1990.[17] Mass atrocities have also shown marked recent declines. The number of episodes of very large-scale killing decreased in a jagged pattern from the end of the Second World War until about 1995. This was followed by a precipitous decline: reductions in the average level of violence targeting civilians in countries that have had at least one intrastate conflict;[18] fewer onsets of mass killing events and a reduced scale of ongoing incidents;[19] and a declining number of minority groups being victimized by governments.[20] This global decline varies by region: in East Asia, it began in the mid-1970s, following the withdrawal of international forces from the region's conflicts and the death of Mao[21]; in Africa the reduction began in the late 1980s.[22]

War, dictatorship and genocide were associated with 75 per cent of the episodes of great and calamitous famines and 75 per cent of the mortality. If countries emerging from armed conflict are included, this rises to 79 per cent of episodes and 76 per cent of deaths respectively.

Some paradigmatic cases

How are we to analyse these? Of the 58 famine events in the dataset, few have been considered by any scholars of genocide or mass atrocities. Of the pre-First World War cases, only a handful have been framed in this way, and then only in the writings of select analysts. Cases include the Congo (1885–99) and most particularly, the genocide by starvation of the Herero in Namibia (1904–7). If we are also to include the starvation inflicted on indigenous people by settler colonists in North America and Australia, the number of scholars is larger, and the convergence between genocide and forced famine is closer.[23]

In the era of total war and totalitarianism, the eastern marches of Europe suffered a uniquely destructive sequence of wars, mass atrocities and famines. Timothy Snyder has described the swathe of land from the Baltic to the Black Sea as the 'bloodlands',[24] and Thomas de Waal has urged for a comparable history to be written for eastern Anatolia and the Trans-Caucasus region.[25]

The Armenian genocide of 1915–16 began with a large-scale massacre and deportation. The meticulous account by Raymond Kévorkian documents numerous massacres, with occasional references to the fact that many also died of hunger. For example: 'Of all the deportees who had set out in the various convoys from Kiği, some 3,000 arrived at Ras ul-Ayn. A month later, no more than 700 were left; famine and typhus had carried off the rest.'[26] About 880,000 survivors found themselves in transit camps in Syria and Mesopotamia, of whom about 300,000 died of famine conditions.[27] The survivors were then relocated to concentration camps, after which the Young Turk Central Committee launched the 'second stage' of liquidation and killed 195,000, while an additional 100,000 died of hunger and disease.[28] Undoubtedly, more continued to die from hunger, including a further 200,000 in the 1919 famine that struck newly independent Armenia, struggling to cope amid the violent chaos of the region.

The 1932–4 famine in Ukraine and parts of southern Russia inhabited by Ukrainians (notably Kuban) was created by political decision. In Ukraine, the famine is known as the Holodomor, and Ukrainian nationalists insist that Stalin was using hunger as a tool in pursuit of genocide. Their claim has an impressive pedigree: no less an authority than Lemkin himself described it as a classic case of Soviet genocide – not only for its lethal intent but also because Stalin's goal was the imposition of a new sociopolitical order.[29] It is no coincidence that the Holodomor is rare among famines in that the Ukrainian state officially memorializes its victims as part of its nationalist narratives. Other scholars of the Soviet Union have argued that the famine was the product of the anti-Kulakization policy, pursued with ruthless indifference to the fate of the peasantry, an explanation lent credibility because it also affected non-Ukrainian areas of Russia and Kazakhstan where the same policies were imposed. Historians now concur that both explanations have their place, and the famine is best explained as having occurred in two stages. At first, starvation was the result of a reckless policy of collectivizing agriculture and destroying the richer peasants (*kulaks*), alongside high quotas imposed to feed cities and export grain. These were errors of economic policy, implemented in draconian fashion. But once a famine had become apparent in the middle of 1932, Stalin's paranoia over Ukrainian nationalist resistance, supposedly abetted by Polish intrigue, led to a new policy of concentrating and deepening the famine as a tool of punishment and control. In the second stage, therefore, famine was rigorously administered in Ukraine and Kuban, both to extract more food for the cities and the army and to snuff out Ukrainian nationalism.[30]

Stalin's deportations are a third case that could well meet the threshold of a great famine. Birgid Brauer describes how, in 1943–4, 644,778 people of different nationalities (meticulously counted by Soviet party officers) were deported to Kazakhstan and Kyrgyzstan and faced conditions which she describes, with some understatement, as 'extremely difficult':

> In Kazakhstan, on September 1, 1944, 64,000 families lived in crowded conditions, the rest under the open sky. In Kyrgyzstan, 31,000 families lived under 5,000 roofs. Families of 10 people living on 6–12 square meters were considered to be among the better off. As a result of all the material shortages, some of the deported nationalities had a total death rate of 50–70% during the years of exile.[31]

The Hunger Plan

Historians' accounts of the Second World War have described mass starvations within the story of total war. Such accounts were also produced as evidence in post-war trials of Japanese and German officials and hence found a place within the legal lexicon. Nonetheless, the Hunger Plan has been less generally accepted as an act of genocide, not necessarily because of a detailed examination of the intent of the perpetrators of those specific crimes, or the nature of the policies they carried out, but rather because they fall within the ambit of the Holocaust, which dominates our understanding of this entire era.

The Hunger Plan is paradigmatic for starvation as a weapon. It has been unjustly neglected in the historiography of famine and mass atrocity. It is hard to reconstruct the often obscure and perhaps confused thinking of the Nazi leadership.[32] However, theories of race and population, and economic and military calculations, all intersect in rationalizing what would have been, if it had been carried through, the greatest atrocity of the century.

The general underpinning of the Hunger Plan was the concept of *Lebensraum* – the need for the German race to occupy enough territory to assure its future, combined with the calculation of the resources Germany would need to challenge the Anglo-Saxon powers in war. Nazi planners were haunted by the way in which food scarcity had undermined Germany's effort in the First World War. Hitler had read Malthus while writing *Mein Kampf* and concluded that 'hunger abets the sword' as a means of conquest, and that surplus populations of

lesser races had no entitlement to exist.[33] He dreamed of a vast programme of agrarian settlements stretching as far as the Volga, repli-
cating the American settler colonial expansion to the Mississippi.[34]
He characterized Jews and Slavs as 'useless eaters' whose elimination
would free up resources for Germans. It is undeniably the most frightening appearance of Malthus's zombie.

The immediate rationale for the Hunger Plan was Operation Barbarossa – the invasion of the Soviet Union – and the enormous food
supplies the Wehrmacht needed to feed its soldiers and auxiliaries.
The German High Command calculated that the war could be sustained only if the army fed itself from the conquered territories and
the home population remained well nourished. In the words of Herman
Göring, it was 'necessary that all should know that if there is to be
famine anywhere, it shall in no case be in Germany'.[35] Operation
Barbarossa and the Hunger Plan justified one another.

State Secretary Herbert Backe of the Reich Ministry for Food and
Agriculture drew up the Hunger Plan in the weeks prior to the launch
of Operation Barbarossa on 22 June 1941.[36] The Economic Policy
Guidelines for Economic Organization East, issued a month earlier,
were explicit:

> As Germany and Europe require [grain] surpluses under all circum-
> stances, consumption [in the Soviet Union] must be reduced accord-
> ingly...In contrast to the territories occupied so far, this reduction in
> consumption can indeed be implemented because the main surplus
> territory is spatially starkly separated from the main deficit terri-
> tory...The population of these territories, in particular the population
> of the cities will have to face the most terrible famine...Many tens of
> millions of people in this territory will become superfluous and will
> have to die or migrate to Siberia. Attempts to rescue the population
> there from death by obtaining surpluses from the black earth [surplus]
> zone can only be at the expense of provisioning Europe. They prevent
> the possibility of Germany holding out until the end of the war; they
> prevent Germany and Europe from resisting the blockade. With regard
> to this, absolute clarity must reign.[37]

The Nazi leadership had no clear idea of how many people would
starve. One high-level memo simply noted 'x million will doubtlessly
starve'.[38] However, Backe calculated that the Ukraine's potential surplus
was being used to feed 30 million Soviet city-dwellers, and if that
food were to be consumed by the Wehrmacht, they must of necessity
starve. The siege of Leningrad and the deprivation of food to the
German-controlled cities of Minsk, Kiev and Kharkov, which suffered
levels of starvation comparable to Leningrad, were the consequence.

Backe, Himmler and Göring all used the figure of between 20 and 30 million starvation deaths as their target.[39]

Barbarossa was ill planned, the army sent east on astonishingly optimistic and simplistic assumptions. Infamously, the soldiers did not even have winter clothing, so confident was the high command of a rapid victory. Similar thinking underpinned the Hunger Plan. Alex Kay has argued that 'there was no clear idea among the economic planners as to how [the plan] was actually to be implemented.'[40] Snyder compares the Nazi administration of famine to Stalin's. Just eight years earlier, Stalin had starved the Ukraine's villages using a massive intelligence and coercive infrastructure reaching down to every village. Massive forced starvation needs a lot of detailed organization and effort, which the German occupiers did not apply. They seemed to believe that simply isolating a population from its former food supply would lead to famine. Unlike during Stalin's Holodomor, villagers could escape using back roads and could barter avoiding town markets. The German plan of starving Kiev, Kharkov and other cities proved harder than expected: shutting off these cities from their agricultural hinterlands would have required a security operation for which the German Army was not logistically prepared. The siege of Leningrad showed how much determination and patience was needed to starve a million city-dwellers to death over 900 days.

Without downplaying the role of racism in Nazism, recent scholarship on German war policies has highlighted the role of extreme agrarian ideology.[41] From this, the agronomist Backe emerges as an important architect of Nazi occupation policy, and not just an implementing technocrat. His alimentary economic calculations – heroically simplistic and misleading, as it transpired – of how many people could be supported by the conquered territory provided a logic for reducing the population by mass murder.

Lizzie Collingham synthesizes writings on this question, describing how in 1941 the systematic murder of Jews in the USSR began with a food supply rationale:

> The quartermaster-general reported that he expected the annihilation of the Jews in central Lithuania, which began in August, to significantly alleviate the food supply problems for Army Group North. In August, 15,000 Jews were shot in Polesje (Prijetsümpfe). Task forces moved through northern Ukraine massacring the inhabitants of village after village. Particular targets were Jews in urban areas where the civilian population was starving, especially in the towns where food and shelter were a problem for troops moving up to the front. In Kharkov 15,000 Jews were murdered that winter, supposedly in order to alleviate the food situation. In Kiev the German authorities claimed that a systematic

massacre of Jews on 29 and 30 September had alleviated the food and housing conditions for the rest of the civilian population.[42]

Another group easily annihilated, with similar rationale, was Soviet prisoners of war. Among them, the death rate was fully 57.5 per cent, mostly due to the death marches, death transports and overcrowded camps that lacked any form of shelter. In Stalag 352 near Minsk, 109,500 prisoners of war died. In the camps of the Polish General Government, some 45,690 people died in just ten days, between 21 and 30 October 1941.[43] This was starvation with annihilatory intent. But it was illogical. The need to incorporate slave labour into the German war economy forced a modification. Indeed, labour shortages soon became more of a concern than 'surplus' population – a problem that had already arisen with Nazi policies towards Poland in 1939–40. The Germans needed people to work the fields and guard the concentration camps, and some of the prisoners of war, having just escaped starvation themselves, were pressed into service as accomplices in the Final Solution.

The starvation policy was impossible to implement at the scale intended. The need for labour was just one of its shortcomings. Another was the impossibility of controlling the black market, especially in light of the formidable famine-survival skills that Ukrainians and Russians had learned; a third was the extreme logistical difficulty of controlling local populations so profoundly antagonized by the ubiquitous deprivation. And lastly, by early 1942, eliminating 'useless eaters' by starvation proved slower and less efficient than Backe had promised. The numbers weren't adding up: Ukraine was not delivering the food that the Wehrmacht demanded and the population wasn't shrinking at the rate required. Indeed, there is an argument that the 'disappointing results of the Hunger Plan' directly contributed to the Nazis' switch from starvation to gas chambers as their preferred method of extermination.[44] The Hunger Plan itself became a set of opportunistic policies whereby the German armies were instructed to live off the land. Starvation was practised 'where it seemed a useful thing to do'.[45] It is impossible to put a number on the death toll of the Hunger Plan. Following the calculations of leading historians, I use a figure of 4.7 million, which should be considered a minimum number for those who died of hunger, disease and cold on account of Nazi policies.

The Germans intended to starve the *entire* USSR, and almost succeeded in that too. Deprived of its major food-growing areas and with its resources diverted ruthlessly to the war effort, the USSR's food production collapsed by two-thirds between 1940 and 1942, and it itself suffered a constant, low-grade famine throughout the war years, causing further uncounted numbers of Soviet citizens to die of hunger. That most survived at all was due to the skills of collecting famine foods, illegally gleaning the remnants of harvests, maintaining private plots and the revival of local collective markets.[46]

As important as the scale of the Hunger Plan and its satellite atrocities is what it tells us about the intimate connections between starvation and massacre, between famine and genocide. Mass death through hunger was not only a product of war and atrocity but was one of its objectives; starvation was one of the preferred instruments of mass killing, interchangeable with other more directly violent methods.

The Soviet treatment of German prisoners of war in 1945 was less atrocious only by the extreme standards of inhumanity that the Wehrmacht had set. More than a million died, a death rate of 35 per cent. The aim was vengeance and exploitation. They were worked to death rather than starved as such, and for this reason this case is excluded from our list of mass starvations, but it is nonetheless instructive. The Soviet bureaucracy enumerated every human life, but none of them counted for anything. In his account of the continuing savagery in Europe after 1945, Keith Lowe remarks, 'The principal reason why so many prisoners died in Soviet captivity was because virtually no one who looked after them cared whether they lived or died.'[47] These words could stand for the entire period of European famines of this era, and indeed as the common thread linking famine crimes.

Less well-known famine crimes

The famine crimes in Asia during the Second World War have garnered even less scholarly attention than those in Europe. Important famines include Bengal, China (Henan and Guangdong), Burma, Vietnam and Indonesia, as well as the Japanese treatment of prisoners of war, Japanese troops and local people in the occupied islands of the Philippines, the Indonesian archipelago, Papua New Guinea and the South Pacific, and the occupation of Manchuria and the expulsion of Japanese settlers there. The total numbers of dead from starvation exceeds 10 million. Japanese occupation policies were brutal and extractive and undoubtedly contributed to famine, notably in Vietnam.[48] But *disruption* was the distinguishing feature of the imperial advance: Collingham writes that 'much of the chaos was caused by mismanagement rather than a malicious, premeditated policy.'[49]

This reached its extreme in the provisioning arrangements – or rather, the absence thereof – for the imperial army itself, whose soldiers were dispatched on operations with food for just a few weeks, woefully inadequate supply lines and instructions to provide for themselves. After the surrender of Japanese forces in Guadalcanal, their commanders estimated that of the 20,000 fatalities, three-quarters had starved to death and just one-quarter had died in combat. Comparable figures perished elsewhere and, overall, an estimated 60 per cent of the 1.74 million Japanese soldiers who died during the war were killed by hunger or related causes.[50] Meanwhile, the American strategy of leaving isolated Japanese garrisons to 'wither on the vine' meant also that the local inhabitants of these outposts, and any prisoners of war, also starved. The combined naval and air blockade of the Japanese mainland also generated hunger, which would have become mass starvation had the Japanese army not surrendered when it did.

In the post-1945 period, only about half of the cases in our catalogue receive any serious scholarly discussion – even then it is inconsistent – of how the acts might constitute genocide or mass atrocities. These include: Chinese government policies; the Nigerian civil war; Indonesian assaults against East Timor; Cambodia under the Khmer Rouge; the Ethiopian famine of 1984–5; and famines in the 'ethics-free zone'[51] that constituted Sudanese civil wars since the 1980s. As for the rest of the famines on the list, they simply do not cross over into the discourse of genocide and mass atrocity.

Classifying faminogenic acts

The third and final part of my famine-as-atrocity argument turns to a case-by-case analysis of each of the 58 instances, treating each one individually, as political historian and, within that context, occasionally as prosecutor. The question to ask for each famine is: What is the responsibility of the governing authorities for the event? We investigate cause and effect by examining the intent of the authorities (political, military, criminal) and the link between their actions and the outcomes.

To do this, I draw upon David Marcus,[52] who classified 'faminogenic acts' on a four-point scale of degree of culpability. Marcus took the notion of a 'famine crime' seriously to explore what it would mean for international law to treat faminogenic acts as crimes against humanity. The categorization can be used to identify *political* intent and responsibility.

A *first-degree famine crime* is committed, according to Marcus, when a person 'knowingly creates, inflicts, or prolongs conditions that result in or contribute to the starvation of a significant number of persons. A first-degree famine crime is committed by someone determined to exterminate a population through famine.'[53] There are three first-degree famine crimes in the catalogue. One is the Armenian genocide. A second is the 1932–4 famine in the USSR. This was initiated by a brutal process of collectivization that affected a large swathe of the southern USSR but, when Stalin realized this, he intensified starvation in Ukraine as an act of persecution, making that element – the Holodomor – into a first-degree famine crime. The third is the Hunger Plan and associated mass starvations. The genocide of the Herero in Namibia was a first-degree famine crime, but it fell short of the threshold of 100,000 dead. First-degree famine crimes in the catalogue killed 8.3 million people, 8 per cent. One feature of first-degree famine crimes also warrants mention, which is the high ratio of killings by massacre to killings by starvation. All the war famines in the catalogue involved lethal violence against civilians but, in these cases, massacre lay at the very centre of policy.

A *second-degree famine crime* is committed by a person 'recklessly ignoring evidence that his or her policies are creating, inflicting or prolonging the starvation of a significant number of persons. A second-degree famine crime is committed by an official recklessly pursuing policies that have already proven their faminogenic tendencies.'[54] These constitute the largest number of famine crimes by far. The list contains 33 instances (more than half) with 64 million dead (62 per cent) in all continents except the Americas, and in every time period. These include wartime famines in which governments mounted counter-insurgency campaigns with the objective of a military victory but were ready to tolerate mass death from hunger. A case is Ethiopia in 1984–5. Other cases are famines that were created by blockades, requisitioning or other restrictions justified by military necessity in which military goals were pursued without reference to human cost. Examples include numerous sieges, the Bengal famine of 1943 and the Somali famine of 2011. This category also includes cases in which disastrous economic and social policies were pursued despite evidence that they were creating famine – and were not abandoned even when their outcomes became clear. Instances include the Great Leap Forward famine and the North Korean famine of the 1990s. In most cases, famines occurred alongside war crimes such as massacres, linked fundamentally by disregard for the value of human life and tactically by the violent pursuit of political and military goals.

Ascertaining intent and culpability is not straightforward, and in many famines there were different, overlapping interests and culpabilities or shifts from one category to another. Common are instances of first-degree famine crimes within larger second-degree famines. For example, the Cambodian famine was, as a whole, an outcome of an appalling policy error – the 'Super Great Leap Forward'[55] – but within it there were cases of forced starvation to death of people labelled political enemies. Darfur in 2003–5 was a second-degree counter-insurgency famine crime which included the forced starvation of the village of Keilak, a first-degree famine crime.[56] However, the numbers starved in Keilak did not suffice to make the whole Darfur crisis into a category-one faminogenic episode.

The *third degree of culpable famine causation* is when public authorities are indifferent: their policies may not be the principal cause of famine but they do little or nothing to alleviate hunger. This falls short of a crime, though there may be *political* culpability. An example is the famine of 1984–5 in Sudan, caused by drought and economic crisis, in response to which the government of President Jaafar Nimeiri chose to deny the scale of the crisis and refused to ask for relief assistance. Another case is the Ethiopian famines under Emperor Haile Selassie. There are many instances from the colonial period in which metropolitan rulers simply didn't care enough whether their colonial subjects lived or died, such as India in the 1870s and 1890s and the Sahel in 1913. Third-degree faminogenic acts caused 16 famines, killing 19 million people (18 per cent).

The *fourth category* is *lack* of political culpability. This is when incapable or incapacitated authorities, faced with food crises caused by external factors (climatic, economic, foreign donors' aid policies, etc.), are unable to respond effectively to needs. Thirteen million deaths (12.5 per cent) occurred in famines in which governments were simply incapable or mildly negligent. Cases include the Chinese and Brazilian famines of the 1870s, India (Maharashtra) in 1972–3 and Bangladesh in 1974. These cases are rare and have become rarer.

The framework of 'famine crimes' is agnostic as to whether the crimes in question are political acts or individual criminal acts, though almost always they are committed in pursuit of political goals using instruments of state policy. A causal story can be told for each famine as a singular and exceptional event. Enabling conditions, or circumstances that make it harder to perpetrate famine political crimes, are relevant considerations. But ultimately it is the agency of the men and organizations that commit famine crimes that provides the core of the explanation.

Endings

Mass atrocity endings aren't tidy. This can be seen even for the simplest case of ending genocide, most celebrated in the global narrative of history, namely the liberation of the Nazi concentration camps. One of the most painful passages of Primo Levi's *Survival in Auschwitz* comes right at the end. Many of the prisoners at Auschwitz were killed by their guards during the evacuation as the Soviet army approached. Levi was lucky: he was ill with scarlet fever at the time and was in the infectious diseases hut of the camp hospital section, along with ten other inmates. When the Germans fled, there was a ten-day interregnum before the Russians arrived, during which time the prisoners – freed from the SS but not from hunger, freezing cold and exhaustion – fended for themselves in the ruins of the camp. One of the eleven died of starvation during these ten days, and a further five in the following weeks, at the temporary Russian hospital.[57] These six men surely counted as victims of the Holocaust in the final days, their lives could be saved neither by themselves nor their fellow prisoners, nor Soviet doctors.

From a greater distance, there's no dispute how the Nazi Final Solution ended: despite the Nazi defeat, nineteen out of twenty Jews in Poland were dead, and Hitler in his bunker could claim success in that grim project. How did the Hunger Plan end? The starvation of Soviet prisoners of war and the Warsaw Ghetto concluded as the hunger planners intended. During 1942, the Hunger Plan was modified to take account of realities, such as the German need for labour. The starvation of Leningrad ended when the siege was lifted, with the retreat of the Germans, and mass forced starvation in the occupied territories similarly faded as the Red Army defeated the Wehrmacht. But famine wasn't finished: tens of thousands died of hunger in the chaos, reprisals and forced displacement after the collapse of the Third Reich, and more than a million died of starvation in the winters of 1946 and 1947. German prisoners of war remained in Soviet camps for years, and more than a million of them perished from hunger and exhaustion. The ending was a complicated mix of completing the assignment, military defeat, adapting the Plan under changing circumstances, and a bigger and longer process of society and the economy recovering after the war, including through American emergency aid.

Most mass atrocity endings are complicated – empirically, analytically and ethically. Conley-Zilkic's book, *How Mass Atrocities End*, consisting of six case studies and a quantitative analysis of all 40 cases since 1945 in which 50,000 people or more died, provides a framework for understanding historic endings over time.[58] Her main findings are the following. First, it is national political agendas that determine when and how atrocities end, not international policy or interventions. Forty per cent of cases ended when violence was carried out 'as planned' – that is, until a political goal was achieved. This does not mean that genocide was carried out until the target group was annihilated. In almost all cases, the perpetrator was intent on achieving a military victory or political security and would de-escalate killings when the main political goal was accomplished. The classic case of this was Biafra, in which the federal government, having won the war, immediately announced a policy of 'no victor, no vanquished', and the genocidal killings that Biafrans had feared did not happen. Other examples are Stalin's purges and Saddam Hussein's campaign against the Kurds: in these bureaucratic totalitarianisms, the dictator had the power and capacity to switch off the governmental killing machine with a single memo, from one day to the next. And they did so – retaining, of course, the power to start it up again. Where state power was fragmented, such as in Sudan, the order to halt might be given but not obeyed – or reinterpreted down the command chain.

In approximately one-quarter of cases, the regime responsible for violence was defeated militarily, either by rebellion or invasion, after which atrocities declined, though not always immediately. A good example is the defeat of the Khmer Rouge by the Vietnamese in 1979. Overthrow of an atrocious government did not automatically lead to an improvement, as the case of the defeat of Idi Amin in Uganda in 1979 and his replacement by Milton Obote showed: the pattern of killings just changed. Seven years later, the collapse of the Obote government again didn't end atrocities but changed their location and their victims.

In 35 per cent of cases, internal political factors – often a conflict that had stalemated – or a coup produced a change of policy or leadership that brought about more moderate strategy. The brutal colonial counter-insurgencies in Mozambique and Angola came to an end with revolution in Portugal in 1974. More controversially, a shift in the balance of power within the Sudanese government, to favour military officers over ideological extremists, ended a genocidal campaign in the Nuba Mountains in 1993 but did not end the ongoing war.

Second, the distribution of endings has changed over the decades. During the Cold War, atrocities most often ended when perpetrators successfully used overwhelming force to achieve their political goals. As the Cold War thawed, the geo-strategic context and national political calculi changed. Atrocities generally diminished in scale. Which leads to the third key point: since the 1990s, atrocity endings have become more varied, with governments less dominant and many other actors involved. A final point is that, throughout all periods, mass atrocities are closely associated with war, and ending war goes far in reducing the killing of civilians.

Does a similar pattern hold for famine endings? Most of the mass atrocities in the catalogue also entailed starvation and disease, and so the ending of the atrocity was ultimately associated with the end of the starvation. However, the connection was rarely so neat: it's harder to end famine by executive order, coup d'état or invasion, and this is one big reason why the epidemiology of death in mass atrocity doesn't match neatly with political decisions. The connection is also complicated by two extraneous factors: the weather and international relief aid. Harvests were important to many endings: bad harvests delayed the ending of starvation after the Second World War in some places, while better crops hastened it in some other cases. Relief assistance poses a definitional dilemma: should allowing relief aid be counted as 'moderating' policy? Or is it purely incidental to pursuing political or military policy goals? Either way, it must be factored in.

Table 6.1 is a schematic representation of famine endings.

A pattern emerges that is broadly comparable to Conley-Zilkic's findings. During the Cold War, famine crimes tended to proceed 'as planned'

Table 6.1 Famine crime endings, 1950–2010

Date	Place	Category	Ending
1958	Ethiopia	3	No government action ('as planned')
1962	China	2	Minimal government action ('as planned')
1970	Nigeria	2	Generosity in victory ('as planned' followed by 'moderation' and aid)
1973	India	4	Government action ('moderation')
1973	Ethiopia	3	Revolution ('defeat') with (belated) aid
1974	Bangladesh	4	Minimal action by Bangladesh and US governments ('as planned')
1978	East Timor	2	Counter-insurgency victory ('as planned')
1979	Cambodia	2	Invasion by Vietnam ('defeat') with (belated) aid
1985	Ethiopia	2	Minimal action by government, international aid ('as planned, with aid') (followed in 1991 by defeat)
1985	Sudan	3	Popular uprising followed by relief ('defeat with aid')
1992	Somalia	2	Local efforts followed by international aid ('moderation with aid')
1997	North Korea	2	Government policy change and international aid ('moderation with aid')
1998	South Sudan	2	Government and rebel 'moderation with aid'
2005	Darfur, Sudan	2	Partial victory over insurgency with aid ('as planned with aid')
2006	Northern Uganda	2	Victory over insurgency with aid ('as planned with aid')

unless the government were overthrown. International involvement sometimes exacerbated famines in the earlier period and usually mitigated them in the later period. Since the end of the Cold War, endings are diverse, including instances of 'as planned', 'defeat' and 'moderation', all of them 'with aid'.

This chapter has endeavoured to show that political factors – across the board from electoral democracy to the ending of wars and atrocities – are indeed the likeliest candidates for the principal role in reducing famines. Table 6.1 shows one clear trend: since 1985, all famine endings are 'with aid'. This poses a related set of questions, which are examined in the following chapter. To what extent did the last thirty years witness a spread of these broad democratic principles in the *international* arena, such that the ending of famines was driven by global political factors? To what extent did humanitarian aid serve, like public health, to reduce the human impacts of famine but without addressing its causes? And to what extent has international law – in theory and practice – contributed to ending mass starvation?

7

The Humanitarian International

The Humanitarian Cascade

When the US Marines stormed ashore in Mogadishu in December 1992, mandated by the UN Security Council to create a secure environment for the aid operations, I asked: are they the current-day shock troops of philanthropic imperialism, or the vanguard of the humanitarian international? It was, I believe, the first use of the phrase 'humanitarian international' and it was initially intended as the emancipatory counterpart of the role of foreign aid as an instrument of power projection. I didn't define the term, but it referred to the global apparatus of aid, law and policy concerned with the relief of suffering.

One part of the humanitarian international delivers material relief: it is the international network of national and multilateral agencies and non-governmental organizations (NGOs) that have a prominent role in responding to famines and humanitarian emergencies. Another part promotes law and legal remedies including (most prominently) criminal trials for the perpetrators of atrocities.

The humanitarian international has generated an enormous literature, much of it critical. Looked at up close, each face has many blemishes: uneven professional standards, wastage and an exaggerated sense of self-importance. The most fundamental criticism of the relief aid business is that its clients are not the recipients of its assistance but those who pay its bills. It is not driven by the needs of the hungry but by the political demands of its donors – chiefly western governments. This is a fair point. I heard a criticism of the relief aid to

Darfur in 1985, which went something like this: 'We welcome the food but why does every truckload need to come with an American attached?' This critique boils down to seeing the global relief system as an arm of a global governance system, dedicated to preserving and advancing western (and especially US) dominance. This is a line of argument particularly associated with Mark Duffield.[1] In the aftermath of the September 2001 terrorist crimes, the US Secretary of State Colin Powell validated this position, telling American NGO leaders, 'I am serious about making sure we have the best relationship with the NGOs who are such a force multiplier for us, such an important part of our combat team.'[2]

But if we step back and survey the humanitarian business over a time frame of generations, the record looks rather more impressive. It is true that decisions on international aid are taken by rich governments on the basis of their own political calculations. But these governments are democratic and are influenced by a compassionate public. The donating public and electorate may have simplified and often misguided ideas about who is starving and why, but the very existence of humanitarian aid and the fact that it is subjected to a fairly high level of professional scrutiny means that it can make a difference in the relief of suffering. Most of its instruments work relatively well most of the time. However, one particular tool – what was called 'humanitarian intervention' in the 1990s and 'the responsibility to protect' more recently – has proved profoundly problematic.

In a comparable manner, the legal regimes that deal with war crimes, crimes against humanity and genocide are weak in general and even weaker in how they deal with famine and starvation as such. But there is a growing public intolerance of atrocities so that the limited scope of laws and the small number of international criminal prosecutions can be said to be emblematic of a shift in attitudes. The fact that there isn't strong legislation against starvation per se also looks less problematic if we consider famine within the ambit of atrocities and how these are less tolerated than before.

Humanitarian Aid

The international relief business has become a regular actor in global dramas. Humanitarians are more numerous, active and better-funded than ever before. Official humanitarian assistance (measured in 2014 prices) increased from US$128 million in 1970 to US$13 billion in 2013 and almost US$28 billion in 2015.[3] Emergency food aid – although a small proportion of total official development assistance and an

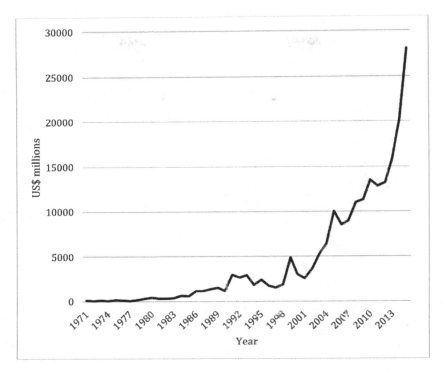

Figure 7.1 Humanitarian assistance budgets (all donors): 1971–2015
Source: OECD QWIDS, Global Humanitarian Assistance Report 2016

even smaller component of international food trade – has also grown in quantity and importance (see Figure 7.1).[4]

This increase in budget has been accompanied by increasing operational complexity, as well as a proliferation of humanitarian organizations. It is still small compared to official development assistance (approximately US$100 billion) and tiny compared to remittances (US$300 billion) and foreign direct investment (US$750 billion). Moreover, financial instruments remain rudimentary – humanitarian action is still funded on a cash budget, with appeals whenever there's a disaster, a system aptly described as 'medieval'.[5]

Supply and demand for humanitarian aid

The rise of the humanitarians coincided with the end of calamitous famines and the beginning of Act Four of our famine story thirty years ago. This is a period in which the number of famines has remained roughly constant but they no longer kill millions. Could it be that both the humanitarians and their critics are right: that the humanitarian international doesn't stop famines but it does save lives? Or is it more complicated?

Gilles Carbonnier, in his *Humanitarian Economics*, is sceptical. He poses the paradox: 'over the past two decades the supply of humanitarian aid (in the form of funding, workers and aid supplies) has rapidly increased, but there is no evidence that this surge was caused by a parallel surge in actual needs.'[6] He observes that the assistance grew while the numbers of people affected by armed conflicts and natural disasters fluctuated wildly but without obvious trends. His conclusion:

> Ultimately, the humanitarian market boom of the 1990s and 2000s reflects the more prominent role of humanitarianism in global governance, next to a post-Cold War rise in peacekeeping operations. Humanitarian responses gained prominence as a foreign policy instrument, often used by default to compensate for the lack of political resolve and capacity to put an end to war crimes and crimes against humanity in the face of domestic pressure to aid distant strangers whose suffering is brought home by instant media coverage.[7]

In short, Carbonnier argues, the massive growth of humanitarianism was driven by the international politics of aid giving rather than by an increase in the numbers of people in humanitarian need. But there are four vitally important caveats.

First, the fact that the increase was supply driven does not mean that there was an oversupply of humanitarian aid or that this aid didn't have significant impact. The *human needs* of people stricken by humanitarian crisis are far greater than their *effective demand*. This is true by definition: if they had the economic resources and the political clout to demand that their needs were met, then these famines simply wouldn't occur in the first place. So it's hard to calculate real need: there is no indication that the fast-increasing humanitarian supply isn't actually necessary. There is certainly inefficiency and wastage, but there are very few crises in which there's a surfeit of aid and many in which there's a serious shortage. What this story tells us is that there was an earlier, massive undersupply of emergency relief, rather than there is too much today.

Second, the most egregious supply-driven component of humanitarian aid – food aid – has been significantly reformed. In their definitive history of food aid, Christopher Barrett and Daniel Maxwell write, 'Food aid programs have traditionally been driven primarily by the availability of the resource rather than by a grounded analysis of food insecurity.'[8] The 'iron triangle' of western farmers, shipping companies and large NGOs were long a vested interest blocking food aid reform. Nonetheless, Barrett and Maxwell contend, food aid has been 'edging towards' a recipient-oriented system responsive to the needs of famine prevention and poverty reduction.

Third, the need for emergency aid has sharply increased in the last few years: the positive trends have gone into reverse. By 2017, the number of people assessed as being in need of humanitarian relief was higher than at any time since systematic records began twenty years earlier.

And fourth, the humanitarian international is a liberal system, subject to democratic demands and internal critique. It is a self-improving system. The fact that aid is governed by politics does not mean it is a malign system, though it has had its share of mixed motives, hypocrisy and outright criminality over the decades.

Humanitarian action in the twentieth century

Emergency relief efforts for the greater part of the twentieth century helped relatively few people who could be reached amidst great suffering and inhumanity. Aid agencies played virtually no role in famine relief during the world wars. Oxfam, founded to bring aid to blockaded Greece in 1942, was able only to provide symbolic assistance. American aid was very substantial after each of the wars. After the First World War, this included the expansion of the Red Cross, the creation of Near East Relief for Armenian deportees[9] and the relief effort for the Russian famine of the 1920s organized by the American Relief Administration under President Herbert Hoover.[10] After the Second World War, there was CARE and the Marshall Plan. However, aid agencies were absent from China under Mao, from Cambodia under Pol Pot, and from East Timor following the Indonesian invasion. The humanitarian international as we know it today only began in earnest during the Biafra war of the late 1960s, where its impacts were controversial.

Food aid as an instrument of state policy started with American assistance to ravaged Europe and East Asia in the 1940s. Public Law 480 ('food for peace') was passed in 1954, setting up a US food aid administration that became one of the cornerstones of American Cold War-era policy towards developing countries. Emergency food aid was only a small part of this, but some nations' food economies became highly dependent on external food aid, such that a disruption to that food aid could contribute to a famine. A case in point is Bangladesh in 1974, when the capacity of the government to manage its subsidized food system – and grain merchants' confidence in that capacity – collapsed due to the co-occurrence of a harvest failure and the withdrawal of most US food aid.

The major decline in famines occurred before the emergence of the humanitarian international. The major *causes* of those famines – wars and dictatorships – couldn't be addressed by humanitarians. But the *impacts* of those famines could be mitigated by relief (even at the cost of distracting attention from the political and military causes of the disasters). And, indeed, there haven't been any calamitous famines since relief aid grew in size and became a normative element of the international scene. In the worst famines of the 1980s, international aid donors, especially the United States, pushed reluctant faminogenic national governments to accept food aid. This happened in Ethiopia when the Soviet-aligned regime denied for a long time that it was suffering famine and refused to appeal for aid, and twice in Sudan when the western-aligned government refused to declare a food crisis in 1984, and four years later when its successor government refused to acknowledge war famine in southern Sudan. Otherwise, these famines would have been far worse. These cases show that the existence of the humanitarian apparatus alone isn't enough: its activities have to be politically initiated. The political dramas and controversies of humanitarian action in the 1990s reprised the same themes on an even grander scale.

Famine relief has become a reason why people survive food and health crises that might in earlier years have killed them. It is an increasingly significant resource that stops food crises and humanitarian emergencies descending into fully fledged famines and in protecting the affected people from the ravages of communicable diseases and the extremes of hunger. Emergency aid also helps people retain assets, stay on their land and recover more quickly. It is tempting to devote a chapter, or a book, to the question of whether humanitarian efforts have achieved their goals, and it would not be difficult to do so, not least because humanitarians like nothing more than writing about themselves. (My book *Famine Crimes*[11] was primarily concerned with the political causes of famine and secondarily with how humanitarian agencies failed to grapple with those, but the interest in the book among students and policy makers has been almost entirely the second, subordinate issue.)

Whatever its marginal role in previous eras, humanitarian aid has now become an important element in protecting people from famine or from the worst impacts of famine. The 2013 'People Affected by Conflict' survey by the Centre for Research on the Epidemiology of Disasters (CRED) examined the impacts of all conflicts for which there are data. The authors reported, 'By and large, our research found encouraging news in terms of lower death rates, indicating that periods of stabilization and humanitarian efforts have succeeded in saving lives.'[12]

Humanitarianism as a learning system

There's another potential causal chain at work. Even while humanitarian agencies tend to depoliticize the crises in which they work, they themselves are the product of a particular kind of politics. The countries that devote significant funds to international humanitarian budgets are democracies, and their electorates have humanitarian sensibilities. The biggest impact of relief agencies may not be in the places where they send their aid workers, medicines and food but rather in their own capital cities, where their public profile and lobbying influences what politicians can do. In so far as the real demand for humanitarian aid is from the donating public and the donor governments they influence, the humanitarians are effective in expanding the size of their own market. But they are also expanding the space for public awareness and debate, which has impacts well beyond donations to charity. Carbonnier implicitly laments the primary role of domestic politics in shaping the scale and nature of humanitarian action. But, arguably, the errors and distortions that arise in the public advocacy and decision making around humanitarian aid are a small price to pay for the ascent of democracy, which is the biggest single element driving the reduction of famines worldwide.

Humanitarian action has not only expanded in scope, it has become more professional and more attuned to its political context and the ethical challenges that arise from trying to work in circumstances of war and political violence. The international disaster relief industry is dominated by a small number of players. They have different philosophies but generally share the same business model. The major consortia, including the bigger church-related agencies, CARE, Oxfam and Save the Children, all rely overwhelmingly on funds from western donor governments and work closely with the specialized agencies of the United Nations and the European Union. There are two big outliers, the International Committee of the Red Cross (ICRC) and Médecins Sans Frontières (MSF), which have foundational commitments to independence (in markedly different ways). These dominant aid agencies have adopted standards and codes of conduct which have undoubtedly increased the professionalism of relief delivery, especially in child nutrition, water and sanitation, and emergency public health. In turn, this has reduced the mortal consequences of famines and humanitarian emergencies such as refugee crises.

These agencies have also shown increasing awareness of the political and ethical issues, particularly following two debacles in the 1990s. The first of these was Somalia, where aid agencies orchestrated what the president of CARE-USA, Philip Johnston, called 'the drumbeat for intervention'.[13] Extraordinarily, it worked. In the dog days of his presidency, George H. W. Bush ordered the US Marine Corps to Somalia in order to establish 'a secure environment for humanitarian relief operations'.[14] The conventional story is that the Marines stopped the famine. It certainly helped in the short term, particularly in bringing aid to some of the worst pockets of extreme hunger. But the intervention could not have ended the famine because the famine was already waning by the time the troops arrived.[15]

As soon as it was announced, I took a strong stand against Operation Restore Hope in Somalia. It was, I argued, a mistaken and dangerous step. I was at Africa Watch at the time. Together with my colleague Rakiya Omaar (1993), I made the case that it was based on a misrepresentation of the situation in Somalia, that Somalis had not been consulted, that alternatives to massive force had not been explored and that there were no guarantees that the intervening troops would not act contrary to humanitarian law and make matters worse. Our parent organization, Human Rights Watch, supported the intervention. Rakiya was fired and I resigned. We were vindicated more quickly than we had expected.

Just six months into the intervention, open warfare broke out between the intervening forces and the United Somali Congress (USC), Somali militia loyal to General Mohamed Farah Aideed. As I was researching a report on violations of humanitarian law by the international forces during that conflict, I was the subject of an order that I be arrested and detained by UN troops.[16] The stated reason was 'supporting the propaganda efforts of the USC'. I escaped arrest because the evening before the instruction was given a Somali friend advised me to leave town immediately as, he said, my life was in danger. I left Mogadishu and arrived in Nairobi the next afternoon to learn the news that four journalists had been killed by an angry crowd just a few yards from the house where I was staying, after a US air strike killed scores of elders who had gathered to consult on a peace initiative.

Aid officials were left reflecting that when they called for international troops, they had not properly grasped that the soldiers would follow military orders and procedures, rather than any purported humanitarian diktat. The occupiers looked after their own security first, were inefficient and reluctant humanitarians, and treated local people with suspicion at best and hostility at worst. However attractive the idea, a military intervention in practice was ugly.

Another shock to the humanitarian system followed quickly: the genocide in Rwanda and its aftermath in eastern Zaire (subsequently the Democratic Republic of Congo – DRC). The mass killing of up to 800,000 people, the great majority of them ethnic Tutsi, was not a famine or humanitarian emergency that fitted into the established categories for aid agencies. But the subsequent influx of hundreds of thousands of people to eastern Zaire was: it resembled a conventional refugee emergency of enormous scale and rapidity, with the sole exception (largely overlooked at first) that the refugees included in their number the political-administrative apparatus of the defeated genocidal government and its army.

This wasn't the first time something like this had happened. The clearest parallel was international aid to Cambodian refugees on the Thai border in the 1980s, which gave material aid and political solace to the Khmer Rouge for a decade following its ouster from power. Cold War realpolitik dictated that western governments continued to recognize Pol Pot and the Khmer Rouge, despite their genocidal and faminogenic record, and deny recognition and aid to the Vietnamese-installed successor government. Aid agencies had also lost impartiality in Biafra and some of them had tolerated manipulation in Ethiopia in 1985, especially around forced resettlement. The aid effort to the Zairean camps – like Biafra and Ethiopia – arose more from naivety than realpolitik. But it was particularly egregious in that, while the *génocidaires* were fed and protected, the survivors of the genocide and the entire ravaged land of Rwanda were neglected by the aid industry and by the narratives that the latter spun.

The major aid agencies began a protracted period of soul searching in the aftermath of Rwanda, from which the most important sets of standards and codes of conduct emerged. A decade later, the results were noticeable. For example, the humanitarian response to the crisis in Darfur was much more impressive in its professionalism and its attention to the political context, largely avoiding the perils of de facto collaboration with the Sudanese government and the shrill chorus of demands for forcible regime change.

Alongside the oligopoly of big agencies, the humanitarian international has a largely unregulated market of start-ups and fringe causes. Each high-profile emergency generates a large number of voluntary efforts, mostly by local people but also by diaspora groups and energetic humanitarian entrepreneurs who are animated by watching a television programme or mounting a local fundraiser. Among these are many amateurs and partisans. But among them are also groups that can be brave and innovative, running physical, professional and ethical risks that more established agencies might not be able to do. Also among them are groups with close links to the affected communities, such as Bosnian and Syrian diaspora groups that took an interest in relieving suffering in their countries' respective civil wars. These people and their organizations usually have much greater knowledge, sensitivity and access than the larger agencies. Counter-terrorism surveillance and legislation have, unfortunately and counterproductively, hampered Muslim charities trying to operate in countries such as Somalia and Syria.[17] Volunteers describe facing questioning and harassment when travelling to Europe, difficulties in making financial transactions and restrictions on how they can operate in the field that mean that their comparative advantage – intimate knowledge of local communities – is the source of suspicion rather than an asset.

Towards a global humanitarian norm

The arc of humanitarian history has bent towards saving lives in crises. The humanitarian system has many ragged edges, including misrepresentation and exaggeration, diversion and wastage and (most seriously) undermining the efforts of local people. Most important, however, is that the norm of prohibiting starvation became accepted by powerful democracies. This had real effects. Two incidents in the 1990s illuminate the shift: Iraq and North Korea.

The people of Iraq in the 1990s suffered a combination of the disruptions of the 1990 war and exceptionally severe comprehensive sanctions.[18] The US Secretary of State, Madeleine Albright, asked for her opinion on a report that half a million children had died, said, 'I think this is a very hard choice, but the price, we think the price is worth it.'[19] She later regretted the statement: public opinion wouldn't any longer tolerate this kind of policy. Albright's regret was the tribute that realpolitik paid to the humanitarian norm. The Iraq sanctions controversy was part of a shift towards making it much more politically difficult for the United States to use the denial of food as a weapon.

When the first signs of famine in the People's Democratic Republic of Korea were apparent to the world in 1997, there was a vigorous debate in American newspaper columns between those who argued that it would be wrong to condition aid on policy change by the regime, notwithstanding its culpability for the famine, and those who implicitly made the case for starving North Korea into collapse, claiming that aid would be fungible and be used to support the military apparatus of a government hostile to its people and to America.[20] Andrew

Natsios was in the pro-aid group, and he concluded his review of that famine and relief efforts by observing that US aid helped make the regime more open to the international community. He also claimed that famines don't overturn dictatorships – generally true but with counter-examples, as in Ethiopia in 1974 and Sudan in 1985.

The sequel to the North Korean aid programme reveals how much the norm was shifting. Natsios took the principle of 'no famine on my watch' into the George W. Bush administration. He explained:

> While I was USAID Administrator [from 2001–6] we, within the Agency, made it a policy that there would be no famines on our watch. I said this was the President's intention though I did not have a specific public document or statement I could quote. The President did say we would never use food as an instrument of diplomacy or deny it as a punitive measure while he was in office. We enforced his policy rigorously.[21]

Perhaps the most remarkable but under-recognized act of USAID during those years was initiating a relief programme for Darfur in September 2003 – six months *before* the humanitarian crisis became headline news. Natsios made this decision, well aware that he would be open to the same critique that was made for aiding North Korea. He did the right thing – relief undoubtedly saved scores of thousands of Darfurian lives.

The norm of humanitarian aid had, it seems, entered the bloodstream of the US government. This norm was tested again in Somalia (2011) and Syria (2012 onwards), against American counter-terrorism law and policy, which restricted aid. On these occasions, the outcome was ambiguous: there were fierce debates within the US government, but aid was delayed to Somalia, contributing to a large-scale loss of life.

The core argument for humanitarian action is that it saves lives,[22] providing some aid to alleviate at least some suffering. David Rieff summed this up with the phrase 'a bed for the night'.[23] More ambitiously, aid agencies have seen their goals as bringing an end to famine and poverty. In the late 1970s and early 1980s, Oxfam staff, noting that a focus on disaster appeals was demeaning to the recipients and that grass-roots development was a more ethical and effective response than emergency relief, tried hard to shift the agency's focus away from famine relief.[24] A wholly different philosophy animated MSF (especially its French section), concerned more with moral solidarity and the duty of 'witnessing' suffering and violations (*témoignage*).[25]

The premise of humanitarian action is that it is good and should not need to justify itself. The more interesting arguments are those *against* humanitarian action. One of the oldest and simplest is that food aid typically arrives late in a famine-stricken area and swamps the market just as farmers are beginning to harvest their post-famine crops. Excess food aid undercuts farmers trying to sell those harvests, drives merchants from the market and changes people's tastes away from local food to imported cereals. Another line of argument introduces the political element: relief aid, particularly food, provides resources that sustain belligerents and authoritarian governments. Even when it is not stolen by soldiers and militiamen, foreign aid shifts the burden of responsibility from the government (where it belongs) to a nebulous and remote international community. In doing this, assistance depoliticizes famine, presenting what is fundamentally a political problem as a technical malfunction deserving charity. Just as Malthus conveniently shifted the blame for famine from the East India Company and its political sponsors in London to their victims, so too humanitarian aid implicitly legitimizes the perpetrator of famine crimes. The culprit in this case is less the material aid itself than the narrative that aid agencies construct in order to obtain funds and justify themselves. The famine story, as told in fundraising appeals and by journalists taken on tours of feeding centres, is one of helpless local victims and foreign saviours, Introducing a criminal culprit – especially one with whom the operational aid giver must of necessity do business – is a complication better left out of the picture. It's easier to blame the weather. So, ultimately, international aid – and the stories aid providers tell to sustain themselves – deceive by pretending to solve a problem that they cannot.

This line of argument can of course be turned against the humanitarian critics: when did emancipatory politics alone halt a famine? And how might it claim to do so without deceiving the hungry? If we examine those instances in which a democratic anti-famine political contract (my proposed panacea in *Famine Crimes*) has indeed emerged, we see that it took decades to effect, and in the meantime short-term humanitarian efforts were needed to end immediate suffering. It follows that frankness about the political contributors to famine is not a substitute for humanitarian action but a complement to it.

Any or all of these objections and critiques may be correct. But they also illustrate the limits faced by humanitarians: they cannot address the causes of famine and they can only act at scale when they are politically able to do so.

Humanitarian intervention

Military intervention is the last, most powerful resource of the humanitarian international. It is also the most problematic and illustrates the limits of humanitarian action as a transformative agenda. The Mogadishu debacle in 1993 burned the hands of those humanitarians who had advocated for intervention, and thereafter relief agencies have not called for troops to serve as the vanguard of famine relief efforts. Instead, the concept of humanitarian intervention was given new clothes as the 'responsibility to protect' (although the proponents of 'R2P' would dispute this identification). The interventionists' new focus was stopping mass atrocity and genocide, not relieving famine.

The number of cases is too small and the singularities of each one so significant that it is difficult to draw general conclusions about the last two decades of military interventions. In a small country such as Sierra Leone, or a limited location such as the Ituri area in the DRC (location for the European Union Operation Artemis in 2003), a deployment of overwhelming military force could provide stability, given enough time. When force was judiciously applied in support of a political process, as in Bosnia in 1995, it could also help achieve positive outcomes, though the soldiers and airmen tend to be given more credit than they deserve vis-à-vis the diplomats. When force was used without a political process (as in Kosovo), the results were disputable; when it was used as an alternative to a political process (as in Libya), the result was disaster. And where force was threatened but not used (as in Darfur), it induced paranoia and stubbornness among the intended targets and inflated hopes and stubbornness among the anticipated beneficiaries to the detriment of peace, peacekeeping and humanitarian action.

A sceptical attitude towards military intervention has served me reliably over these years. The cautionary words of Sir William Harcourt, writing under the name 'Historicus' 150 years ago, to counsel against British intervention in the American civil war stand the test of time:

> [intervention] is a high and summary procedure which may sometimes snatch a remedy beyond the reach of law. Nevertheless, it must be admitted that in the case of Intervention, as in that of Revolution, its essence is illegality and its justification is its success. Of all things, at once the most unjustifiable and the most impolitic is an unsuccessful Intervention....
>
> Intervention may be wise, may be right – nay, sometimes, may even be necessary. But let us not deceive ourselves, intervention never has been, never will be, never can be short, simple or peaceable.[26]

Since the Libya intervention of 2011, the cheerleaders for R2P at the point of a gun have fallen quiet. The intervention was not intended to relieve starvation. Its humanitarian rationale was preventing a massacre in Benghazi, and that may indeed be its sole, if intrinsically unprovable, success. The subsequent failures in Libya are inescapable evidence of the folly of the operation. But the way in which the intervention was decided at the UN Security Council also discredited the concept. The French-British-American plan for military operations in Libya won acceptance at the UN Security Council only by deceiving Russia and the African Union that the air attacks would be conducted in support of diplomatic efforts, not as a means of forcible regime change. The interventionist norm had political traction only when there was a minimum consensus not to obstruct it among the 'permanent five' at the UN Security Council and, when the deception over Libya became apparent, that consensus was blown apart. The Russian-American antagonism over Syria, which blocked concerted humanitarian and political action over that conflict, was a direct consequence.

For humanitarian actors – whether relief workers or human rights advocates – calling for armed intervention crosses a threshold. Instead of seeking to aid and protect people threatened by the misuse of power, they wanted to use power in a transformative manner. Like revolutionaries throughout history, they found themselves subject to two iron laws: the law of unintended consequences and the rule that power corrupts, especially when that power's critical faculties are clouded by strong belief in a virtuous enterprise.

Crimes Without Names?

My central tenet in *Famine Crimes* was that those who cause famines should be held to account in the court of public opinion, if not through legal prosecution. The concept that starvation is contrary to natural law is found in customary codes of law and politics across the world, and most lawyers would argue that acts of famine and forced starvation are forbidden under international law.

Those seeking to criminalize starvation need to answer two intrinsically difficult questions. First, *what kind of crime is starvation?* Is it a crime of murder or extermination? A crime of inhumane treatment? Of persecution? Or is starvation a crime of disproportionate suffering, inflicted on unfortunate civilians as a by-product of military tactics? In the case of peacetime famine, is it the outcome of political, economic or ecological recklessness?

There are three bodies of international law that are relevant: the laws of war; crimes against humanity; and the Genocide Convention (with a passing nod to human rights law). The most signal weakness of these laws is that for the most part they do not specify starvation and famine as such. Nonetheless, the law is good enough for prosecuting most starvation crimes under different headings, should the will to do so exist.

The second difficult question is: *how is culpability to be proven?* Unlike a death caused by an act of violence, a death from starvation is slow and has many actual or potential contributory causes. The only cases in which a simple causal attribution is possible are those where prisoners are entirely dependent on their gaolers for food. Any mass starvation or famine has multiple causes. How is a prosecutor to prove that it was the act of the perpetrator, rather than another factor, such as communicable infections, that caused a person to suffer or die? Even in a besieged city, the attribution of criminal responsibility for deaths by starvation would be extraordinarily complicated.

The warrior's honour

The customs and laws of war have historically been ambivalent about the prohibition on starvation. There has always been a tension between chivalry and codes of honour among warriors and practices of armies living off the land, violating women and girls and using blockade and siege warfare.

One of the earliest modern formulations of humanitarian law was commissioned by President Abraham Lincoln from the legal scholar Franz Lieber in 1863. The Lieber Code was intended to inform the conduct of the Union army during the American Civil War. Article 17 reads: 'War is not carried out by arms alone. It is lawful to starve the hostile belligerent, armed or unarmed, so that it leads to the speedier subjection of the enemy.' While this does not prohibit civilian starvation, it narrows its justification by requiring the condition that it should contribute to a military goal – the defeat or surrender of the adversary.

Part of the reason for the non-prohibition of starvation was that the great powers of the day, notably Great Britain, were maritime powers that routinely used blockade as their preferred method of economic warfare. The British government sought to codify this in 1909 with the London Conference concerning the Laws of Naval Law. The status of foodstuffs in blockade was one of the most vexatious issues in the negotiations.[27] The resulting Declaration re-stated the customary rule that food should be treated as 'conditional contraband', permitting free passage only if it could be shown that the food was intended exclusively for the civilian population. The London Declaration was never ratified, and in both world wars Britain and the United States used blockade against Germany, German-occupied territories and Japan. Winston Churchill was notoriously slow and reluctant to permit the blockade of Greece to be lifted to provide food to relieve the famine there in 1942. The mining of Japanese harbours by the US air force was candidly named 'Operation Starvation'.

Genocide

The horrors of the Third Reich surpassed the reach of the laws of war, leading Rafaël Lemkin to invent the term 'genocide'. Lemkin was, as I have described in chapter 2, concerned with starvation as genocide. But that concern was diluted as his campaign proceeded for getting genocide recognized as a crime.

Lemkin tried to have the crime of genocide included in the Nuremberg Charter of 1945, which set up the International Military Tribunal to prosecute the German leadership. He didn't succeed: the indictments were for war crimes, crimes against peace and crimes against humanity. Three years later, Lemkin was more successful when states agreed on a Convention on the Prevention and Punishment of Genocide. Article II of the Convention reads, 'genocide means any of the following acts committed with intent to destroy, in whole or in part, a national, ethnical, racial or religious group, as such.' Of the five acts enumerated, the third is: 'Deliberately inflicting on the group conditions of life calculated to bring about its physical destruction in whole or in part'.[28] This would seem to provide ample grounds for prosecuting famine crimes.[29] However, this has never happened. Part of the reason is that the question of *genocidal intent* has preoccupied scholars and prosecutors. Proving intent has been the major challenge facing those prosecuting crimes of genocide, and it would be even harder to prove intent in the case of starvation than of massacre.

Crimes against humanity

After the war, Churchill remarked that it would be 'best to leave the past to history, especially as I propose to write that history myself'.[30] The victorious Allies' diplomats and lawyers similarly wrote the international legal codes that followed. The Nuremberg Charter was the first time that the concept of 'crimes against humanity' was codified in law. Article 6(c) specifies: 'Crimes against humanity: namely, murder, extermination, enslavement, deportation, and other inhumane acts committed against any civilian population, before or during the war, or persecutions on political, racial or religious grounds in execution of or in connection with any crime within the jurisdiction of the

Tribunal, whether or not in violation of the domestic law of the country where perpetrated.'

Starvation was subsumed under 'inhumane acts', 'extermination' or 'persecution'. And thus it transpired during the Nuremberg trials. The indictment mentions starvation of Jews, prisoners of war, slave workers and the populations of occupied territories on numerous occasions. Starvation was also specified in the war crimes charge: 'The murders and ill-treatment were carried out by divers means, including shooting, hanging, gassing, starvation, gross over-crowding, systematic under-nutrition, systematic imposition of labor tasks beyond the strength of those ordered to carry them out, inadequate provision of surgical and medical services, kickings, beatings, brutality and torture of all kinds...'[31]

However, in all cases, starvation was prosecuted only as a subsidiary element within other crimes, namely extermination and inhumane acts. Probable reasons include lack of clarity about what kind of crime starvation should be counted as and the difficulty of proving cause and effect. The stripping of foodstuffs from occupied territories was prosecuted under 'plunder of public and private property'.[32] The Tribunal's decision about Hans Frank, Governor General of the occupied Polish territory, reads:

> Frank was a willing and knowing participant in the use of terrorism in Poland; in the economic exploitation of Poland in a way which led to the death by starvation of a large number of people; in the deportation to Germany as slave laborers of over a million Poles; and in a program involving the murder of at least 3 million Jews.[33]

The difficulties of classifying starvation crimes and the challenges of proving cause and effect were probable reasons why starvation faded into the background during the trials. Another reason was prosecutors' ambivalence about whether starvation should qualify as a war crime at all.

International humanitarian law

The uncertainty around the prohibition on starvation was evident in the post-Nuremberg 'High Command Trial' of Field Marshal Wilhelm von Leeb and twelve other generals, primarily for war crimes. Von Leeb was the commander of Army Group North on the Eastern Front and, as such, responsible for the siege of Leningrad. The American prosecutors argued that von Leeb knew of and approved an order to fire artillery at civilians attempting to leave the city with the aim of maintaining the pressure of the siege.[34] The judges concurred: 'We find this was known to and approved by von Leeb. Was it an unlawful order?'[35] They then cite Charles Hyde, the foremost American authority on international law (who in turn drew on the Lieber Code):

> A belligerent commander may lawfully lay siege to a place controlled by the enemy and endeavour by a process of isolation to cause its surrender. The propriety of attempting to reduce it by starvation is not questioned. Hence the cutting off of every source of sustenance from without is deemed legitimate. It is said that if the commander of a besieged place expels the non-combatants, in order to lessen the number of those who consume its stock of provisions, it is lawful, though an extreme measure, to drive them back, so as to hasten the surrender.[36]

The judges then delivered their decision: 'We might wish the law were otherwise, but we must administer it as we find it. Consequently, we hold no criminality attaches on this charge.'[37]

After the Second World War, the laws of war were updated. But the 1949 Geneva Conventions remained conspicuously muted on questions relating to starvation. British and American tolerance of inflicting hunger through blockade was slow to fade. Twenty years later, Michael Stewart, foreign secretary at the time of the Nigerian civil war, steadfastly and notoriously defended Britain's support for the Nigerian blockade of the secessionist enclave of Biafra, which created famine, saying, 'We must accept that, in the whole history of warfare, any nation which has been in a position to starve its enemy out has done so.'[38]

Nonetheless, the war famines in Biafra and Bangladesh contributed to the expansion of the scope of international humanitarian law, resulting in the protracted negotiation and adoption of two Additional Protocols to the Geneva Convention in 1977. For the first time, a specific prohibition on starvation entered the law book. The ban on the starvation of civilian populations contained in Article 54 of the First Additional Protocol begins as follows:[39]

1 Starvation of civilians as a method of warfare is prohibited.
2 It is prohibited to attack, destroy, remove or render useless objects indispensable to the survival of the civilian population such as foodstuffs, agricultural areas for the production of foodstuffs, crops, livestock, drinking water installations and supplies and irrigation works, for the specific purpose of denying them for their sustenance value to the civilian population or to the adverse Party, whatever the motive, whether in order to starve out civilians, to cause them to move away, or for any other motive.

Paragraph 1 is superbly categorical and paragraph 2 makes it clear the prohibition holds, regardless of whether or not the intent is starvation (in marked comparison to the Genocide Convention). The weaknesses of this paragraph are elsewhere. One is the failure to prohibit restrictions on *activities* indispensable to the survival of the civilian population, such as trading or foraging. A second is that the provision relating to relief 'retreats in the face of military necessity of blockade'.[40] Third is the weak protections afforded to humanitarian workers. Remedying that deficit was the principal focus of subsequent initiatives to expand the laws of war for humanitarian crises. Finally, the provisions in the Second Additional Protocol, concerned with wars 'not of an international nature' (i.e. civil wars), are much weaker.

Tribunals

Despite all that had occurred in the intervening half century, the 1998 Rome Conference that established the ICC echoed Nuremberg and Tokyo in how it handled starvation.[41] The delegates were not intrinsically conservative. On the contrary, they were pioneers and were ready, for example, to elaborate the law concerning gender crimes. Article 7 of the Rome Statute expands the scope of crimes against humanity from the Nuremberg list, but without explicit mention of starvation. Article 7(1)(b) prohibits the crime of 'extermination' and defines it to include 'inflicting conditions of life calculated to bring about the destruction of part of a population'. Article 7(1)(c) prohibits 'inhumane acts', defined to include inflicting 'great suffering, or serious injury to body or to mental or physical health, by means of an inhumane act'. But starvation was still a crime whose name remained unspoken.

At the Rome Conference, there was a single attempt to prohibit economic embargo as a crime against humanity. The Cuban delegate, Dr José Peraza Chapeau, proposed that 'other inhumane acts' should include 'economic, financial and commercial blockades intentionally causing great suffering or seriously injuring physical integrity or mental or physical health', and that 'extermination' should include 'the infliction of conditions of life, inter alia, deprivation of access to foodstuffs and medicines, calculated to bring about the destruction of a population'.[42] He didn't garner enough support. In his closing remarks, Peraza Chapeau thanked those countries that had supported his unsuccessful proposal and promised to continue to 'denounce the genocidal war waged against the Cuban people by an economic blockade'.[43] If that statement did not make the politics of the proposal sufficiently clear, we should also remember that negotiations occurred at the height of the controversy over international sanctions against Iraq, with the US government vigorously defending a policy that was reported to have caused the deaths of hundreds of thousands of Iraqi children. So perhaps we should be less surprised that great power unwillingness to legislate against blockade and starvation had still not faded.

While the delegates in Rome were negotiating over the ICC statute, the International Criminal Tribunal for the former Yugoslavia was prosecuting cases. Blockade and starvation had been well documented as elements of the war tactics pursued in Bosnia-Herzegovina. But the tribunal did not bring any charges for starvation crimes. The massacres following the fall of the 'safe area' of Srebrenica were prosecuted as acts of genocide, overshadowing the deprivation and starvation that had been perpetrated beforehand during the siege. The blockade of food and other necessities to Sarajevo, while it generated a great deal of attention as an instance of the use of hunger as a weapon of war, did not lead to any proven deaths from starvation, as a consequence of which General Stanislav Galič escaped prosecution on that charge – while he was convicted of war crimes associated with sniping civilians and shelling the city.[44]

The fact that the intended victims did not in fact starve to death does not make Galič any less guilty of using hunger as a weapon, though it does make the charge even more complicated to prove. Diana Kearney has, however, claimed these are not insuperable obstacles.[45] She takes the case of the Israeli siege of Gaza and analyses it as an instance of persecution. At its height during Operation Cast Lead of 2008–9, the blockade entailed tight control of basic supplies to the territory. The UN was permitted to transport just a fraction of the assistance it considered necessary for humanitarian purposes.[46] The insult to human dignity of the Gazans was extreme, and the homes and livelihoods of the population were thoroughly degraded, but the line into mass starvation appears not to have been crossed. Dov Weisglass, an advisor to Ehud Olmert, the Israeli Prime Minister, is reputed to have said, 'The idea is to put the Palestinians on a diet, but not to make them die of hunger.'[47] Kearney argues that this amounts to a crime against humanity, regardless of whether the outcome was starvation deaths: 'The deprivation of food was systematically planned, pursuant to state policy, intentionally carried out, and targeted a group based on national identity...Because persecution envelops both death and suffering, mass starvation deaths do not have to result – it is enough to demonstrate that the actions caused large-scale anguish.'[48]

Kearney's position is of course controversial. It points, however, to the way in which there are multiple prosecutorial options for bringing a charge of a famine crime. If it is not murder, it could be persecution or inhumane acts. But starvation still remains subordinate to other charges.

Other options for criminalizing famine

A recent opportunity for revising the law was the Rome Statute review conference in Kampala in 2010. Finally, 101 years after the negotiations in London, when the crime of aggression was added to the Rome Statute, naval blockade was included as an act of aggression.[49] While aggression is traditionally seen as a crime against sovereignty rather than against individuals, the tribunals at Nuremberg and Tokyo had also condemned it as the infliction of mass death without justification.[50]

None of these bodies of law deal with political actions that can create, intensify or prolong famine in peacetime. There are three possible approaches to this. One is to use human rights law. Parallel to the legal developments just recounted, there has been a longstanding initiative at the UN to have the right to food enshrined in an international convention. Its progress is disappointing, and the failures are best understood by looking at who is opposed and why. Notably, at the 2002 World Food Summit, most states wanted to specify a mandatory right to food, but the United States – standing alone – insisted on a watered-down version of the final document that referred only to establishing a working group 'to elaborate a set of voluntary guidelines to support Member States' efforts to achieve the progressive realization of the right to adequate food in the context of national food security'.[51]

A second approach is to use the law of crimes against humanity, as advocated by David Marcus, Diana Kearney among others.[52] A particularly significant case occurred with the long-awaited establishment of the Extraordinary Chambers in the Courts of Cambodia (ECCC) in 2006 to prosecute crimes under international law committed during 1975–9, the period of Democratic Kampuchea (DK) when the Khmer Rouge was in power and inflicted starvation on its own people. Randle DeFalco has argued that the ECCC could use three enumerated crimes against humanity – extermination, other inhumane acts and persecution – to indict Khmer Rouge leaders for famine crimes.[53] He writes that this is not only a possibility but a necessity: 'how the ECCC addresses important yet complicated issues such as famine, starvation and living conditions during the DK period may be decisive in the overall perception of the Court as a success or failure.'[54] Starvation was mentioned many times in the Court's proceedings. However, the Court's convictions of senior Khmer Rouge leaders, Nuon Chea and Khieu Samphan, found them 'individually criminally responsible for murder, extermination, persecution on political grounds, and other inhumane acts (comprising forced transfer, enforced disappearances and attacks against human dignity)'.[55] Starvation as such did not figure, save in so far as it was subsumed under other crimes. Cambodia provided a rare opening for judicial activism to achieve a fundamental alteration in the law. Thus far, prosecutors have not set the precedents for which we might have hoped.

In the absence of special courts such as the ECCC, progress will be even more difficult. With reference to North Korea's state-made famine of the 1990s, Rhoda Howard-Hassmann argued that it could be considered a crime against humanity, especially with reference to the systematic deprivation of food to 200,000 prisoners.[56] However, in the absence of a court with jurisdiction, she more pessimistically concluded that there is little recourse under international law to punish the perpetrators. Similarly, it is very improbable that any accountability for the enormous starvation perpetrated during Mao's Great Leap Forward famine of 1958–62 will ever be obtained.

A third option is to link famine with ecocide, which is the destruction of the natural environment so as to make human habitation impossible. Ecocide is not yet prohibited under international law, but it is nonetheless a useful framework in two respects. First, ecological destruction can cause famine, and indeed has been an instrument for genocide including through starvation,[57] and, second, because the efforts to criminalize ecocide in international law provide a template which is useful to consider in developing similar approaches for famine. The proposal that ecocide represented a war crime was first developed by Richard Falk in opposition to the US despoliation of the natural environment of Vietnam, Laos and Cambodia.[58] Others have subsequently expanded the concept outside armed conflict to apply to anthropogenic widespread, severe and long-lasting harm to the ecology of a location committed with or without intent to inflict such harm.[59] For example, ecocide can be the by-product of economic or commercial development, or committed recklessly, by disregarding available information and nonetheless proceeding, regardless of knowledge. It is also a 'slow crime' par excellence: it is low visibility, attritional and dispersed, and its impacts can often be measured only over decades, making the perpetration remote from the ultimate harm.[60] These are precisely the same considerations that would need to be taken into account in criminalizing faminogenic acts.

A challenge for humanitarian activists

This cursory review of the criminalization of famine ends with a paradox. There is enough international law to prohibit and prosecute most of the actions that lead to famine. Indeed, if mass starvation is at once a variant and an outcome of mass atrocity, then the existing law should be sufficient to stop it. Yet the laws themselves are reticent on naming starvation and famine as crimes and, specifically, framing the instruments for prosecuting famine perpetrators.

There is an instructive parallel with gender crimes. Before the 1990s, existing laws all prohibited rape, sexual slavery and virtually all gender-based crimes. Indeed, some of the earliest uses of the term 'crime against humanity' were in reference to rape as a weapon of war. But efforts to prohibit and prosecute gender crimes in wartime were weak. Hence gender activists took up the cause of advocating for these crimes to be mentioned specifically in the statutes of international criminal tribunals, notably the ICC, in order to increase their visibility and put pressure on prosecutors to bring cases on these charges. Singling out sexual and gender-based violence and exploitation served the indispensable function of putting these crimes at the top of the agenda. This speaks directly to the agenda of famine crimes: they may be (mostly) prohibited but will be actively prosecuted only when there is a clamour for this to happen. We need an international treaty that prohibits famine crimes.[61] If famine is to be criminalized effectively, activists need to take up the cause.

When I used the term 'famine crimes' twenty years ago, I did so without a proper theorization of what it would mean to bring famine into the arena of international criminal law. The challenges that follow have not been resolved and will not be resolved soon, but I hope they can at least be seen more clearly.

8

Ethiopia: No Longer the Land of Famine

Good News Is No News

It is hard to tell a good news story in the media. In March and April 2016, while Ethiopia was in the midst of its worst drought for more than half a century, there wasn't much media interest. In the lobbies of the major hotels in Addis Ababa, I met a handful of journalists who had come to report on the drought. All of them had a mental storyline in their heads: they had come to uncover the scandal of the hidden famine, the starving children whom the Ethiopian government wanted to conceal from the world. They were disappointed and annoyed that they hadn't yet found them but were seizing on any whisper of where they might find the secret starvation. When I challenged foreign journalists with the argument that there was no evidence for any substantial increased mortality, I was told that it wasn't as rosy as that, and aid agencies were reporting some hotspots of serious malnutrition. Probably they were right. But even such pockets of acute hunger and their concealment do not stand comparison with the horrors discovered by Michael Burke and Mohammed Amin in 1984 or Jonathan Dimbleby in 1973. Journalistic memories are short.

The Ethiopian government can be its own worst enemy. It had mounted an extraordinarily effective drought relief programme. But it was also restricting independent newspapers, jailing journalists and bloggers, and refusing to discuss anything except its own pedestrian and frankly boring account of the drought and relief response. I succeeded in placing an opinion piece in the *New York Times*.[1] But this was among very few articles on the Ethiopia success story published by a major newspaper.[2] And the government's own official data are often suspect – polished to make the record seem better – so the story may not be as good as it claims. The zero-deaths claim is unlikely to stand up to scrutiny. Nonetheless, Ethiopia's record is a considerable success.

Chapter 3 opened with the observation that, as the global population has increased, the number and lethality of famines has decreased. This chapter describes how this has happened – and may continue to happen – in one of the world's poorest and historically most famine-afflicted countries, Ethiopia. It explores this story through the hypotheses examined in chapters 5 and 6, looking at Ethiopia's modern history of famines through the lenses of population, climate change, poverty, markets and political decision.

Malthus and Famines in Ethiopia

My article in the *New York Times* elicited twenty-two comments.[3] Of these, nine disagreed with – or simply didn't understand – the central argument. One wrote simply, 'Too many people, too little food causes famine. We need less people.' A second castigated Ethiopia for letting its population explode, predicting disaster around the corner. A third answered the question in my article's title, 'Is the era of great famines over?', by writing, 'No, the era of famines is not over! When the population on this planet reaches 10, 12 or 15 billion by 2050 or 2075 or 2100, a threshold breaking point will be reached & there will be famine and pandemics on a global scale...'

Malthus's zombie plagues Ethiopia. David Attenborough, as an addendum to his Royal Society of Arts lecture that I critiqued in chapter 3, produced Ethiopia as the knock-down argument for over-population causing famine. He said, 'What are all these famines in Ethiopia?',[4] to which the response must be, 'What famines in Ethiopia?' Droughts, undoubtedly; food crises, arguably; but great famines – no longer. Consider Table 8.1.

An expanding population in Ethiopia is associated with lower infant and child mortality and increased life expectancy, as shown in Table 8.2.[5]

Of course, these trends may suddenly reach their limit and a Malthusian calamity may kick in. The current government has vigorously promoted family planning and other measures, such as girls' education, that reduce population growth, fearing that the productive capacity of the land is strained by a high population.[6] But despite repeated, confident predictions, no calamity has happened. Over half a century, Ethiopia's population has increased fourfold, and famine deaths have declined to close to zero.

Table 8.1 Famines and food crises in Ethiopia

Date	National population	Death toll
1958	23.2 million	100,000
1966	27 million	50,000
1973	31.5 million	200,000
1984–5	40 million	600,000
1999–2000	69 million	19,900
2002–3	71 million	Thousands
2015–16	99 million	Near zero

Table 8.2 Life chances in Ethiopia

Year	Infant mortality	Child mortality	Life expectancy
1985	132	223	44.6
2015	41	59	64.0

Sources: Population and mortality figures: UN Inter-agency Group for Child Mortality Estimation (UNICEF, WHO, World Bank, UN DESA Population Division), http://www.childmortality.org/; Famine death toll: World Peace Foundation 2016

A Brief Catalogue of Ethiopia's Famines

Emperor Haile Selassie's Ethiopia was a hybrid of a thin veneer of a modern state and a feudal, slaving empire built on conquest, subjugation and a steep hierarchy of peoples with different values attached to their lives. Until the late nineteenth century, the imperial capital roved around the country, living off the forced contributions of local landowners and their serfs, until its appetite had eaten all within striking distance. The emperor's armies pillaged the frontier regions and the lands of any notables or peasant movements in rebellion against his authority. Even when more stable governance came to this multi-ethnic imperial territory, farmers were compelled to pay a third, sometimes more, of their harvest to landlords, and the inhabitants of the western and southern marchlands were treated as savages and slaves. Some of the most marginal peoples survived by making themselves invisible to the imperial authorities, which meant having few material possessions worth stealing.

In line with Tawney's remark about the peasantry, not only were rural Ethiopians standing up to their necks in water, but their overlords were repeatedly jumping on their backs and making them stumble under the waves. The sequence of famines recorded by Ethiopian historians is the result of this.[7]

Throughout the feudal era, famines were commonplace, especially in the northern highlands.[8] The most infamous was the 1888 famine, caused by a lethal combination of a rinderpest infection that killed most of the cattle, including plough oxen, and drought and war. Local famines were frequent and often unrecorded. In 1958, famine killed 100,000 people; in 1966, famine killed 50,000. In 1973, drought and feudal exactions caused a famine that killed about 200,000 people, which became a scandal and helped cause the revolution of the following year that brought down the imperial regime of Haile Selassie.

The Ethiopian population in those years was much smaller – though accurate statistics are hard to come by. The emperors weren't interested in counting people. There's an apocryphal story that an Ethiopian aristocrat, visiting London in the 1930s, was asked by his equally aristocratic host how many people there were in Ethiopia and replied, 'about a hundred families'. The rest, he implied, didn't count – as the derogatory names for entire populations, such as *baria* and *shankilla*, meaning 'slaves' or 'enslavable people', indicated. Subsequent demographic work estimates that the population increased from 23.2 million in 1958 to around 31.5 million in 1973.[9]

The 1973 famine helped catalyze popular opposition to the imperial regime and its lavish lifestyle. The following year, revolution unleashed armed conflict across almost the entirety of the Ethiopian highlands, as peasants took the slogan 'land to the tiller' into their own hands, and diverse sociopolitical forces, from feudal lords to revolutionary students, took up arms to defend their privileges or fight for their ideals. The disruptions caused by the turmoil of the revolution, and the Somali invasion (repulsed after an enormous military mobilization) and the Red Terror campaign against leftist parties opposed to the military junta, might have been expected to lead to widespread famine. But Ethiopia's farmers had just shed the crushing burden of feudal levies and dues to landlords, nobles and the church, so the class of people who had historically been most vulnerable to famine were, for the first time, cultivating for themselves and eating their own produce.

The revolutionary junta, known as the Dergue (Amharic for 'committee'), ruled from 1974 until its defeat in 1991. Despite early measures that enhanced food security and protected from famine, such as the creation of a Relief and Rehabilitation Commission and land reform, the Dergue's coercive central planning, its diversion of national resources into sub-Saharan Africa's largest military and its numerous and brutal counter-insurgency campaigns contributed to recurrent food crises and occasional famines. The entire period of military rule was one of civil war, in which the Dergue fought numerous provincial rebellions. The most significant of these were in Eritrea, where the Eritrean People's Liberation Front (EPLF) fought for independence, and in Tigray, where the Tigray People's Liberation Front (TPLF) fought for the rights of the Tigrayan people and to transform the state.

Just as the Dergue prepared to celebrate ten years of the revolution, a combination of drought and relentless counter-insurgency created an even worse famine than that of 1973. The most visible and convenient culprit for the 1984–5 famine was rainfall failure, but careful examination of how the famine unfolded – which areas were worst hit and when – shows close association with the offensives mounted by the Ethiopian army, including the latter's forced displacement of people, destruction of crops and villages and looting of livestock. For example, the first major alarm bells for famine were sounded in February 1984 when people arrived, hungry and desperate, in Korem in northern Wollo province.[10] The government had tried to conceal the harvest failure, not wanting to admit that ten years after famine had discredited the imperial regime, it was now facing an even greater crisis. It then admitted the drought but refused to acknowledge its own role in the famine. The army had just completed an offensive, right into the heart of the largest food-producing area under the control of the rebel TPLF, and much of the distress migration was a direct result of that.

In December 1984, Acting Foreign Minister Tibebu Bekele said to the US Chargé d'Affaires, 'probably with more candor than he intended', that 'food is a major element in our strategy against the secessionists.'[11] Throughout the war, the army destroyed crops, fed itself off the land and requisitioned food supplies, including using World Food Programme (WFP) wheat to feed the militia. It disrupted trade by mounting roadblocks and bombing markets. It used food aid as an enticement to control the rebellious population, including drawing people for a forcible resettlement programme. It denied food relief, so that Tigray, with up to one-third of the total people affected by famine in 1984–5 received just 5.6 per cent of official international food assistance.[12] To the extent that they received any relief aid at all, Tigrayans were instead supplied by a covert cross-border relief operation.

The Ethiopian famine of 1984–5 was not a natural disaster, it was a second-degree famine crime. The military regime of Colonel Mengistu Haile Mariam created and sustained the famine as part of its counter-insurgency. Its objective was to crush the TPLF, and one of its tools was famine. Had the aim been to destroy the Tigrayan

population as such, through mass starvation, it would have qualified as a first-degree genocidal famine crime, and indeed at times the
actions of military administrators and generals did appear to show
that level of bitter determination. Overall, however, famine was a
tool, not an objective.

This famine killed at least 600,000 people and caused Ethiopia's
GDP to contract by nearly 3 per cent in 1984 and almost 12 per cent
in 1985.[13] At that time, the population of Ethiopia was estimated to
be slightly more than 40 million.[14]

In 1989, the TPLF became the central component of a coalition
of parties, the Ethiopian People's Revolutionary Democratic Front
(EPRDF) which, together with the EPLF, defeated the Dergue in 1991.
The EPRDF formed a new government, which brought internal peace
and development to the country. The end of the civil war in 1991
saw the end of major famine. The great majority of the country,
including all the historically most famine-prone areas in the highlands,
has been at peace since then. The absence of killing famine from the
Ethiopian highlands for an entire generation – something unprecedented
in the country's history – is a direct outcome of this absence of war.

Ethiopia as a whole, however, has not been at peace. There was a
massive conventional war with Eritrea in 1998–2000. It was triggered
by a border dispute and was fought along the two countries' common
border. Tens of thousands of people were displaced out of the zone
of the fighting, but there was no famine in this area – in fact many
of them benefited from military salaries, either by enlisting or from
the local boom that followed the deployment of hundreds of thousands of soldiers in the vicinity. It was a conventional inter-state war
involving organized, mechanized armies fighting for fixed positions.
In many respects, it was an anachronism, even in previous eras of
conventional wars, in that tens of thousands of young soldiers died
on each side but very few civilians. The war was an enormous blow
to the national economy.

In the midst of the war with Eritrea, a concatenation of events
caused the worst famine to afflict Ethiopia under the EPRDF. In
1999–2000, a food crisis struck south-east Ethiopia, a region inhabited
by Somali-speaking people. Its epicentre was Gode. One cause was
drought. Another was a protracted low-level conflict in which the
army fought insurgents and imposed tight economic restrictions on
the affected area. A third factor was that the border war with Eritrea
damaged Ethiopia's standing with international donors, who were
reluctant to provide aid for the humanitarian crisis on the grounds
that Ethiopia itself should have been spending its resources on fighting
poverty and hunger, not war.

The famine was not great in magnitude, but severe in its impact. Between 19,900 and 25,000 children perished.[15] One of the by-products of this crisis was a vigorous debate in which the Ethiopian government and the WFP declared 'famine averted', and the food security and nutrition experts pointed to the data on livelihoods and mortality to make the case that a famine had indeed occurred. This controversy led to the development of an agreed metric for measuring the magnitude and severity of food crises, resulting ultimately in the IPC scale used by the UN.

This was followed two years later by a severe nationwide drought, which led to a food crisis, with 14 million people in need of food assistance. This was a major challenge to the EPRDF government, which had prided itself on a decade in power without any such emergency and was pushing for donor policies to transition away from emergency relief to development assistance. The combination of an effective national disaster response and rapid provision of food aid by foreign donors, led by USAID, averted a crisis. The American position had changed since 1999 because Ethiopia was seen as a major ally in the 'war on terror'. For the EPRDF leadership, Ethiopia's dependence on donor generosity was not only an embarrassment but also a strategic vulnerability.

During this food crisis, there were 'hot spots' of increased malnutrition and mortality in various parts of the country but no measurable increase in mortality among the general population.[16] There is no agreed figure for mortality, and even a marginal increase in child deaths among the very large affected population would imply tens of thousands of excess deaths spread, more or less imperceptibly, across the country. National GDP contracted by 2 per cent. At that time, the population of Ethiopia was just over 70 million (bearing in mind that Eritrea, with 3.5 million people, separated in 1993).[17]

This brings us to the recent crisis with which I opened the chapter. In 2015–16, the most severe and widespread drought in more than half a century cut the rate of GDP growth from about 10 per cent to somewhere between 4 per cent and 7 per cent, but did not cause any noticeable increase in deaths. At that time, the population of Ethiopia had reached almost 100 million.

Climate Change

The eclipse of famine in Ethiopia is a remarkable success story. One of the mutant children of Malthus's zombie will surely appeal, 'What of the impact of climate change on Ethiopia? Ethiopians have been living on borrowed time and the relentless logic of too many people and too few resources will catch up with them!'

Let me reassure Ethiopians that this day of reckoning is not in sight. Climate change will slow Ethiopia's economic growth, with impacts expected to begin in about 2030,[18] but there is no sign of any apocalyptic collapse of the country's ecology or food system. Lower rainfall between 1991 and 2008 has led to a loss of 13 per cent of agricultural productivity, with a further 6 per cent fall predicted.[19] These were substantial losses, but they were offset by growth in other economic sectors.

Predicting Ethiopia's future climate is particularly difficult because the country lies at the intersection of different climatic systems, which means that some parts of the country are likely to get drier and other parts wetter. Modelling suggests northern Ethiopia faces a future of lower rainfall during the long rains, while eastern Ethiopia is becoming wetter with higher risks of floods.[20] Some parts of the country will have improved productivity, others will face losses,[21] with the adverse impacts on the economy driven more by flood damage than by drought.[22]

Because of the proactive interest of the government in studying and responding to the issue,[23] the data are relatively good and the mitigation policies are well developed. Ethiopia has a pioneering 'green economy strategy', the Climate-Resilient Green Economy strategy, which addresses both climate change adaptation and mitigation objectives.[24] It a rare example of a country that has combined its aims of a green economy and climate change resilience within a single policy framework that is also consistent with its overall economic goals.

Poverty and Growth

The earlier famines in our catalogue – 1973 and 1984–5 – struck the poorest people in a desperately poor country. After 1991, the EPRDF government adopted a programme of equitable development as its priority. Alongside peace, the leaders assumed that famine was no longer a threat. As a result, the food crises of 1999–2000 and 2002–3 came as a severe shock. At the same time, a split in the ruling party led to a political realignment, with Prime Minister Meles Zenawi emerging ascendant. He reaffirmed the commitment to a developmental state but changed its focus to the single-minded pursuit of accelerated economic growth. In the Marxist-Leninist language of the EPRDF, he shifted from seeing rich peasants as a strategic ally in the political-economic struggle to embracing them as the vanguard of development. Defending his enthusiasm for regulated capitalism as the engine of growth, Meles argued that, should the country remain poor, its very survival was in question.[25] At a time when the consensus among international development agencies was 'poverty reduction' – reflected in the Millennium Development Goals – Ethiopia was unabashedly seeking rapid growth, explicitly trying to emulate Taiwan and South Korea.

Ethiopia has pursued a strategy of accelerated economic growth that aims to lift the country to middle-income status. Central to this are policies for industrialization led by the agricultural sector, the provision of basic services and the construction of ambitious infrastructure projects, notably for transport and hydropower. This aims to decrease the share of agriculture in GDP from 40 per cent to 30 per cent and thereby reduce the likelihood that fluctuations in farm productivity will lead to famine. But in the overall picture of Ethiopia's future, population is not the determining factor, and famine is fast disappearing as a significant threat, as shown in Figure 8.1.[26]

The 2002–3 crisis revealed that a substantial number of Ethiopian farmers were chronically dependent on food aid, even in a year of good rainfall. In response, government and aid donors formed a 'New Coalition for Food Security'. The government quickly took control of the agenda, and obtained donor pledges to establish a 'Productive Safety Net Programme' (PSNP).[27] It was intended initially as a

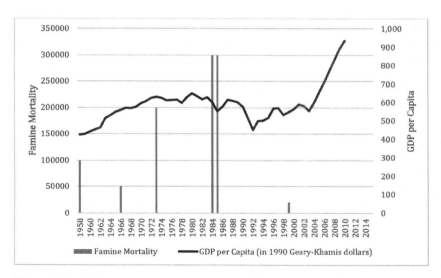

Figure 8.1 Ethiopian GDP per capita and famine mortality, 1958–2010
Sources: GDP estimates, Maddison Project 2013; famine death tolls, World Peace Foundation 2016.

short-term measure to substitute for emergency food aid. Beginning in 2005, it was rapidly rolled out to five million people, thereby becoming the largest such programme in Africa, at a cost of approximately US$170 million per year.

Most of the funds were from donors: the government was directing its own money to programmes, such as infrastructure, industrialization and resettlement, which donors would not fund. National and international NGOs were embraced, provided they remained in the restricted role of service provision and steered clear of politics and human rights.

The PSNP aimed to bring seven million people out of extreme poverty and dependency within five years. It did not meet its goal: perhaps 500,000 graduated by 2010. A second five-year programme aimed to reduce enrolment to 1.3 million by 2015. By that date, however, the emphasis was shifting. The PSNP, which had been de facto a social protection programme, could now be explicitly recognized as such and could be linked to a newly adopted national social protection strategy that included, among other things, a component in urban areas.[28] And an even more severe drought in 2015 affected 18 million people.

The PSNP operates on the basis of a series of early warning systems which have also been put in place by the Ethiopian government. These try to estimate the impact of drought shock and livelihood crises and are called the Livelihoods, Early Assessment and Protection (LEAP) tool and Livelihood Impact Analysis Sheet (LIAS) tool. LEAP and LIAS, when combined with monthly food security reports and identification of those administrative areas (*woredas*) which are likely to be most affected, allow the Ethiopian government and its partners to target the PSNP resources where they are most required. This is not to say that the PSNP is an unmitigated success. Critics argue that the PSNP has been used to entrench political control at the local level but acknowledge that there has been significant positive change in food security as a consequence.[29]

The PSNP and its associated social protection programmes have proved to be an essential counterpart to the strategy of accelerated development, cushioning the poor from the impacts of downward shocks as the economy as a whole grows.

Markets

Disrupted or malfunctioning markets can cause famine or make it worse. Well-functioning markets help farmers get better prices in normal times and can mitigate price shocks in bad times. But Ethiopia's experience suggests that better-functioning cereal markets, on their own, wouldn't be sufficient to prevent a food crisis causing famine.

Ethiopia's mountainous terrain is a challenge to road builders, most especially in the northern highlands. Even today, large numbers of people live many hours', or even days', walk from the nearest roads, and a generation ago most of the rural population was remote from markets.

One of the first, pioneering analyses of markets and famines in Ethiopia was by John Seaman and Julius Holt.[30] On the basis of (admittedly patchy) market price data, they identified a ripple in increased food prices from the epicentre of the 1973 famine in northern Wollo. This they used as an indicator of the level of distress. The fact that prices rose meant that the famine was not strictly a 'slump famine' (in Sen's terminology), as price increases meant that effective demand existed, albeit driven by sales of assets, such as plough oxen, by desperate farmers.

Stephen Devereux re-examined the 1973 Wollo famine, arguing that a much finer-grained examination of how rural markets actually functioned was needed. He wrote: 'In fact, in rural Ethiopia, there is not one famine region surrounded by a perfectly functioning set of markets, but thousands of fragmented, almost isolated communities, each with their own food supply problems and poor transport and communications links with neighbouring villages and districts.'[31] His re-analysis showed how the fragmentation of markets meant that it was not profitable – at least, it was not reliably profitable – for traders to supply small-town markets with food, however high the prices might be, because the small size of those markets and their disconnectedness from the wider market meant the price signals were an unreliable guide to real demand. The price might be extremely high on the basis of just a few purchasers, and even a single lorry load of grain might be enough to flood the market and leave grain unsold. Even if there was a windfall profit to be made, the trader would also have forgone a smaller but more reliable return in a regular market and, in failing to supply that market, might jeopardize his niche.

The implication of Devereux's analysis was that preventing or mitigating famine required a better-integrated market. However, the following decade, the reverse happened: war visited disruption on this already weak market network. To be precise, the counter-insurgency mounted by the Ethiopian army, which involved closing markets (often bombing them) and setting up roadblocks on rural roads to either tax grain traders or confiscate their goods altogether, brought the rural food trade nearly to a halt.

In the late 1980s, I studied food prices in war-stricken northern Ethiopia in areas controlled by the rebel TPLF.[32] Historically, the price of grain in Tigray was between 30 per cent and 100 per cent higher than in north-central Ethiopia and three times higher than in eastern Sudan. Along the main roads, grain prices reflected the price in the nearest grain-producing area (either north-central Ethiopia or eastern Sudan) plus increments for transport and other transaction costs. In the off-road market segment, prices were much more variable for the reasons explained by Devereux. During the war, these differences were exacerbated, due to the TPLF control of the rural markets and the government's counter-insurgency. Astonishingly, many of the TPLF-controlled areas were better integrated into the cross-border grain markets of Sudan a few hundred kilometres away than into the garrison towns that were sometimes just a stone's throw away but almost totally isolated from movement and trade.

I calculated the cost per kilometre of transporting a sack of grain by main road, by unpaved country road and by donkey. A 100 kilogramme sack of sorghum (known as a quintal), bought in the eastern Sudanese town of Gedaref (the main grain-growing region) for distribution in a village close to the small town of Chilla in central Tigray, would have to travel 437 km. The first 205 km would be on an articulated lorry, driving by daylight along the main paved road to the border town of Kassala. The cost: 0.30 Ethiopian birr per quintal. The next 202 km would be on a four-wheel-drive truck over rough roads to Chilla via the TPLF centre of Sheraro by night, at a cost of 69.4 birr per quintal – more than 200 times more expensive per kilometre. The quintal would be transported its final 30 km by donkey, at a cost of 28.2 birr – still more expensive.

The country roads were rough, some of them hewn out of the mountainside by the TPLF itself. Transport was only by night because of the risk of air raids. I remember travelling on a truck which had to do five-point turns on the hairpin bends, with a precipice below and with the truck's tyres scrabbling for traction and small rocks and pebbles shooting off into the darkness. Nonetheless, as the TPLF-controlled territory expanded and lorries replaced donkeys, the markets of Tigray became integrated and the price of grain fell, food security improved and people stepped back from the brink of famine.

In its dying months (March 1990), the Mengistu government liberalized grain marketing, lifting all forms of quotas, fixed prices and forced deliveries. At the time, most of the grain surplus-producing areas were under government control, and the impact was rapid and immediate. Prices paid to producers rose and those paid by urban consumers fell as provincial wholesale cereal markets became more closely linked to the single biggest market in Addis Ababa. The end of the war further reduced the costs and dangers of trading in grain, while the benefits of liberalization spread to urban markets in the formerly war-affected areas. Using data for 1987–93 (the period spanning the transitions from central planning to economic liberalism, and from war to peace) for markets outside the war zones, Stefan Dercon found that the combination of liberalization and peace improved the functioning of markets, as shown by increased prices paid to producers and the reduction in price differentials between markets. 'The conclusion is that market liberalization increased the prices paid for teff [the main cereal] in the main producing areas, and that liberalization and, to a lesser extent, peace, improved the functioning of markets through increased short-run integration.'[33]

Ethiopia's infrastructure was still in very poor shape, and this was just the beginning of the growth of Ethiopia's market economy. In 1991, Ethiopia had a total length of 19,000 km of all-weather road. Twenty-five years later, this had grown sixfold, connecting three-quarters of all villages and reducing the average walking time to a road from 10.2 hours to 1.7 hours.[34] Looking at the period 2001–10, Seneshaw Tamru measured the speed of the transmission of price information among cereal markets and the transaction costs of moving grain between markets and found a significant improvement. Tamru attributes this to 'improvements in roads, mobile phone availability, income growth, and urbanization leading to bigger commercial flows'.[35]

Traders are mainly involved in buying food grains in producing areas and selling them in the towns, not selling them in rural areas that are chronically in deficit. Both Dercon's and Tamru's main concern, like most economists studying cereal markets, was the efficiency of the market in terms of incentives for producers and traders. Rural markets in Tigray, the largest deficit region, remain less integrated.[36]

The resilience of the market in vulnerable and food-deficit regions to price shocks, and the supply of affordable food to the poor and hungry, was tested during the 2015–16 drought. A review of food markets found precisely the kinds of impacts one would expect: food markets struggled. There were overall national price rises, but more so in the worst-affected areas, and big shortages of food reaching markets in remote areas. But the review is also remarkable in showing that the price effects were modest, far less substantial than would be expected during a nationwide food crisis.[37] The reason for the resilience was the combination of a stronger market infrastructure, a stronger economy and prompt public action in response to the food crisis – massive imports of food.

Political Decision: Democracy and Public Action

Ethiopia moved from feudalism to garrison socialism in the 1970s. Since the EPRDF won power in 1991, it has officially been a multi-party system. But it is not a democracy, and its moves towards political liberalization came to an abrupt halt in the aftermath of the 2005 general elections, when opposition provocations were met with a wide-ranging government crackdown, and reversion to de facto one-party government. The press, which had been growing in freedom and confidence, was intimidated. A highly restrictive law on civil society organizations forbade them from engaging in advocacy. In 2015, just as serious drought struck, protests against the government spread rapidly in small towns across the country, and the scale of the discontent and the lack of any organized constituency speaking on behalf of the ruling party and its record indicated a collapse of legitimacy. If Ethiopia's performance on democracy and human rights were a guide to its record of eliminating famine, the country's progress on preventing famine would have gone into sharp reverse since 2005.

This did not happen. In fact, during the highly effective drought relief programme of 2015–16, the EPRDF government entered its most repressive phase to date, imposing a state of emergency which granted extraordinarily wide-ranging powers to the security services. But there is a nonetheless a link between political legitimacy and action against famine, which is best explained by exploring how the EPRDF came to be committed to famine prevention, and for what reason.

The EPRDF is a multi-ethnic coalition that grew out of the TPLF, a guerrilla movement founded in 1975 in the immediate aftermath of the revolution. The TPLF from the outset had to struggle, not only against the military regime but also against competing armed movements in the highlands of Ethiopia. Lacking the financial resources and highly connected leaders of its rivals, the TPLF instead took the longer and more demanding route of mobilizing the peasantry. They won the confidence of rural people by following a strict code of personal behaviour and consulting with villagers on issues such as local government and land reform. In the mid-1980s, the people of Tigray were the epicentre of the great famine. The TPLF leadership identified its strategic advantage, and hence its strategic priority, as sustaining the confidence and support of the peasantry. It could not hope to defeat the Ethiopian army militarily, but it could consolidate its popular constituency so that the province was ungovernable by any force other than itself. Central to this strategy was fighting famine. The

TPLF organized a mass evacuation of people to refugee camps in Sudan, then a mass return when the rains came. The guerrillas mounted military operations to overrun the government's food storage centres where the Dergue was allocating relief food to government militia and to people who were compelled to join a resettlement programme – the food was 'liberated' and distributed to the locals by the locals. The TPLF mounted operations to protect the supply lines for clandestine relief convoys driving by night from Sudan into the liberated areas. The front adapted its economic policies and development programmes to the demands of the villagers, abandoning price-fixing in local markets and tolerating some regulated money lending. In due course, this commitment to the welfare of the people – and its 'anti-famine political contract' – was reciprocated by a solid show of support for the TPLF and readiness to make enormous sacrifices in pursuit of its armed struggle.

The TPLF's theory of 'revolutionary democracy' drew upon its principles and practice of mass mobilization as a form of direct democratic participation. The TPLF (and from 1989, EPRDF) was a vanguard party, representing the interests of the people (as they saw them) and acting in a centralized, strategic and decisive manner on their behalf. There was no liberal democracy, no open voting for the highest political offices.

When the EPRDF marched into Addis Ababa in 1991, its secretary-general, Meles Zenawi, was asked his ambition for his time as leader of Ethiopia. He replied that he hoped that Ethiopians could all eat three meals a day – a remark that disarmed the sceptical press corps. The EPRDF in power has demonstrated a commitment to public action against hunger and in support of broad-based development and poverty-reduction measures that has no rival in Africa. Among these are the rapid mobilization of relief, the PNSP and (recently) mechanisms for insurance against future droughts.

The commitment to preventing famine also arose from a strategic analysis of threats to Ethiopia's national security, based on the history of the previous regimes. One of the sparks for the 1974 revolution had been that the emperor failed to stop a drought turning into a famine and then denied the seriousness of that famine. Colonel Mengistu's failure to prevent the 1984–5 famine had not only undermined his domestic legitimacy and capacity but had forced him to open the door to humiliating international interference. The EPRDF leadership was determined that Ethiopia would be strong and able to chart its own course. From its earliest days in government, it decided to reduce the size and cost of its army, setting a ceiling of 2 per cent of GDP for defence spending and making development the priority.

In 1998–2000, those commitments were tested by war with Eritrea – a war that began with Eritrea taking the offensive against an ill-prepared Ethiopian army. A vocal group within the EPRDF leadership argued that victory against Eritrea should be achieved at all costs and that the country should fight until its last drop of blood was spilled and last dollar spent. Meles argued back that the primary enemy remained poverty, not Eritrea, and that Ethiopia's war aims were to defend its sovereignty, not to destroy its neighbour. He reminded his comrades that a large and well-funded army was not a guarantee of national security – after all, the TPLF/EPRDF had defeated precisely such an army – but rather that prosperity and democracy were the central pillars of national security. In late 2002, after the war, and just as the country was receiving its first shipments of USAID food to prevent drought turning to famine, Meles wrote Ethiopia's Foreign Affairs and National Security Policy and Strategy, which formalized the EPRDF's adherence to its earlier principles, and re-stated arguments he had made to the EPRDF's Central Committee. Condemning previous regimes (and his critics) for 'jingoism with an empty stomach', the paper argued that 'The real source of our national humiliation in our time is poverty and backwardness.' Meles challenged his critics, writing that 'our defense capability should not be built in a way that would have a detrimental influence on our economy.' The paper concluded, 'The failure to realize development and democracy has resulted in our security being threatened. It means we have remained impoverished, dependent and unable to hold our heads high. The prospect of disintegration cannot be totally ruled out.'[38]

Ethiopia's 'economy first' national security strategy illustrates the 'war causes famine' hypothesis in reverse. A sound analysis of national security in a famine-prone country, placed famine prevention at the centre of the security strategy. The EPRDF 'anti-famine political contract' was a revolutionary democratic commitment in the sense of a Leninist vanguard party acting on behalf of the people. In more conventional political science terms, it was a strategic political commitment, not a liberal-democratic sensibility. That has been a strength because it means that responses to threats of famine occur regardless of the democratic context. It is a weakness because the contract can be revised by the leadership without the people having any recourse.

This explains the paradox that, even while popular protests unfolded across the country in 2015–16 and the EPRDF was subjected to unprecedented criticism for its democratic failings, it still mobilized the country's largest-ever drought relief programme, primarily using its own resources. The scale of the drought became evident in August 2015, when the El Niño effect caused a widespread harvest failure.

In many areas, there had also been harvest failures in the previous two years. In addition to the existing PNSP caseload (7.9 million people), just over 10 million people were assessed as needing food aid. After a few weeks' hesitation, the government acted boldly. It was fortunate in that it had set aside more than US$1 billion as a petroleum reserve in case the price of oil rose, which didn't happen. The Ministry of Finance made available US$700 million to import food aid, of which US$300 million was spent in four months.[39] This early response ensured that the food pipeline was quickly filled. International donors could not respond that rapidly, but their growing pledges – US$700 million by March 2016 – helped give the government the leeway to pursue its ambitious programme. The government also imported trucks and used the working parts of its new railway from the port of Djibouti, still incomplete.[40] Total government relief spending was US$735 million, and international donors spent US$985 million.[41]

Food aid was the single-biggest element in the relief programme. Emergency relief reached about 8 million people. It was delivered primarily through the PSNP, which also engaged nearly 6.6 million people in public works activities and provided those who couldn't work with direct support. The programme included trucking water to communities where wells had dried up and providing fodder to keep livestock alive. While food aid was a government effort supported by the WFP, the other components were also implemented by an array of NGOs.[42]

The relief programme worked. Not only was no excess mortality reported, but livelihoods were relatively well protected. After the 2016 harvest, the number of people needing food aid was cut back to 5.6 million.[43]

The prompt and capacious relief response was politically smart, probably more so than the government realized at the time. The map of anti-government protests in 2015–16 and the map of drought relief efforts do not overlap: those in receipt of food rations evidently thought better than to riot and destroy infrastructure. Moreover, the history of food price hikes inflaming political discontent is too strong to need repeating. The fact that basic food prices in Ethiopia rose only 28 per cent (and, in the case of wheat, didn't rise at all)[44] during the country's harshest food crisis and its biggest opposition mobilization may be the reason why the EPRDF survived.

The strategic commitment to prevent famine is not evenly distributed across all Ethiopians. Since 1991, relief efforts have been better organized and more generous in the TPLF/EPRDF heartland of Tigray than elsewhere. In the politically marginal areas of south-east Ethiopia, particularly during counter-insurgency operations, the army tends to revert to faminogenic practices.[45] Treating food security as national security also puts key elements of the strategy in the hands of national security institutions. The 2002 national security white paper called for transparency and public participation in national security issues, but in practice the reverse has happened. Much of the information that is needed for an effective anti-famine political contract (let alone a functional democracy) is tightly controlled.

Over the last half century, the single most important reason why Ethiopians have suffered famine is repressive government, indifferent to the welfare of its people. The EPRDF reversed that. Remarkably, its deepening authoritarianism, including the 2005–6 crackdown on the opposition and the heavy-handed, security-led response to widespread protests in 2015–16, has thus far neither undermined the government's drought relief programmes, nor contributed to food insecurity and hunger. The other side of the coin is that the relief programme appears to have won the government some grudging acceptance from the population, not any deep support. If the commitment to preventing famine is to become a genuine social-political contract with the citizens, it must be part of a democratic process. That isn't happening. On the contrary, the repressive turn is cause for concern, both in itself and because it may yet spell a retreat from the leadership's commitment to preventing famine. That commitment is only as robust as the leadership's historic analysis of the political and national security threats posed by famine, which can of course change. There are no other guarantees. To date, the abandonment of policies that protect against famine has not happened, but there is need for vigilance.

Conclusion

The most compelling story of famines in Ethiopia is that each is caused by a concatenation of shocks acting on underlying vulnerabilities, and that political decision has emerged over time as the most important element. Ethiopia has historically been poor and isolated, with many of its communities anomalously late in emerging from subsistence. In earlier decades, neglect and indifference exacerbated food crises, making localized famines worse than they would otherwise have been. Under the Dergue, political decision and military strategy turned a food crisis into a great famine. Under the EPRDF, a strategic political commitment to preventing famine, alongside internal peace, a strong programme of economic development and generous aid donors, has meant that Ethiopia has been free of famine to a degree without precedent in the country's history. The economic transformation of the country means that any famine in Ethiopia today could occur only through an act of commission by the government. The weakness in the Ethiopian anti-famine political contract is that it entirely depends on the political decision of those in power.

I presented Ethiopia as a case study for three reasons. First, because I have followed these issues for thirty years. Second, because it is credible to argue that if famine is disappearing from Ethiopia, surely it is vanishing from the world. Third, the Ethiopian case also reveals how public policy can be instrumental in overcoming famine. Crucial to the effectiveness of Ethiopia's policies has been the political analysis underpinning them, especially the understanding – born of bitter experience refracted into political theory – that famine is a threat to national security.

Part III

The Persistence and Return of Famines

9

The Famine that Isn't Coming

New and Newer Famines

Bill McGuire opens his sobering little book, *A Guide to the End of the World*, with the observation: 'The big problem with predicting the end of the world is that, if proved right, there can be no basking in glory. This has not, however, dissuaded armies of Cassandras from predicting the demise of our planet or the human race, only to expire themselves without the opportunity to proclaim "I told you so".'[1] Famine – or to be more precise, Malthus's global 'Famine' – is one of the Cassandras' favourite harbingers of the apocalypse, if not as protagonist then with a walk-on part. There's little indication that such a Famine is in prospect.

A benefit of having spent more than three decades working in the Horn of Africa, one of the most turbulent and famine-prone parts of the world, is that it is a good vantage point for measuring world disaster trends. The veteran of the Horn treats scare stories with a big sceptical pinch of salt. Whenever a journalist, diplomat or activist claims that some disaster is unprecedented, it's not difficult to find a similar event that was worse during this time span, especially the 1980s. On almost every indicator, things are better in Sudan, Ethiopia and Somalia than they were thirty years ago. But sceptical optimism doesn't warrant a routine dismissal of concerns.

It is too soon to conclude that famines and episodes of forcible mass starvation have been banished. In a prescient book, Stephen Devereux wrote about 'new famines' in the era of globalization[2] and there may yet be 'newer famines' as different patterns of violence and deprivation emerge. Famines remain singular and exceptional events, and (fortunately) there are too few recent cases for us to draw definitive conclusions about today's trends. But we can still explore what is happening: this chapter does so.

Recalling my recurrent use of Tawney's image of a man standing up to his neck in water, this chapter is organized around the following questions. First, how much has the water receded (or indeed, deepened)? What waves do we face? And, next, what actions might force the man to stoop, kneel or fall? What are the famine crimes of the twenty-first century?

These questions correspond to two distinct kinds of famines. One threatens in places where globalization and poor public policy have already led to severe chronic deprivation and may yet lead to peacetime food crises. To understand these, we need to examine the perils posed by multiple sources of turbulence for the poorest people in the weakest countries. Throughout, as we discard monocausal accounts of what might create future famines, we need to attend to a seed of caution: a succession of different cautionary notes could stack up to something more serious.

The second kind of potential famine is concentrated in places with the most virulent and intractable conflicts, namely parts of Africa and the Middle East. Some of these converge with the economic marginalization that has caused chronic peacetime deprivation, but others do not. To understand these, we need to study the wars that cause them and the political and ideological projects that turn armed conflicts into famines. That is the subject of chapter 10.

Trends in global hunger, poverty and inequality

The early twenty-first century is the best time in history to be alive. Around the world – with very few exceptions – young people have better health, nutrition, education and life expectancy than their parents and grandparents. Measures for global hunger show immense improvements across the board, albeit with some gaps and recent reversals. From the 1980s to the mid-2000s the picture was one of steady improvement.[3] Hundreds of millions of people, especially in East and South-East Asia, are better fed and healthier than before. The signal exception is countries at war. The 'People Affected by Conflict' report indicates that levels of acute malnutrition (wasting and/or nutritional edema) have been rising since 2008 as a result.[4]

There's a parallel story of vast progress for the first and most important of the Millennium Development Goals: poverty reduction, with an encouraging trend but complicated footnotes (see Figure 9.1).

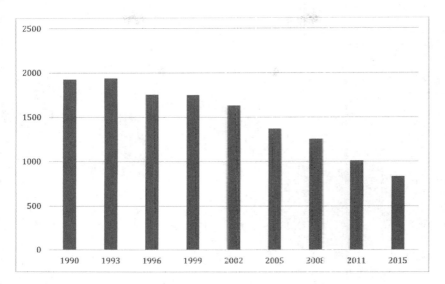

Figure 9.1   Number of people living on less than US$1.25 a day worldwide, 1990–2015 (millions)
Source: Millennium Development Goals Report 2015

The impressive headline masks the fact that the increase in the incomes of the poorest has been uneven. Hundreds of millions of people have been left behind as global inequality has increased. This is shown in Branko Milanovic's celebrated 'elephant chart' (Milanovic 2016) (see Figure 9.2).

Milanovic identifies three points of interest on this chart. Point A is near the median of global income distribution, a point at which people had the highest income growth. This is in middle-income countries. Point B is well to the right: a richer group, but who have had no real income growth for a generation. This is what Milanovic calls 'the lower middle class of the rich world'. Point C is the global 1 per cent, the elephant's trunk whose aggregate income growth is as large as the aggregate growth represented by the body of the elephant.

But our concern is what Milanovic *doesn't* draw attention to. This is the far left of the chart. The lowest quartile's income growth is insufficient for them to escape definitively from the zone of poverty and vulnerability. For the lowest 5 per cent, income growth is insignificant. Moreover, this category includes people who have become poorer over this time, particularly because of armed conflict or forced displacement. It's a small number overall but a very important category

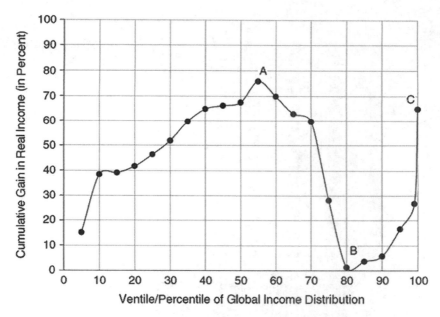

Figure 9.2 Relative gain in income per capita by global income level, 1988–2008
Source: Milanovic 2016

for the study of famine. Many of these people are all but invisible to policy makers.

In 2013, the Centre for Research on the Epidemiology of Disasters (CRED) estimated that 172 million people had been affected by conflict in the previous year.[5] The great majority of these belonged to a group to which humanitarian policy makers had not been paying much attention: 'conflict-affected residents'. These people had stayed in their homes and hadn't fled to become refugees or displaced persons. They numbered 149 million, including 28 million in Pakistan and 19 million in Nigeria, and were often faring even worse than refugees and displaced people.[6] CRED found that levels of acute malnutrition had been rising since approximately 2009, and the cases of Syria and Yemen – examined in the next chapter – will have added to these numbers.

We are only beginning to become aware of the wider impacts of crime, gang violence, brutality by state enforcement bodies and intimate-partner violence. Data for the global burden of armed violence show that armed conflict accounts for only a relatively small proportion of violence globally.[7] Of the estimated 780,000 people who died each year during 2004–9 from violence and its immediate effects, 66 per cent were killed in non-conflict settings (mainly crime), 27 per cent died from hunger and disease due to conflict, and just 7 per cent were combat deaths and civilian fatalities in war. Of the fourteen countries with annual violence death rates of more than 30 per 100,000, just six were war affected. The other eight – with El Salvador at the top of the list – suffered from the effects of high rates of violent crime. Researchers are only just beginning to appreciate the scale of this problem. A pioneering study in Uganda found a wide range of major and lasting impacts of serious crimes on households: those who had suffered these crimes were poorer, with worse food security and worse access to health care, education and water, and they were more vulnerable than others to becoming victims of further crimes.[8] Across the world, there has been no significant humanitarian response to the communities worst affected by crime.[9]

Infectious diseases – especially chronic, debilitating illnesses that affect adults such as HIV/AIDS, tuberculosis and cancers – can similarly contribute to deep pockets of localized deprivation. With respect to the HIV/AIDS epidemic in southern Africa, I suggested that this threatened a 'new variant famine' characterized by a 'Swiss cheese' pattern of vulnerability. I will explore this hypothesis later in the chapter, but the key point relevant to this discussion is the way in which such individual or family adversities can cause a level of vulnerability to starvation that is dispersed across society, socially imperceptible and not captured by conventional indicators of food insecurity.

One of the features of historic famines and episodes of forced mass starvation is that they can be defined geographically. Not everyone in the affected area starves, but mapping an 'affected area' makes sense. The IPC scale uses a territorial framework to determine the extent to which a community – defined by location – is food insecure. The possibility of converging, intensified inequalities opens the disturbing possibility of acute food crisis that meets all the criteria of magnitude and severity to count as a famine, except that it is sufficiently dispersed to be invisible to policy makers.

The global food crisis

In 2007–8, the price of cereals in the international market suddenly and unexpectedly spiked – the 'global food crisis' (see Figure 9.3). The spike was repeated three years later. Does this portend a new age of famines?

As explored in chapter 5, open markets are a double-edged sword when it comes to preventing famine. Global economic liberalization

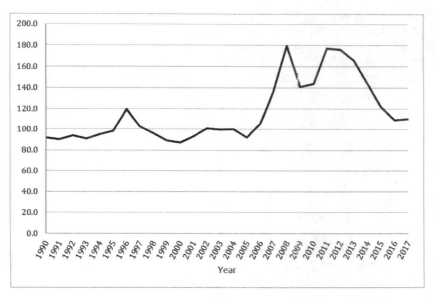

Figure 9.3   Global cereal prices, 1990–2017
Source: FAO, annual global cereals price index, with 2002–4 = 100

has brought both prosperity and vulnerability in its wake. This was seen in the unexpected turbulence in the international food market. The global food crisis had numerous causes, including the diversion of agricultural land to biofuels production, rising prices of fertilizer and oil (energy prices are a significant supply cost in mechanized cereal production as well as transport), production falls in some countries, low food stocks and speculation in the food market.[10] The United States, which dominates the global market in wheat, maize and sorghum, played an outsize role, notably in the repercussions of increased demand for biofuels and in commodities futures markets. Once the food price rises reached a significant level, many governments responded with panic buying and protection measures, driving prices even higher.[11] It was a bubble, not a long-term shift: prices came down in due course. But the immediate consequences were dramatic and could have been fatal. In every continent, people were compelled to spend more of their household budgets on food, pushing ⸲30–155 million into poverty.[12] There were food riots in many countries. The biggest countries (China and India) were insulated by public stocks and restrictions on trade, and effects in the most remote communities in parts of Africa were mitigated by a high proportion of local production compared with imported foodstuffs: it was the people in the middle, exposed to global markets but without strong state intervention to protect them, who suffered most.[13] In 2008, there was no famine resulting from the higher food prices. In fact, aggregate global food security appears to have increased over 2007–9 because of continuing economic growth in Asia.[14] Moreover, at their 2008 peak, cereal prices were still below the average prices prevailing in the 1970s (inflation adjusted), and far below those prevailing more than fifty years ago (see Figure 9.4).[15]

The long-term downward trend is expected to continue.[16] Even if the improvement in food production productivity is reduced to just 60 per cent of its recent rate and, with the adverse effects of climate change taken into account, global food production will outpace population growth well into the middle decades of this century.

Even though many agricultural and food security policies have adjusted and the trends are again optimistic, the global food crisis sounded a warning. As Derek Headey and Shenggen Fan observed, 'the nature of this crisis is not how expensive prices are relative to their historical trend, but how quickly they have risen, together with the related problem of behavioral adjustments by consumers and producers.'[17] The volatility of global markets can, through a series of unfortunate events, suddenly push scores of millions of people into poverty and raise the risk of famine. Steve Wiggins and his colleagues wrote: 'With so many factors combining, the [food price] spike can be seen as an unusual event – 'a perfect storm' – and hence unlikely

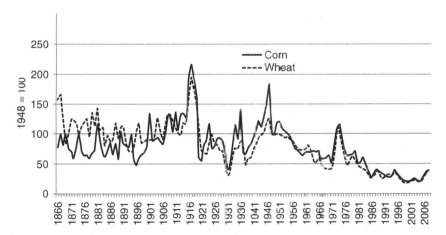

Figure 9.4 Index of real cereal prices (US), 1866–2003
Source: Sumner 2009, p. 2051

to arise frequently. That said...changes in the future may make spikes more likely, so this is not an argument for complacency.'[18]

Wiggins's concern was validated more rapidly than he could have feared. The second wave of price increases in 2011 duly fulfilled that grim possibility in one place: it aggravated the food crisis in Somalia at that time and was one key factor pushing that country over the edge into famine.[19] The 2011 food price spike also contributed to bread riots across the Middle East. Ever since there have been food markets, high food prices have caused protests, and they have been implicated in numerous riots and upheavals, including the French Revolution. In contemporary times, there's a well-documented relationship between increases in food prices and social unrest.[20] And, in so far as political upheavals can in turn lead to conflict and repression, they increase the risks of famine in a vicious feedback loop.

Weak national economies in a globalized economy

Perhaps even more important in terms of overall numbers of people at risk of hunger, the global economy is volatile, and small open economies at the margins of the global economy, especially those dependent on the export of primary commodities and reliant on the goodwill of aid donors, are vulnerable to fluctuations in international markets and donor policies.[21] Many countries in Africa have no comparative advantage in *anything*: their agriculture cannot compete with the subsidized mechanized farming of Europe and North America; their manufacturing cannot compete with China. Whatever opening they appear to have, whatever niche they are exploiting, can vanish overnight as a small change in the global economy or regulatory system reshuffles the deck. An illustration is the 2005 liberalization of the international textile market. It allowed China to displace African exports to western countries and also opened up African markets to Chinese textiles, forcing draconian retrenchment and restructuring on an entire African industry at the cost of an estimated 250,000 jobs.[22] National economies are often not sufficiently resilient to withstand such shocks without external aid – especially when combined with any other shocks that may occur – and, when donors are unsympathetic, hunger can follow.

Aid donors have not been sensitive to this predicament. In the 1980s and 1990s, the 'Washington Consensus' policies pushed countries to reduce social spending and scale back on important national food security measures such as counter-cyclical intervention in grain markets. Today, the rules of trade and aid are stacked against any country that wants to protect domestic industry and agriculture, or to treat food security as a national security issue rather than a question of efficiency on the assumption of a functioning market. There are good reasons to be cautious about protectionism and still better ones to be suspicious of national security rationales for policy, but a doctrinaire swing to the opposite extreme can also be damaging. As the OECD Development Assistance Committee's International Network on Conflict and Fragility notes, 'Despite the diversity of their political-economic structures and legacies, liberalisation policies and measures are still regularly applied to fragile states as blueprints, with no adaptation to context.'[23]

In Malawi in 2002, a combination of local shocks and donor-enforced economic liberalization contributed to the first food security crisis in that country for fifty years. This led to between 46,000 and 85,000 deaths.[24] Another case was the Niger emergency of 2005, due to crop failure and chronic poverty, but also to a dogmatic insistence on the virtues of economic liberalization. This caused an estimated 13,000–48,000 excess deaths.[25] If Ethiopia had followed the conventional path of economic liberalization, it might well have faced something similar but on a bigger scale.

These hunger crises are readily predicted and averted – it just demands policy making more sensitive to the frailties of small, poorer countries and a readiness to plan ahead for the inevitable shocks and create the right responses in good time. In the words of Daniel Clarke and Stefan Dercon, it's necessary to 'dull disasters'.[26] The appeals-based humanitarian response should be the backup, not the first line of response. There is increasing attention to using financial hedging mechanisms for risk management in developing countries, which is a promising avenue for helping countries weather setbacks, including food production and price shocks.[27] But the underlying vulnerability demands more strategic policy making and an activist state ready to create the conditions for economic development. Ethiopia's success in economic growth in the first fifteen years of the twenty-first century is an example.

This book has shown that the cause of famine is not a shortfall in global food production with respect to the world's human population. The world can feed many, many more people than it does at present. This does not mean we should be complacent about the world's food economy. There are serious problems with the global food industry: it is inefficient, it does not serve the needs of the poor or the planet and it contributes to global warming and environmental despoliation. What this means is that the food industry should not use fear of global food crisis or famine as a justification for its production methods and its business models. Further improvements in agricultural and food technologies are welcome and may make a modest improvement to protection from famines in so far as they contribute to lower poverty and better food systems.

'The coming plague' and famine

Pandemic disease ranks second to gigantic famine as one of the spectres of the apocalypse. There are hyperbolic claims to be debunked and real fears to be parsed.

In the 1990s, there was a fear that 'the coming anarchy' (in the words of the journalist Robert Kaplan), which included infectious disease as both metaphor and purported actual vector of chaos, would also bring global catastrophe, including famine.[28] Kaplan wrote, 'It is Thomas Malthus, the philosopher of demographic doomsday, who is now the prophet of West Africa's future. And West Africa's future, eventually, will also be that of most of the rest of the world.'[29] In the 2000s, Jared Diamond wrote about societal collapse, pointing to the Rwanda genocide as an example of catastrophic violence brought about by resource scarcity: 'Modern Rwanda illustrates a case where Malthus's worst-case scenario does seem to have been right.'[30] Those with deeper knowledge of the societies in question ably fought against those reappearances of the Malthusian zombie,[31] but the populist invocations still have more public resonance than the scholarly refutations.

Laurie Garrett warned of 'the coming plague' as new and resurgent infectious diseases overwhelmed a neglected public health infrastructure.[32] I also beat an alarmist drum in this band and can explain where and why I was wrong. I predicted that the HIV/AIDS epidemic in Africa would send economic development and governance into reverse, causing societal crises, in particular including 'new variant famine'.

As mentioned, famines have usually been followed by epidemics of communicable diseases, which often kill more people than hunger itself. The converse fear that epidemic disease would cause famine has also intermittently reared its head. This is important and has lessons for how we should analyse our fears about coming famines.

The prelude to the story of health crises leading to societal disaster was the unexpected fact that the sole US government agency to predict the end of the Cold War was the US Census Bureau, whose analysts detected a rise in infant mortality rate in the Soviet Union in the early 1980s and foresaw that this might portend a crisis of state legitimacy.[33] They were proven right, and the standing of demographers as intelligence seers was reinforced in the mid-1990s by the findings of the

State Failure Task Force (SFTF), which was set up in the wake of the fears, fanned by Kaplan, that Haiti, Liberia, Somalia and Yugoslavia signalled a new kind of foreign policy challenge – anarchy. The SFTF found that three variables from its list of 75 were the best predictors of state failure: openness to trade; democracy; and infant mortality.[34] The political significance of health and demographic indicators was validated.

And in due course, a few years later the US National Intelligence Council (NIC) issued a report on infectious disease as a threat to world peace and security.[35] Then, at American instigation, the United Nations Security Council held its very first session of the millennium on the topic, with particular focus on HIV/AIDS. The risks of pandemics of new or resurgent infectious diseases, such as new strains of influenza or highly drug-resistant tuberculosis, are real, but experience of HIV/AIDS shows that predictions of their disastrous societal, political and security impacts are easily overstated. The US NIC, having in 2000 and 2002 warned of the impending social breakdown in sub-Saharan Africa, Asia and Russia caused by HIV/AIDS, was by 2008 advising the US government that global public health was instead an arena for effective American diplomacy.[36]

The reasons for the optimistic turn, following eight years of intensive research into the subject, are important in their own right and also relevant to the question of why global scare stories are so often exaggerated.[37] The forecasters of doom tend to think in a linear way, aggregating one adverse factor on top of the next, thereby generating a worst-case scenario. What they overlook is that all modern societies and human ecologies are complex, non-linear and possess both redundancy and resilience. Redundancy refers to the fact that one mechanism or set of people or factors can be knocked out but the overall system can still function. So, for example, one of the AIDS-and-security fears was that high rates of HIV among the officer corps of national armies would strip those armies of the skills and experience they relied upon. It turned out that estimates of much higher levels of HIV among soldiers in general and officers in particular had been exaggerated, generalized from a few extreme cases. But, more significantly, armies are designed with built-in redundancy: in peacetime, senior officers are retired routinely and their subordinates promoted and, in wartime, armies need to be able to function even with casualties among their commanders. Resilience refers to the ability of the system to adjust to a shock. One of the main findings of research into famine – cited right at the beginning of this book – was the ability of agrarian societies to withstand acute food crises by adopting coping strategies. Much the same held for the impacts of HIV/AIDS. For example, the high numbers of parents who were facing illness and premature death did not translate into commensurate numbers of orphans growing up without care or socialization because of the capacity of extended families to care for those children.

The other major reason why HIV/AIDS did not lead to global calamity was that there was a vast and remarkably effective response. The scientific and public health communities rose to the challenges of the disease.

There was also a specific fear that HIV/AIDS would cause famine. This is where I enter the story: I alerted the reading public to that particular fear, including coining the phrase 'new variant famine'. The occasion for the warning was the fear that the southern African drought of 2002–3 would combine with the impoverishing impacts of HIV/AIDS on rural households to create a new pattern of famine.[38] The rationale for the name 'new variant' was that previous famines had been driven by disasters that hit an entire geographic area at a specific time, creating visible and acute hunger across a territory, whereas the impact of HIV/AIDS was scattered across an entire population, creating pockets of chronic hunger household by household. While households in which a breadwinner was suffering from AIDS tended to grow less food, the disease did not lead to an aggregate fall in agricultural production, leading those who still adhered to the 'food shortage' theory to an unfounded confidence that there could not be famine. Without question, there were pockets of deepening poverty and worsened hunger across southern Africa at that time. But despite these household-level deprivations, with their terrible human cost, there was no evidence that it had contributed to hunger-related mortality.[39] The main reason for this: families and communities still had the resources to cope, albeit at a cost.

Even the most feared contagious disease of recent times, ebola, did not lead to a societal crisis or famine. The main reason for that was not the medical and humanitarian response – a mixture of the heroic, the incompetent and the irrelevant – but was chiefly because West African communities adapted rapidly to the threats it posed and applied their own skills.[40] Again, that response came at a cost.

Would the public health officials' greatest immediate fear – a worldwide influenza pandemic – cause famine? It would probably not cause production shocks, but it could well cause huge disruptions to global markets, exacerbating instability in commodity markets.

Two more cautionary notes are in order. The first is that we must be alert to invisible hunger, such as that caused by a chronic and burdensome disease and its possible interaction with other sources of stress. The second is a reminder that the biggest cause of the reduction in famine deaths has been public health improvements. We are not likely to see a resurgence of the common famine diseases of the past, such as smallpox and typhus, but the intersection of the societal disruptions and migration caused by famine with new or re-emerging infectious diseases, could create newer patterns of famine mortality.

Will Climate Change Cause Famine?

Climate change is a fact. We have every reason to be extremely worried: this may indeed be the occasion on which McGuire's Cassandras are finally vindicated. But we have less reason to be worried that climate change will lead to famine than might be supposed. The trend lines for extreme poverty and vulnerability to food crisis remain in the right direction, for decades to come, under all climate change scenarios. What we have reason to fear is that climate change increases the risk of the conjuncture of exceptional events, both climatic and political, that could lead to famine.

The 2016 annual report of the FAO on climate change and its impacts, provides an excellent and up-to-date synthesis of climate change and food security.[41] The FAO structures its analysis around the four pillars of food security: food availability; food access (Sen's 'food entitlement' in layman's terms); food utilization; and the stability of food systems. I will pose these as four questions and then add two more. The fifth is whether climate change will cause armed conflict, and the final one is whether government policies arising from *fears* of climate change and resource scarcity could lead to famine. My answer: the sixth question addresses the greatest danger.

First: *will climate change be disastrous for food supply?* The FAO report summarizes a vast amount of evidence about how climate change will impact farming, livestock and fishing. The evidence is that, in the short term, the positive and negative impacts more or less balance each other out. There are productivity gains in agriculture because of the positive effects of CO_2 fertilization (the stimulatory effect of increased levels of atmospheric carbon dioxide on plant growth) and increased rainfall in many areas. But, as global warming advances after about 2030, the negative effects outweigh the beneficial ones, especially for tropical countries.[42] Negative impacts include higher temperatures, flooding (especially in Asia), drought (especially in Africa and the Middle East), more pest infestations and greater variability and uncertainty in weather patterns. Very substantial impacts on crop yields are predicted by the year 2100 in a range of 10–35 per cent reduction for maize, of 5 per cent improvement and 15 per cent reduction for wheat, and of 5–20 per cent reduction for rice.[43]

Without any adaptation of farming and food supply systems, this spells upward pressure on food prices. For the poorest, vulnerability to famine increases. The loss of land to rising sea levels will be a huge problem for certain historically food-insecure countries such as Bangladesh. But predictions this far into the future, especially regarding complex systems that include factors of human resilience, are fraught with difficulty.

A subsidiary but no less important question is: *will climate change adversely affect food supplies in certain poor and vulnerable parts of the world?* Numerous scholars have predicted that the localized impacts of climate change will cause famine, focusing on increasing drought and higher temperatures in already food-insecure areas in Africa and parts of the Middle East. The evidence on this is ably summarized by Kevin Trenberth and his colleagues,[44] who have demonstrated that droughts are likely to be more frequent, more severe and less predictable as climate change intensifies. This seems surely correct, but it is wrong to extrapolate from more drought to more famine. Unfortunately, this is routinely done. For example, Bryan Walsh wrote an article in *Time Magazine* under the title 'Climate Change Could Cause the Next Great Famine'.[45] His main point of reference was the Irish famine of the 1840s, the proximate cause of which was potato blight (nothing to do with drought) and the underlying cause was English misrule.

Climate change also makes some dry, poor places wetter and more productive, among them the Sahelian belt in Africa, location of famines in the 1970s and 1980s, including in Darfur.[46] However, increased evaporation, greater fluctuations and the difficulty of predicting beyond the short term indicate that the increased rainfall is unlikely to translate into improved prospects for agriculture.[47] Grasslands will benefit more than farmland and livestock herders more than farmers.

Second: *will climate change intensify poverty?* Peacetime famines in the modern world are, as we have seen, failures of demand rather than failures of supply. Famine is the lowest end of the poverty spectrum. And indeed, as numerous economic studies have concluded (usefully summarized by the FAO[48]), global warming is an obstacle to reducing poverty. The FAO report summarizes: 'With climate change, however, the population living in poverty could increase by between 35 and 122 million by 2030 relative to a future without climate change.'[49] Note, however, the qualification: we are talking about *a slower downward trend, not an absolute increase.* Also, different economic growth scenarios are by far more important as drivers of

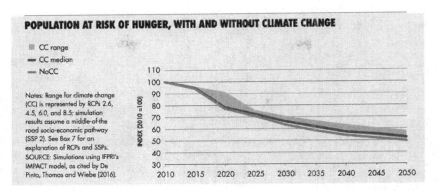

Figure 9.5 Global population at risk of hunger, without climate change and with median and high scenarios for climate change
Source: FAO 2016, p. 36

the rate of poverty reduction compared to climate change. Figure 9.5 shows the best estimates for extreme poverty in the world under a range of scenarios from no climate change to the worst case.

Two things jump out: one, poverty is reducing under all scenarios, even the worst case; and two, the poverty reduction scenarios all lie within a relatively narrow band. Given that at the 2010 baseline famines are rare, the trend of reducing poverty predicts further reductions in vulnerability to famine. It is just that the reduction is slower than would have been the case without climate change.

Third: *will climate change make food utilization deteriorate?* This is an often overlooked element in food security: if food is contaminated, poorly processed or poorly prepared, it is less nutritious. This is a particular concern in the ecology of urbanization, as water supply and hygiene systems often struggle to cope with the combination of fast-growing cities with overstretched infrastructure alongside pollution and a shrinking availability of drinking water.[50] For example, we may see greater prevalence of water-borne infections in shanty towns. This is not a contributor to famine in a clear way, but if hungry, distressed migrants converge on places where low food and water quality is already a problem, it could contribute to further hardship.

Four: *will climate change cause instability in food systems?* The answer to this question is undoubtedly yes. One of the best-demonstrated impacts of global warming is the increasing number of extreme weather events, including droughts, storms and extremes of temperature. Instability in the weather is a problem for all farming systems that rely on predictable weather patterns. But the central point that it is apparently necessary to repeat ad nauseam remains the simple truism: drought is not famine! And neither are storms and floods equivalent to famines either.

A supplementary question is: *could all these factors interact to increase the risk of famine?* This is where generic predictions tend to break down and trend lines can mislead. We should again recall that modern famines are exceptional events, and we should ask not about averages but about risks of catastrophic failures of a complex and generally robust system. What is the risk of a concatenation of factors that together cause a disaster, even while each one singly is unproblematic, or even in smaller combinations don't pose a danger? The cautionary answer to this is: yes, *extreme multi-causal events become less unlikely.*

Climate change makes some poor and vulnerable populations less food secure. But the risk of these insecurities turning into famine will depend on political decisions. It follows that we need to pose the question: might climate change also make faminogenic political decisions more likely?

Climate change, conflict and famine

The basic thesis of this book is that better politics have led to fewer famines. There are good reasons to fear that the global increase in democratic, open political systems is stalling. We cannot take for granted that political systems will have the key features necessary for maintaining the current successes in overcoming famine. That is particularly so because contemporary political orders have a mixed record in providing global public goods and have been notoriously bad at planetary climatic management.

Will climate change cause armed conflict which then creates famine? War is a possible pathway to food crisis that the FAO report neglects but which has animated others. But there isn't much evidence for this either – at least not in a simple or non-linear manner. An examination of the cases that are most often cited shows how a zombie concept can team up with sensationalism, selectivity and the politics of attempted exoneration to create a fallacy.

One example is the process whereby Darfur earned the label 'the world's first conflict caused by climate change'.[51] The source of this was not any expert on Darfur or climate change,[52] but UN Secretary-General Ban Ki-moon, who in June 2007 wrote a column for the *Washington Post*[53] in which he claimed, 'Amid the diverse social and political causes, the Darfur conflict began as an ecological crisis, arising at least in part from climate change.' The reason for his opinion piece was that he wanted to persuade sceptical Americans that the UN and the African Union had got a good deal when they agreed to send a hybrid peacekeeping mission to Darfur. To do this, he needed to make the case that Darfur was not a genocide inflicted by an evil government on innocent civilians but a rather more complex civil war with the usual complicated mix of causes. (This was a theme he stressed in a subsequent article, in which he wrote, 'Darfur is a case study in complexity.'[54]) Among those causes, Ki-moon selected a story about how the rains had failed twenty years earlier, and nomads and farmers began violently competing for food and water. He then quoted an article by Stephan Faris, who was using the Darfur case to illustrate a wider argument about the perils of climate change.[55] And, in turn, Faris's piece opens with a vignette provided by me.

My story concerned an elderly sheikh with whom I stayed during the depths of the famine of 1985.[56] Sheikh Hilal Mohamed Abdalla told me how drought and desertification were upending the established order, and how the world as he knew it – of reciprocal relations between farmers and herders – was coming to an end. In my article, I fast-forwarded to the then-present of massacres of villagers by the infamous Janjawiid militia, whose leader, Musa Hilal, was the old sheikh's son. It was a compelling anecdote, and it pointed to the way in which that famine spelled the end of the social order as Sheikh Hilal and his generation had known it.

The stresses on livelihoods, communities and the governance of Darfur contributed to a crisis and conflict in 1987–9, which in turn sowed the seeds of societal tensions that led to war a further fifteen years on. However, we should note that the rains returned to Darfur in 1985, ending a fifteen-year period of comparative aridity.[57] There were numerous conflicts between camel herders over dilapidated water points, which were caused partly by larger numbers of animals congregating around wells and reservoirs, whose ownership was disputed and which didn't have the capacity to slake all those animals' thirst. Some of the herders demanded a *dar*, or homeland, to call their own, coming into conflict with other herders and also forcibly displacing farmers. New nomadic groups arrived from Chad, fleeing the civil war and repression on the other side of the border. Meanwhile, the mechanisms for maintaining social order, such as inter-tribal conferences backed by an impartial government, were either neglected or politicized in a partisan way.[58]

There is some controversy over whether Darfur's farmland, pasture and forests are sufficient to support its growing human and animal populations. Agronomists disagree over the extent of soil degradation and erosion. The fluctuations in rainfall – accentuated in recent times

– mean that in some years the whole region is semi-arid, while in others the desert blooms. But there is no question that the inhabitants of Darfur can see the landscape changing before their eyes: massive deforestation and disruption to the ecology are evident to all. People *believe* that there is climate change and ecological crisis, and this in turn makes them ready to mobilize to seize land or to protect it. A fearful uncertainty is abroad. In so far as climate change contributes to war and massacre, it does so through those fears – some exaggerated, some manipulated, but all of them real – which are then seized upon by political leaders.

Climate change and environmental decay cannot explain the Darfur crisis and still less are they good alibis for the politicians who created that crisis. But they provide one contributing factor that increased social stresses and made the Darfurians more fearful and more susceptible to political intolerance and extremism.

In fact, for fifty years or longer, the connections between conflicts over natural resources, especially land, and armed insurgencies have been recognized in the Horn of Africa.[59] Some resource conflicts date back to the 1950s or earlier, when large tracts of land were confiscated from their customary users (pastoralists and smallholder farmers) for use as commercial farms and plantations. These are exemplars of a sorry history of central planning with serious adverse unintended consequences or commercial land grabbing. Climate change is a latecomer to the rogue's gallery of likely culprits for these conflicts.

A comparable story can be told for Syria and the origins of its war. The fact that the Arab Spring coincided with high food prices (a global market phenomenon), and that the north-east of Syria was suffering a multi-year drought, has led some to speculate that climate change is an underlying cause of the crisis. Specialists on Syria recognize that these elements contributed to the slide to civil war but find that their caveats about the way in which food crises are refracted through political decisions, and their insistence on the primacy of political agency, are often obscured as soon as they mention drought or climate change.[60] No respectable writer wants to be a climate change denier, but it is also problematic to see simple causal links where complexity rules.

These cautionary tales are important. A lot of research on the societal impacts of climate change does not meet standards of scientific rigour. For example, a series of studies that correlate temperature, rainfall and violent incidents in Sudan and Somalia makes the mundane point that episodes of conflict tend to correlate with the drier and hotter periods of the year, a fact known to everyone who has lived in a pastoral zone in these countries.[61] In the dry season, herds congregate around water holes. Animals and their herders are stressed and in close proximity. Violence is more likely than during the cooler, wetter season, when livestock and their owners are more healthy and dispersed. This correlation also holds when there are droughts that extend over several years, which cause greater stress, longer migrations and greater pressure on water resources. But these findings cannot be taken to imply that an overall rise in temperature or a further drying of the climate will lead to a comparable increase in levels of violence. The results are not scalable or extendable to different circumstances. Yet this is precisely the kind of research finding that makes its way through peer review into the literature. Many of these pieces of research have been shot down by more rigorous review.[62]

Climate change and political panic

The dangers of a climate change denialist in government contributing to famine are not difficult to spell out. Failing to mitigate or adapt to climate change increases vulnerability to natural adversities and their economic consequences. It is also likely that any government that is hostile to intellectual globalism in this manner will also be authoritarian, bellicose and xenophobic, increasing the possibility of faminogenic political decisions. The overpopulation zombie often appears in racist clothing and could even be invoked as an alternative to climate change and political economics as an explanation for social crises, including famine and mass migration from stricken places.

Less obviously worrisome are those who accept climate change as a fact but respond inappropriately. For example, we need to be alert to the danger that large-scale climate change *responses* – whether centrally planned or commercially driven – could generate social and economic tension and even conflict. Therefore, the final, supplementary question is: *could mistaken policies, animated by fears of climate change, cause famine?* And the answer to this is: yes. This is why scaremongering isn't an innocent pastime or a harmless means of raising awareness. Crying wolf can create panics, bad policies, worse political decisions, conflict and hunger. And it explains why Malthus's zombie can be so malign.

A widely repeated claim, which dates back to a remark by Egyptian President Anwar Sadat after the signing of the Camp David accord with Israel, is that the next war will be over water. In fact, the evidence is that transnational river basins are more often the cause for cooperation than conflict, with the Jordan and Indus valleys being cases in point of where otherwise hostile countries are able to cooperate in sharing water resources.[63] The Nile waters have often been identified as a likely cause of armed conflict, given the inequitable allocation of water resources by the Nile Waters Agreement of 1959 and Egypt's deep concern about preserving its access to its share of the water.

In 2013, there was a scare that the Egyptian government, then led by President Mohamed Morsi, might threaten Ethiopia with military action over the construction of the Grand Ethiopian Renaissance Dam on the Blue Nile. This was an act of desperation in which the government sought to distract attention from its domestic political crisis by lashing out at an external adversary. Resort to such stratagems in future cannot be discounted by governments in the region and elsewhere. Control of water resources can be used as a bargaining chip in inter-state diplomacy.

The Nile Basin Initiative has demonstrated the potential for win–win solutions to the common management of the Nile Waters, and the 2015 Khartoum Agreement involving Egypt, Ethiopia and Sudan, signed by President Abdel Fatah el Sisi, recognizes the common benefits to the three countries arising from the dam, properly and cooperatively managed. As the pressure on the Nile Waters intensifies and technocrats in the riverine countries increase their knowledge of the possibilities for mutually advantageous water-sharing regimes, cooperation is likely to increase. This is not to argue the impact of climate change on scarce water resources isn't important: quite the opposite. But it doesn't help to make simplistic arguments. And – to repeat – providing a climatic alibi for political crimes does not help in trying to stop famines.

Malthus's zombie is not only wrong, it is dangerous. There *is* a link between resource scarcity, conflict, state crime and genocide, and it runs through the fearful imaginations of politicians and gullible publics. People who believe that there is an impending global scarcity (of food, fuel, land, water, etc.) may act on that fear, regardless of its empirical foundation. And the actions that follow can make matters worse.

The 2008 world food crisis was worsened by some of the protectionist measures taken by panicked governments. But the crisis was contained without causing famine or major conflict. There's no expert commentary on the food crisis that invokes overpopulation, and science journalists felt it necessary to make pre-emptive strikes against this argument by prefacing their explanations by clearly asserting that population size had nothing to do with it.[64]

But Malthus's zombie is remarkably difficult to kill, and we need to be vigilant to make sure that it doesn't re-enter at moments of intellectual laziness. One regrettable lapse was made by Timothy Snyder, the historian whose book *Bloodlands* I cited extensively for the account of the Holodomor and the Hunger Plan.[65] In *Bloodlands* and his follow-up, *Black Earth*,[66] Snyder describes how Hitler's rudimentary Malthusianism contributed to his conviction that the German race could feed itself only through geographical expansion (*lebensraum*), not through progress in agricultural technology or trade. So far, so good: I am sympathetic to this rereading of Nazi ideology, bringing agrarian extremism and alimentary economics back into focus.

Where Snyder strays is his extended conjectures on what this may mean for the contemporary world in the book's concluding chapter and in an opinion piece in the *New York Times* entitled 'The Next Genocide'.[67] The core of Snyder's argument is correct: fear of scarcity, for example taking the form of an 'ecological panic' induced by climate change, could lead to a global land-grab or resource-grab that could turn violent – just as large-scale land seizures for commercial farms caused rebellions in earlier decades. So far, so good. But then Snyder himself succumbs to some bad social science. As if following Robert Kaplan or Jared Diamond (whom he doesn't cite), he sees African crises as harbingers of a future zero-sum world of ethnic conflict over resources and attributes the genocide in Rwanda and the famine in Somalia to resource scarcity, albeit (in the Rwandan case) cynically manipulated to other political ends. Moreover, his explanation for the demise of famine is an old-fashioned supply-side one: 'The Green Revolution has removed the fear of hunger from the emotions of electorates and the vocabulary of politicians.'[68] Snyder then stirs the fear of impending global food crisis: 'The Green Revolution, perhaps the one development that most distinguishes our world from Hitler's, might be reaching its limits.'[69]

In short, having espied defunct alimentary economics lurking within the Nazi project, Snyder then ushers that spectre back on stage through repeating popular misconceptions about famine and Africa. He correctly identifies the route to disaster as through the *misreading* of the social science of scarcity – but then he himself misreads the African cases he brings up. That a historian of Snyder's rigour and acuity would succumb to a distressingly superficial narrative is testament to Malthus's insidious influence.

Population increase, natural disasters, climate change and shocks to the global food supply are all problems. None of them, on their own, threaten famine. It requires a combination of many factors, including shocks, of which at least one must be political decision, to create a famine. Among those who have studied the topic, the concept of 'famine' has gradually shed the misleading and dangerous associations with 'overpopulation' and food shortages per se, and instead famines are now correctly seen as political decisions acting on or against vulnerable populations. Nonetheless, Malthus's zombie still marches on among the general population and public intellectuals who should know better: it is the responsibility of those who *do* know better to spare no effort in slaying it, again and again.

10

The New Atrocity Famines

The Resurgence of Great Famines?

In February 2017, the Famine Early Warning System Network (FEWSNET) warned that the number of people in acute need of humanitarian assistance had risen to 70 million, up from 45 million in 2015, and that 20 million people in four countries – Nigeria, Somalia, South Sudan and Yemen – faced 'a credible risk of famine' during the year.[1] This marked an alarming reversal of the positive trends of the previous thirty years. A few weeks later, using the same data, the UN declared that famine had struck South Sudan. On 10 March, Stephen O'Brien, head of the United Nations Office for the Coordination of Humanitarian Affairs, told the UN Security Council that, 'We stand at a critical point in history. Already at the beginning of the year we are facing the largest humanitarian crisis since the creation of the United Nations.'[2] As this book has shown, O'Brien's claim was hyperbolic but nonetheless he was correct that 2017 marks a critical turning point, a moment at which famine could return. Also, O'Brien's recommendations to the Security Council were appropriate to the real causes of the famines. Instead of an appeal to charity, he called for quick action aimed at '[p]reserving and restoring normal [market] access to food and ensuring all parties' compliance with international humanitarian law'. He called for expanded humanitarian operations and for stopping the fighting.

Today's famines, actual and threatening, have in common that they occur in virulent and intractable conflicts. More than that, they occur as the product of wars in which the belligerents deny the right of the other to exist, and in which those directing the fighting are ready to discount the lives of people – civilians and soldiers alike – in pursuit of their political and military ends. And, worse, these wars have no apparent end.

The previous chapters have used a crude measure of excess deaths to identify famines. In this chapter, I will also use the recently developed Integrated Food Security Phase Classification (IPC scale) for measuring food insecurity and 'humanitarian emergencies', those somewhat anodyne but nonetheless useful terms of art designed to address crises that demand action by international humanitarian agencies.

The major part of this chapter is an outline of seven major humanitarian emergencies of the twenty-first century, all of which qualify as episodes of famine or forced mass starvation, either by magnitude (100,000 or more excess deaths) or by severity (level five on the IPC scale). Two occurred in the first decade, namely Darfur, Sudan (2003–5) and northern Uganda (2003–6). These are conventionally called 'humanitarian emergencies' rather than famines but they met the 100,000 deaths threshold. These crises demonstrated the political salience of numbers and the need for an objective and apolitical criterion for defining famine. In 2011 in Somalia, the IPC scale was used for an official international declaration of 'famine' for the first time. South Sudan in 2017 was the second.

These seven famines reprise old themes and also illustrate new ones. In all cases, belligerents have imposed sieges, destroyed livelihoods and food production, blocked aid and attacked humanitarian facilities. These are nothing new. In fact, just about every armed conflict in sub-Saharan Africa causes forced displacement and humanitarian crisis. This was the case in south-east Ethiopia in 1999–2000. In Angola in 2002, the final military campaign in the long war to defeat the rebellion by the National Union for the Total Independence of Angola (UNITA) led to forced starvation in the camps for UNITA prisoners of war and demobilizing soldiers and their families, with excess deaths in the thousands.[3] The numerous conflicts in the DRC caused enormous displacement and suffering. So too did the crises in the Central African Republic and Mali and the war in the Sudanese regions of the Nuba Mountains and the Blue Nile.

But war famines are new in the contemporary Middle East. Yemen heads the list of countries in terms of the proportion of the national population deemed by the UN to be in need of food, nutrition or livelihood assistance, at 51 per cent. Syria is in fourth place.[4] New also is the legitimacy of counter-humanitarian ideologies and strategies such as wholesale blockades and prohibition of humanitarian operations.

Who Cries Famine and for What Purpose?

Famines are political, and crying 'famine' is a political act.[5] Throughout history, there have been no objective criteria for determining what counts as a famine. Civil servants, missionaries, journalists and aid workers have all cried 'famine', using different and inevitably subjective assessments of what is happening and what counts as 'famine'. Politicians have responded on the basis of political calculus, including public outcry. Only within the last decade has there been a measure that sought to address the technical challenges of 'crying famine' in a manner that provides a starting point for a policy debate that is not irretrievably dependent on subjective political calculus. That is the IPC scale, and in this chapter I will explore its strengths and shortcomings.

But, first, a short digression into how the aid debate reached the point at which a common definition of famine was felt to be needed and could be agreed. Throughout this book, I have been specifically concerned with famines and not with the broader phenomena of hunger, human distress and suffering, for example among war-affected and migrant populations. The solutions to the problem of famine are very different to the solutions to the problem of world hunger or the needs of people affected by war or driven from their homes by repression or natural disaster. But the lines between (smaller) famines and fluctuations in chronic hunger, and between famines and crises of forced displacement and distress migration, are blurred. As great famines have declined, this blurred zone has become more significant: this is where we need to focus our concern.

In the 1980s – first of all in Mozambique – aid agencies began speaking about 'complex emergencies', which were crises with multiple causes and different dimensions. People were affected by a combination of natural and human adversity (e.g. drought and war) and were hungry, in need of health care and often displaced. Like much of the vocabulary of professional relief action, it deliberately erased the political dimension of the problem, so that aid workers could do their jobs. That's a useful oversight, as long as scholars and policy makers don't forget that it is an oversight. Some practitioners and analysts smuggled the word 'political' back in to create the composite 'complex political emergency', which served as shorthand for a crisis created by armed conflict. It has since become common to use the term 'humanitarian emergency', a phenomenon defined by the fact that international humanitarian agencies are concerned with it.

The fact that humanitarian emergencies were so diverse made it difficult to standardize definitions and measurements. Paul Howe and

Stephen Devereux took the lead in exploring a set of criteria for establishing a standard set of categories for them.[6] The scale they developed had two dimensions: magnitude and severity. The magnitude element – numbers of deaths – is the one I have used for historic famines. But, for obvious reasons, a metric based on the number of people who are already dead isn't much use when a crisis is imminent or actually occurring.

International agencies needed an operational toolkit, and for this the severity dimension was the most salient. The outcome was the IPC scale,[7] initially developed in Somalia by the FAO's Food Security Analysis Unit in the early 2000s. The first version of the IPC scale and toolkit was adopted for north-east African countries in 2006. A revised version was adopted in 2012 and has been applied in 26 countries and by most major donors.

The IPC scale has five categories: none/minimal; stressed; crisis; emergency; and humanitarian catastrophe/famine.[8] The first is 'minimal' (in the first version of the IPC, 'broadly food secure') when more than 80 per cent of households can meet basic food needs 'without engaging in atypical, unsustainable strategies to access food and income'. Already we see that the scale is designed with poor and mostly rural populations in mind. Also, the scale is mixing an objective, measurable criterion with a situation-specific one because it refers to what is 'typical' for a community. This will be subjective, and we could read it as 'acceptable in terms of retaining the longer-term viability of the household livelihood and its social dignity'. Category two is 'stressed' (in version 1: 'borderline food insecure'), which occurs when at least 20 per cent of households are reducing food consumption and cannot protect their livelihoods. Category three, 'crisis', occurs when at least 20 per cent of households have significant food consumption gaps, leading to high levels of acute malnutrition, or they can meet minimum food needs only by endangering their longer-term livelihoods. Category four is 'emergency', an accentuated version of the above. The final category is 'famine or humanitarian catastrophe'. This is defined as at least 20 per cent of households in a specific area facing a complete lack of food and other basic needs, a situation in which starvation is evident, with more than 30 per cent of children acutely malnourished and death rates heightened to exceed two per 10,000 per day. The IPC manual stresses that its purpose is 'not to classify various degrees of famine...but to inform real-time decision-making', and that in particular 'the IPC thresholds for famine...are set to signify the beginning of famine stages.'[9]

As this book has demonstrated, achieving a standard definition of famine, let alone an operational categorization of different kinds and severities of food crisis, is extraordinarily complicated. It is no surprise that it took a very long process of technical discussion among governments and international agencies to reach agreement on the IPC scale. Its criteria are of course an operational compromise, but the scale serves its purpose: for the first time, there is a common standard for assessing when a society is approaching famine.[10]

For our purposes, the most important things about the IPC scale are that it is agnostic as to the cause of the emergency, works across diverse kinds of crisis and is based upon information that all can agree upon. That's a considerable achievement and could, in principle, achieve the goal of making a declaration of famine a purely technocratic exercise. But it still needs agreement among international actors as to how to interpret the information (and whether they have enough information) to make the call – and that is a political decision. As we shall see in several of the humanitarian emergencies described, perhaps a better way of posing the question is: 'Who *refuses* to cry famine, and for what purpose?'

Darfur: Famine as Counter-Insurgency

The crisis in Darfur in 2003–5 isn't often described as a 'famine', but this book's expansion of the definition to include all episodes with heightened mortality associated with hunger means it falls within our set of cases. It is a political famine par excellence

The Sudanese government's intent in Darfur was a counter-insurgency to defeat a rebellion. It achieved its immediate goal of neutralizing the major threat posed by the rebels but at vast human cost and unanticipated political repercussions – including the international ostracism of Sudan and an intractable low-level conflict. The debate on whether it was genocide is a fruitless one and a diversion from the political and humanitarian issues.[11] The debate on the numbers who perished also became extraordinarily heated, with advocates of the higher figures sometimes implying that those whose analysis indicated lower figures were somehow exonerating the government of its culpability. The best evidence is that the army and militia violently killed about 30,000 people, mostly civilians, and that a further 200,000 died of a combination of hunger, disease and exposure as a result of the war and mass displacement.[12] At the height of the conflict, about 2.1 million people were forcibly displaced within Darfur and a further 250,000 fled to Chad as refugees.

In some respects, the Darfur crisis is a humanitarian success story. The relief programme for Darfur was initiated in August 2003, shortly after the first government offensive caused mass displacement, six months before the first alarm bells were rung by the United Nations and eight months before the creation of the Save Darfur Coalition. The administrator of USAID, Andrew Natsios, had decided that the US government should provide aid, even though it was on antagonistic terms with the government in Khartoum and there would surely be accusations that aid was being diverted to the government's war machine.[13] That aid took about six months to arrive, which meant that when the government and rebels signed a ceasefire in April 2004, a well-resourced relief effort could be mounted at once. Death rates in the displaced camps peaked early and fell rapidly. Ironically, after two or three years, health and nutrition levels in Darfur's huge displaced camps were better than they had been before the war. The aid agencies managed to operate their programmes despite deep suspicion and occasional outright hostility from the government, negotiating access by making uncomfortable compromises on where they could go and what they could say. They sensibly distanced themselves from the more lurid narratives of American advocacy groups. Nonetheless, when the ICC issued an arrest warrant for President Omar al-Bashir in 2009, the government expelled thirteen international agencies. Most of their operations were taken over by Sudanese partners (a transfer prepared in advance) or other international agencies in their networks. When compared with comparable counter-insurgency famines in southern Sudan (1988 and 1998), the Darfur emergency was less severe than one might have feared.

Northern Uganda: Famine as Counter-Insurgency

Northern Uganda, by any sensible measure, was another political famine. In January 2004, the UN Humanitarian Coordinator, Jan Egeland, wrote:

> As the world turns its gaze toward the horrors in Darfur, an equally terrible situation in northern Uganda continues virtually unnoticed: the actions of a fanatical rebel movement, the Lord's Resistance Army (LRA), have displaced over 1.6 million people, even more than in Darfur. The conflict has destroyed lives, communities and rich cultural traditions. This conflict, surrounded by an inexplicable international silence, cannot be allowed to continue. The international community must help to end it and staunch the haemorrhage of human suffering.[14]

Egeland was right but was silent on the culpability of the Ugandan government in the crisis of mass displacement. As in Darfur, the international community as a whole took sides but this time with the stronger actor, the Ugandan government, against the insurgents. It is also striking how official reports on the crisis in northern Uganda are bereft of estimates for mortality, and UNICEF stopped counting mortality in 2000. Numbers of abductees and displaced people are routinely mentioned but not the numbers of dead.[15] However, there is every reason to suppose that excess deaths breached the 100,000 threshold.

During the conflict, an estimated 68,000–100,000 people were killed violently and a further 63,000–100,000 people forcibly abducted, mostly by the LRA and most of whom never returned.[16] We don't know what the abductees died from, but for many held by the LRA it would have been exhaustion, hunger, disease and untreated wounds – all of which count within the category of forced starvation. At the peak of the conflict in 2005, 1.84 million people were forcibly displaced, due to both LRA attacks and the Ugandan counter-insurgency by means of emptying the rural areas. The Ugandan army and air force routinely used lethal force, or the threat of such force, to compel people to move and, once moved, to stay in the camps. For an agricultural population, separation from farmland is a sentence of hunger.

Rigorous estimates of overall mortality in northern Uganda are striking for their scarcity. One of the few surveys covers the Acholi region (the worst hit) in the first seven and a half months of 2005. It found overall death rates of 1.54 per 10,000 per day, short of IPC stage five but clearly a severe humanitarian emergency. Estimates for excess mortality in that period, due to all causes (disease, malnutrition, AIDS, violence) were 24,000–33,000.[17] Of these, 10,000 were children under five, and 9.4 per cent of deaths were attributed to violence. These kinds of conditions changed little over at least two years. It follows that it is very likely that, over the course of this war, excess deaths due to hunger, disease and displacement surpassed 100,000. The war and humanitarian crisis ended in 2006, when, as part of an effort to negotiate a political settlement, the LRA withdrew its forces from northern Uganda to a base on the border between southern Sudan and the DRC and began peace talks under the mediation of the southern Sudanese leadership in Juba.

In contrast to Darfur, the United States actively supported the Ugandan government. It had designated the LRA as a terrorist organization in 2001 and provided military advisors and training to the Ugandans. Humanitarian agencies cooperated with official policy. These double standards animated critics. Adam Branch writes: 'It was not the aid agencies' need for access, but the Ugandan government's international alliances and reputation as a responsible state that allowed it to blatantly instrumentalize humanitarian aid, with devastating consequences.'[18] He argues that the humanitarians were an accessory to the brutal counter-insurgency. The United States reluctantly and half-heartedly backed the peace talks and supported a Ugandan military attack on the LRA headquarters in the DRC borderlands just as those talks stalled – definitively closing off the prospect of a negotiated end to the insurgency and dispersing the LRA into a long, low-level campaign of banditry and atrocity in the borderlands of the DRC, southern Sudan and Central African Republic. The ICC issued its first arrest warrants for the leaders of the LRA, and many in the international community, especially in the United States, were profoundly sceptical about the possibility or value of negotiating peace. The narrative of heroes and villains, beloved of the media and some advocacy groups, demonized the LRA leader Joseph Kony and drew attention to his atrocities. Kony is without question a brutal person who is guilty of many crimes, but that should not be reason to overlook the crimes of his enemies.[19] The simplistic international narrative did precisely that, ignoring or exonerating the Ugandan government's counter-insurgency, although that was equally responsible for the displacement and hence the food crisis and the elevated death rates.

Placing Darfur and northern Uganda side by side highlights the importance of the political lens through which a crisis is seen and poses the question of how information on death rates is collected, calculated and used. It underscores why we need objective metrics for humanitarian emergencies – the function of the IPC.

Somalia's Multi-Causal Famine

The 2011–12 famine in Somalia was a 'complex emergency' in the classic sense and a collective failure of Somali political systems and the international community.[20] One cause was severe drought and a food production shortfall across central and southern Somalia. A second was a squeeze on remittances, a critical source of income for Somalis, more important in aggregate than international aid, caused by US measures against money laundering and to combat the financing of terrorism which placed huge obstacles in the way of the functioning of the *hawala* money transfer system.[21] And the third, critical shock was the global food crisis which caused cereal prices to double. The background to these shocks was war – or, to be precise, several overlapping wars. Over decades, the Somali civil wars had consisted of fights between militias, mobilized along clan lines but with their political and military operations organized as political business ventures, which sought to control sources of wealth and revenue. They fought over control of the most fertile land along Somalia's rivers and the lands in between, over control of ports and airports and key roads, and over urban real estate. The headline war, however, was the conflict between an Islamist movement Harakat al-Shabaab al-Mujahideen, commonly known as al-Shabaab, and the combined forces of Somalia's Transitional Federal Government (TFG) and its African backers, especially Ethiopia and Kenya, alongside (and increasingly part of) the African Union Mission in Somalia (AMISOM). The TFG was internationally recognized but was corrupt and ineffective. Al-Shabaab was ostracized internationally and placed on the US list of terrorist groups in 2008, but it was efficiently run. Al-Shabaab exacted onerous taxes and contributions from the population under its control and also tried to prevent them from fleeing to become refugees in neighbouring countries. It was also profoundly suspicious of international aid agencies which it accused of espionage and supporting western anti-Islamic agendas. Al-Shabaab harboured a particular animus against food aid, which it condemned as a deceitful stratagem in which foreign agencies (of both the aid and intelligence variety) conspired to undermine people's self-reliance.[22]

The famine caused between 244,000 and 273,000 deaths.[23] It need not have done so. The UN-led early-warning system gave ample notice of the crisis. Despite the war and the extreme difficulty of working with al-Shabaab, an international relief programme could have reached most of the affected population, and the simple fact of providing food aid to southern Somalia would have depressed food prices and blunted the impact of the famine. However, US counter-terror legislation (specifically the PATRIOT Act) prohibited relief agencies (or any individuals) from undertaking any activities that might provide support, material or symbolic, to an organization labelled as 'terrorist' – including even the inadvertent support that would occur if aid was stolen and ended up in the hands of a terrorist group. The agencies affected by the prohibition included not only American organizations but any organization that received US funds, or expected to do so, or did any kind of business with the United States – a group that included the UN agencies and just about every sizeable international aid agency.

The UN belatedly broke this impasse with a declaration of 'famine' in July 2011. This was the first occasion on which the IPC scale – which had of course been developed with Somalia in mind – was applied in this manner. It had the desired effect: over the previous six months, aid officials had worked with US administration lawyers to try to find a way to work around the PATRIOT Act provisions, and the formula was found quickly after the famine declaration. This succeeded to the extent that relief could finally reach the affected parts of Somalia. But it was a failure to the extent that six months was a fatal delay for scores of thousands of Somalis.

The Darfur and Somalia crises show the importance of US political action to provide humanitarian aid in complex and unfriendly situations. In Darfur, a perceived humanitarian imperative overrode antipathy to the Sudanese government and fears about what might happen to aid. In Somalia, that didn't happen until very late in the day.

In early 2017, Somalia was once again on the list of countries at risk of famine. The possible crisis arose from the intersection of several factors: drought, high food prices and the inability of humanitarian agencies to reach populations in need, all against the background of a rural economy that had not recovered from the calamity of 2011.

Yemen: a Nationwide Famine, Ignored

The Yemen famine that began in 2015 was unusual among contemporary humanitarian crises in its scale, and in the fact that it extended far beyond its epicentres in the fiercely war-affected areas to affect the majority of the country. It also developed with scarcely a tremor of public or political concern at the highest levels of the international community. One UN official described it as 'a forgotten crisis, with millions of people in urgent need across the country'.[24] There are no published mortality estimates for the Yemen crisis: press reports refer only to the numbers of civilians known to be killed in air raids and other acts of violence, not the much larger numbers who surely are dying from hunger and disease. The silence on these numbers is doubtless because Saudi Arabia and western nations bear the greater responsibility for reducing the population to destitution and probable starvation. There's no indication that the Saudis intended anything other than a short, victorious campaign, and they certainly have no interest in a humanitarian catastrophe in another neighbouring country. But, as so often, it seems that arrogance and miscalculation was compounded by the logic of military escalation, creating a march of folly into disaster.

The background to the Yemen disaster is that the country was poor – the poorest by far in the Arab peninsular – and highly dependent on imports of food, fuel and other essentials. Following the Arab Spring uprisings of 2011, Yemen slowly slid into civil strife, which was worsened by economic austerity measures. One measure of this is that agriculture increased as a proportion of GDP, from 12.1 to

14.7 per cent over the years 2010–14. Political conflict escalated in 2015 with a fast-spreading rebellion by the Houthi minority, which overran the capital Sanaa and most of the highlands of the country. Identifying this as an Iranian-backed insurrection, Saudi Arabia led a coalition of Gulf Cooperation Council (GCC) countries, plus Egypt, Sudan and Eritrea, into a war against the Houthis in March that year.

The war directly caused humanitarian disaster, resulting from the sieges of cities, the destruction of the health-care system, the bombing of markets and disruptions to food supplies brought about by fighting and by the destruction of roads and bridges. For example, the Houthi forces' siege of Taizz, and the 200,000 people trapped there, caused starvation and the collapse of the medical infrastructure in the city.[25] The WFP finally brought food to the last besieged enclaves in July 2016, using an innovative voucher programme with local traders.[26] In the Houthi province of Saada, declared by the Saudis as a military target in its entirety,[27] coalition bombing destroyed all the functioning markets and brought trade – including in food – to a standstill. But the extent of the crisis reached far beyond those directly affected by war. In November 2015, the UN estimated that 82 per cent of the population (21.2 million out of 26 million) needed assistance, a much greater number than the 12.4 million in conflict-affected areas.[28] These numbers were largely unchanged in early 2017.[29]

The bigger reason for the collapse was economic warfare. As it launched its intervention, the GCC with US and UK support closed Yemeni airspace and imposed a naval and land blockade. UN Security Council resolution 2216 followed on 14 April. Its stated intent was an arms embargo on the Houthis, but its effect was a near-total blockade,[30] with only one exception, which is that the UN Secretary-General was requested 'to facilitate the delivery of humanitarian assistance and evacuation, including the establishment of humanitarian pauses, as appropriate, in coordination with the Government of Yemen'. Stronger language, proposed by Russia, which had mandated 'humanitarian pauses' in the coalition air strikes, was struck out.[31] Coalition bombing raids also severely damaged the port of Al-Hudeidah, the entry point for 60 per cent of pre-crisis imports. The bombing destroyed the container capacity at the port so that offloading of ships had to be done manually, leading to long delays and low efficiency.[32]

War and blockade led an already shaky economy into disaster.[33] According to the Ministry of Planning and International Cooperation, the GDP contracted nearly 35 per cent, from US$13.3 billion in 2014 to US$8.7 billion, in 2015. More than 2.5 million people lost their jobs. Inflation surged. The government was only able to pay some salaries, with no resources available for supplies or maintenance of essential infrastructure including hospitals and water supplies.[34]

Recognizing the severity of the mounting suffering, in July 2015 the UN declared Yemen a phase 3 crisis on the IPC scale. This set in motion a substantial UN humanitarian response. But the UN agencies were careful not to place any explicit blame on the GCC blockade for the disaster. Press releases and reports studiously attribute the destruction of Al-Hudeidah port facilities only to 'hostilities'. On occasions where the Houthi militia are responsible, such as the siege of Taizz, the UN has been ready to be more candid and single out the culpable party. The kinds of data that would be necessary for declaring a phase 5 crisis – famine – either do not exist or are suppressed. In January 2017, the IPC assessment was bolder: a likely famine affecting more than 10 million people.[35] Without explicitly mentioning the GCC blockade and its authorization by the UN Security Council, the assessment emphasized that, '[t]o mitigate severe, ongoing food insecurity and prevent Famine over the coming year, the international community and local actors must protect the ability of private traders to import staple food.'[36] Humanitarian access was mentioned as a secondary measure. Stephen O'Brien, head of UNOCHA, expanded on these points in a statement to the UN Security Council in March, in which he pointedly called for 'all parties' compliance with international humanitarian law' and for a stop to the fighting.[37] Without mentioning any names (and referring to the other three crises as well as Yemen), he said, 'To continue on the path of war and military conquest is – I think we all know – to guarantee failure, humiliation and moral turpitude, and [those who continue on that path] will bear the responsibility for the millions who face hunger and deprivation on an incalculable scale because of it.'

Should a famine rage in Yemen, the culpability for creating it and covering it up will lie primarily with the Saudi-led military coalition and its use of indiscriminate economic warfare.

Forced Starvation in Syria

Syria has been the most spectacular and visible humanitarian disaster of the decade. But it is not seen through the lens of food security and famine, and there has been no UN effort to classify it on the IPC scale. Syria may not meet the magnitude criterion for famine but the starvation in besieged towns and enclaves is surely severe enough.

Before the war, Syria was a middle-income country with a GDP per capita of US$1700, 70 per cent of its people living in cities and agriculture responsible for one-sixth of GDP. In five years of civil war, the Syrian government and opposition, armed, financed and actively supported by nearby countries and foreign powers, have reduced it to ruin. At the epicentre of the country's destruction are besieged enclaves where starvation is used to break down resistance, possibly even with the aim of eradicating communities. More widely, there is generalized abject poverty, hunger and immiseration. Syria's famine is all these things.

Besieged cities have suffered the worst horrors, where starvation is used as a weapon of war. During 2014–16, about 400,000 people were trapped in these enclaves.[38] Amnesty International documented sieges in Eastern Ghouta,[39] Yarmuk in the Damascus suburbs,[40] Daraya and Madaya,[41] and their effects. They described people eating leaves or going without food for days, cases of outright starvation and food items so scarce that they were selling at prices inflated a hundred times or more. For example, for the 42,000 people trapped in besieged Madaya in late 2015 and early 2016 – a siege described as a 'war crime' by the UN Secretary-General[42] – rice and flour were selling at US$120 per kilogramme, prices 90–150 times higher than in Damascus.[43] In these enclaves, profiteers made small fortunes trading bread, fuel, water and medicine across the battle lines.

Syrians also faced a wider crisis of destitution. More than six million people have lost their homes or livelihoods due to the war – to be precise, due to the way in which the war has been fought in populated areas – and struggle to find enough food. At the beginning of the war, 0.7 per cent of the population lived in 'abject poverty', but by 2016 it was fully 35 per cent.[44] This includes the great majority of the 4.5 million people defined by the UN as 'hard to reach' for humanitarian agencies, but also large numbers of others rendered destitute by economic collapse.

The third level is the wider 'in need' population, estimated at 13.5 million people by the UN in 2015, a level unchanged in 2017.[45] This includes displaced people, their local hosts, people in hard-to-reach areas, handicapped people and refugees from Palestine and Iraq. The UN uses functional 'in need' categories rather than estimates for poverty, but the scale of the economic and food security crisis is not in question.

Syria's economic collapse is appalling. According to the World Bank, GDP has been contracting by an average of 15.7 per cent each year since the war began.[46] The loss of infrastructure and assets is in scores of billions of dollars. The Syrian pound has lost over 90 per cent of its value against the US dollar. But to understand what this means for hunger and starvation, we need to appreciate that the collapse has been selective – geographically, politically and socio-economically. Already in 2010–11, the drier north-eastern parts of the country were affected by drought and the mismanagement of water resources, and the price of bread was increasing.[47] The Syrian state had provided extensive food and fuel subsidies and had an extensive public sector payroll, and as the political, security and economic crises hit, the government selectively withdrew these benefits through a process of 'subsidies rationalization', lay-offs and simply not paying salaries.

The most comprehensive data and analysis of the Syrian economy is a survey by the Syrian Centre for Policy Research.[48] This shows how the manufacturing sector has been reduced to just 35 per cent of its pre-war output, internal transport is 27 per cent and the state-controlled oil sector is just 2 per cent – with the Islamic State controlling most of remaining production. Unemployment is 57 per cent, with 3 million jobs lost. Syria has been regressing towards a subsistence, barter and extortion economy. Agricultural production has declined, but nonetheless is a larger share of GDP, up from 17.4 per cent in 2010 to 28.7 per cent in 2015, with a modest rebound in farming in 2015 due to good rains. Inflation has eroded households' purchasing power, with approximately three- to fourfold increases in flour and rice prices in the first year of the war. Economic activities have shifted to the war itself: a sixth of the active population is estimated to be involved in the war economy, and the share of 'semi-public expenditure' – spending by entities outside government control such as rebel forces – is 13 per cent of GDP.

How many have died? There have been major efforts to calculate war fatalities, but little comparable on deaths attributable to hunger. For example, the *New York Times*' otherwise comprehensive assessment of war deaths in Syria in 2015 enumerated just 565 deaths from starvation, dehydration or lack of medical care – an absurdly low figure.[49] The Syrian Centre for Policy Research estimates 400,000 deaths from violence and 70,000 from hunger, disease and lack of medical facilities since the war began.[50] The death rate has risen from 4.4 per 1,000 per year before the crisis to 10.9 per 1,000 in 2014 and 2015. Life expectancy has plunged from 70.5 years in 2010 to 55.4 years in 2015. Birth rates have also fallen. Within the wider crisis of civil war and the mass destruction of Syrian society, tens of thousands of people have died from starvation: famine in severity if not in magnitude.

South Sudan's Famine Crimes

In February 2017, the UN made its first real-time declaration of famine for six years, announcing that parts of South Sudan were in famine, and others were likely to follow. The famine is caused by the civil war that broke out in December 2013. South Sudan is a particularly significant case because famine has occurred in a place where international humanitarian actors have a long-standing presence. There are no good figures for mortality in South Sudan. One UN official used the figure of 50,000 dead (without specifying the causes), while another said that number 'may well be an underestimation'.[51]

The background, and part cause, of the civil war was economic collapse in South Sudan. At independence in 2011, South Sudan was a middle-income country, with 60 per cent of GDP and 98 per cent of government revenue from oil, although the benefits of these riches were monopolized by a political and military elite, while the majority remained poor. The political leadership in the South Sudanese capital Juba was determined to assert its power vis-à-vis the government in Khartoum, its former master and adversary. This required military action on the border and in support of a rebellion in the 'two areas' of Southern Kordofan and Blue Nile. In turn, military action against Sudan would have been futile, given that South Sudan's oil was pumped along a pipeline that ran through Sudan, which would of course have instantly taken the oil for its own purposes. In January 2012, therefore, South Sudan shut down its entire national oil production. Its calculation was that Khartoum would be brought to its knees, financially and militarily, before Juba. I described it at the time as an 'economic doomsday machine'.[52] So it turned out, and South Sudan collapsed first. Although most of the country's riches had been consumed by a relatively small elite, much had also trickled down in the form of government salaries and (especially) payroll and pay-off to the 745 generals of the national army – the Sudan People's Liberation Army (SPLA). Poverty intensified, especially in small towns. Also, as the kleptocratic system of government ground to a halt without the funds needed to grease the wheels of patronage, the protagonists turned to an increasingly bitter power struggle, and then to violence.[53]

As soon as the first shots were fired, the SPLA split apart along ethnic lines. There were reciprocal massacres and the sudden displacement of over 1.5 million people, of whom nearly 200,000 took refuge in the base camps for the UN Mission in South Sudan (UNMISS). The main immediate causes of death were violence and the dangers associated with flight, such as drowning in rivers and children and elderly people becoming lost or abandoned. As would be expected, these traumas were followed by infectious diseases and hunger. In the UN camp in Bentiu, displaced people were living in a flood zone, sometimes forced to sleep sitting or standing because the water had risen.

There were a few attempts to collect data on which to estimate mortality. One of them was by UNOCHA.[54] A survey of 2,150 households with 19,321 people found 866 deaths over the previous year from violence, drowning and other causes, with a considerable additional number of people lost or their fate unknown. Overall, this put the death rate well above the famine threshold of two per 10,000 per day and, given that things were getting worse and a fundamental rationale of the IPC scale is to anticipate and thus prevent such a worsening, this would appear to be ample justification for declaring famine. But the IPC country team – consisting of UN and donor agencies and the host government – hesitated to declare famine. Instead, they declared a phase 4 emergency, adding an exclamation mark to indicate that it would be phase 5 without humanitarian assistance.

The technical reason – or pretext – was that the number of deaths from hunger and disease alone did not bring the mortality rate up to the threshold. The survey found that violence was responsible for 78 per cent of the deaths among those aged six years and older, while among children of five and under, 30 per cent of deaths were from violence, 29 per cent drowning and 41 per cent 'other' – i.e. so-called 'natural causes' of hunger and disease. Men and boys were much more likely to be killed violently (79 per cent of deaths) than women and girls (44 per cent). Clearly, a battle or massacre is not a famine as such, but the dividing line between different causes of death in a massive, complex humanitarian emergency is arbitrary. And one reason why the vocabulary of 'complex humanitarian emergency' was indeed adopted in the first place was precisely so that these kinds of arbitrary distinctions did not need to be made.

The political reason why the IPC team declined to declare famine was the sensitivities of the South Sudanese government – which was of course represented in the team. The UN had to deal with a national ruler, President Salva Kiir, who was becoming paranoid about international engagement in the country. The government expelled the UN humanitarian coordinator, Toby Lanzer, in 2015. Government soldiers assaulted and raped national and foreign aid workers on more than one occasion and fired on embassy cars at other times. Throughout, the UN humanitarian agencies had to negotiate their public stand with peacekeepers and mediators who were worried that the host government would reject their troops or their peace proposals. Thus

President Kiir – arguably a famine criminal – had a veto over whether the world declared famine in his country. And at that time none of the UN agencies had the courage, or the political backing, to challenge him. There was no alternative international political strategy, rather a sense of confusion about what, if anything, could be done to salvage a moribund peace process and a deepening crisis of hunger, disease and displacement. In the meantime, South Sudanese children were dying.

By early 2017, the government's calculus had changed. It was now so desperately short of resources and foresaw (correctly) that humanitarian aid would be a new source of plunder, and cynically agreed to the IPC analytics.[55] The UN declared famine in February. This achieved the immediate goal of putting South Sudan's crisis onto the international news cycle: whether it provides the political stimulus to end the crisis is unclear at the time of writing.

Northern Nigeria's Insurgency Famine

A final case is the emergency in north-eastern Nigeria as a result of the protracted war between the Nigerian army and the extremist group Boko Haram. Northern Nigeria has been historically prone to periodic food crisis, caused by the dislocations and exactions of incorporation into the colonial and neo-colonial economy, and periodic drought.[56] Nigeria's fabulous oil wealth and dynamic middle class ought to have ensured that, from the 1970s, famine was consigned to history. But corruption and mismanagement kept Nigerians poor and the north-east of the country poorest of all. This was also the location of the militant Islamist Boko Haram insurgency, and, in due course, Nigeria's first fully fledged humanitarian emergency since the Biafran war of 1967–70.

From 2009, Boko Haram's irregular forces controlled significant parts of Maiduguri, Bornu State. Their presence had brought many normal trading activities to a halt. Remarkably, sub-Saharan Africa's largest army failed to roll back the insurgency, a failure widely attributed to extraordinary levels of corruption in military procurement and payroll and the readiness of some individuals within the army command to tolerate an insurgency that undermined the political prospects of President Goodluck Jonathan and other members of the ruling elite.

During 2016, when the Nigerian army, supported by neighbouring countries (notably Chad), finally made territorial gains against Boko Haram, their advance revealed a humanitarian crisis. By September

2016, there were 1.82 million people displaced and 5 million in need of emergency assistance. According to OCHA, 3.3 million were in IPC phase 3, a further 1 million in phase 4 (food emergency) and 65,000 in phase 5 (famine). At the time, no 'famine' was declared because the numbers did not add up to 20 per cent of the overall population in the affected area.[57] Later, aid agencies reported that retrospective surveys showed that famine probably occurred in certain localities, causing 2,000 deaths in Bama local government district, for example. They also said that famine might still be ongoing in hard-to-reach areas.[58]

Counter-humanitarianism

Counter-humanitarianism is the rejection of humanitarian norms. It is different from critiques of humanitarian overreach, which flow from the fear that overambitious and politicized actions taken in the name of humanitarianism may undermine objectives such as peace, human rights and feeding the hungry. It is distinct from the belief that the goal of alleviating famine could sometimes be better served by using means that are not explicitly philanthropic, such as promoting the commercial food trade or changing a government policy. Counter-humanitarianism is an array of political and ideological practices that deny the value system of humanitarianism *as such*. Counter-humanitarians may act out of ideology, out of fear or because they have other political or military priorities that, they believe, trump humanitarianism. They may consider some human lives as possessing lower value or no value.

The very fact that we can identify and name 'counter-humanitarianism' is a backhanded tribute to the advance of the humanitarian norm. Over the last decades, incrementally, through myriad negotiations and pressures, it became more difficult for bellicose or repressive governments to obstruct relief. Providing aid to hungry people across battle lines, arranging humanitarian pauses and protecting civilians caught up in armed conflict, became the norm rather than the exception. Humanitarian agencies routinely decried the restrictions on their 'humanitarian space' of operation, but often this complaint reflected the fact that they were extending their operations into more and more difficult places where they would not have been able to tread in earlier years. There was always resistance and obstruction, but we are now witnessing a wider political and ideological backlash. Counter-humanitarianism is sinister beyond its material impacts because it legitimizes political and military conduct that is indifferent to human life or subordinates human life to other ends.

The emergence of counter-humanitarianism coincides with the recent period in which the long decline in armed conflicts has stalled and reversed. The number of wars and conflict-related deaths has increased from an all-time low in 2006[59] and is increasing each year. Today's figures are still well below historic levels, and there have been temporary reversals in the decline in war before, but the upward trend is nonetheless significant. The logic of the long war on terror, including legitimizing military actions that in previous years would have been defined as aggression, has intersected with an array of other realpolitik and security agendas to foment these new wars. It is difficult to disentangle cause and effect, but the parallel increase in war and decline in respect for humanitarianism is reason to worry that episodes of mass starvation may become more frequent and more deadly.

The most visible counter-humanitarian ideologies are militant extremist agendas such as that espoused by ISIS, the disregard for human life in the pursuit of military goals by the Saudi-led coalition in Yemen and by the Syrian government in its civil war, and extremely violent ethnic chauvinism as seen in South Sudan.

The counter-humanitarianism of extremist armed groups has not been sufficiently studied. It is difficult to know the extent to which it stems from ideology and values or from political circumstances and security fears. For example, some hostility to international humanitarianism may derive from a principled belief in self-reliance, to the extent that those who cannot support themselves do not deserve to live. Alternatively, it may arise from paranoia about international relief organizations, which may be labelled as spies or seen as the agents of efforts to make people dependent on western charity.

The counter-humanitarianism of the US-led war on terror is a particularly insidious threat, partly because it materially obstructs relief and partly because it directly assaults the principle of humanitarian neutrality. Its central plank is legal restriction on operating in areas in which groups designated as terrorists are active. The US PATRIOT Act criminalizes any action that provides moral or material support, deliberate or not, to an organization identified as terrorist, unless there is a specific exemption. In the case of Somalia, al-Shabaab is among the proscribed groups, and fear of US legal action contributed to delays in international responses to a famine that was foreseen and preventable.[60] As a result of the outcry, the United States made it possible for humanitarian agencies to operate under licences, but that work-around remains ad hoc and discretionary. The shadow still hangs over humanitarians working in countries in the front line of the long war on terror: they may be accused by the US authorities of crossing the line, and they may be suspected by local people of being agents of the western agenda.

Similar challenges face humanitarian agencies trying to operate in Syria and Yemen.[61] The British Charity Commission has taken on the task of policing voluntary organizations to identify those at risk of harbouring individuals with extremist sympathies, or which might deliberately or inadvertently have dealings with people or groups designated as terrorists. This is acting as an intrusive, much-resented brake on voluntary action by Muslim humanitarians in Britain. It is also removing the particular added value of Muslim relief agencies, as the kinds of close contact that they enjoyed with recipient communities is now perilous in the eyes of the British authorities, whether the intelligence agencies or the Charity Commission.

The counter-terrorist prohibition on talking to terrorists not only rules out negotiating humanitarian access and other measure such as ceasing hostilities but also prevents peace talks. There are very few cases in which insurgencies mounted by groups labelled as terrorists have been ended by military action. Much more commonly, it is necessary to talk to them.[62] The alternative may be indefinite war, which if it is driven by competing counter-humanitarianisms may of course imply indefinite war famines.

National security remains the most commonly invoked justification for obstructing humanitarian efforts. This has a long pedigree, and the limits on humanitarian action in wartime are well recognized. Recent instances include the Sri Lankan government's withholding of aid to the besieged and hungry civilians during its final offensive against the Tamil Tigers in 2009[63] and the GCC blockade of Yemen. In earlier years, these actions would have passed unremarked. Today, their significance is that faminogenic actions that are not condemned internationally help to incubate counter-humanitarianism.

Counter-humanitarianism is also witnessed in xenophobia and hostility towards asylum seekers, refugees and migrants in general. The tightening of laws and practices concerning refugees in Europe and the United States risks creating very vulnerable populations in countries afflicted by war, transit countries and recipient countries. There is a knock-on effect on intolerance across the rest of the world, especially the greater Middle East, where policies to control migration may be materially supported and politically validated by metropolitan chauvinism. Many of the people most at risk of starvation in the coming years may be migrants and asylum seekers who are stuck en route or forcibly returned to places where they are very vulnerable.

11

Mass Starvation in the Future

The History and Future of Famine

The twentieth century's calamitous famines ended with the end of wars of annihilation and totalitarianism. The demographic transition, public health advances and humanitarian action meant that many fewer people died when food crises did in fact occur.

Great famines and episodes of mass starvation continue in the twenty-first century. The recent mutations of wars in parts of Africa and the Middle East may yet herald Act Five of modern famine. The prospect of unending war fought with diminishing respect for humanitarian norms by militant insurgents, regional powers and western counter-terrorists, tolerated by authoritarians and xenophobes elsewhere in the world, could well entail a new era of protracted humanitarian crises – small in magnitude but intractable and intermittently very severe. Political decisions to block or scale down relief aid, or to stop distress migrants or forcibly return them home, could well become complicit in the escalation of crises into mass starvation.

Famines caused by natural disasters and economic shocks remain a very remote possibility, though intensifying inequality and increasing multi-dimensional volatility in the global economy and ecology mean that we need to be alert.

Stopping Famines in a Volatile World

Famines are shapeshifters and the disguises in which they come can readily confuse us. Mass starvation has become remote from the lived experience of a generation of Asians and two generations of Europeans, and for thirty years it has been misleadingly identified as an exclusively African issue. The popular imaginary of famine is still haunted by Malthus's zombie. All the above makes for intellectual laziness and political complacency. The first agenda item for ending famines is understanding them, and I hope this book is a small contribution to that task.

There are multiple parallel trends that increase the risks of a compound extreme event that could lead to famine. There is climate change and the increase in extreme weather events. There is the turbulence associated with economic globalization, which can lead to sudden and unexpected food price rises and equally precipitous losses of jobs and livelihoods. There is mass-distress migration and hostility to refugees and asylum seekers. There is the precarious condition of the global public health system. Our global institutions tend to focus on single issues – trade, agriculture, health, trade, refugees or peace and security. Each one of these is important and needs to be supported, and the whole can be augmented by technocratic measures such as insurance against climatic shocks. Particularly relevant to the risk of famine, there are also no global institutions that can deal with compound threats in an integrated manner or even predict such perils in a cogent way.[1]

The political risks, such as political turmoil and intolerance associated with the long war on terror, are bigger and intrinsically less predictable. The rise of plutocratic populism, economic nationalism and xenophobia may augur political, economic and normative upheavals on an even bigger scale. The waters have not risen to anywhere near the neck of Tawney's peasant, but they are swirling in such a way that there is a greater danger of a freak wave that could swamp him. To extend the metaphor, just as global warming makes severe hurricanes more common, so too does the unstable global political economy make a 'perfect storm' of faminogenic factors less improbable.

The decline in famines is strongly associated with the rise of democratic freedoms and a beneficent multilateral world order. Over the last 30 years, we have assumed benevolent governance – that the default option in the international order is to promote humane values and act against needless human suffering. That era may now be passing, and the default setting for global politics may return to the older premise that faraway human suffering, including mass starvation, can be tolerated or ignored. Sen's thesis that the growth of democratic freedoms has driven the reduction in famines can work in reverse: in a world of resurgent authoritarianism, exclusion and xenophobia, we need to be more worried about famine.

Another way of putting this is that there are multiple pathways to famine, each of them intrinsically unlikely, but growing less so, and each of them including political decision at some point. Many of these pathways are dominated by politics and some them include *only* a sequence of bad political decisions. The likeliest scenarios for famine for the foreseeable future are political crimes, committed in error and fear, in the context of political-economic turbulence, armed conflict including the long war on terror, authoritarian and chauvinist government and counter-humanitarian ideologies.

There is also reason to worry that faminogenic politics may be abetted by unfounded or exaggerated fears of 'Famine', which trigger pessimistic or panicked resource grabbing and exclusionary politics. The peculiar genius of Malthus's zombie is that it often appears in the benevolent guise of preserving the planet's ecosystems and resisting despoliation. It's important that arguments are made for the sustainable management of the earth's limited resources that don't invoke the spectre of 'gigantic inevitable Famine'.[2] It's important that the real tensions and disputes over scarce resources, which will undoubtedly be intensified by climate change, are not politically discoloured by invoking the dangerous simplifications of alimentary economics.

During the writing of this book, some European and American electorates embraced the politics of pessimism and scarcity, creating new openings for those who would pursue exclusionary, chauvinistic, misogynistic and zero-sum politics. These are the conditions in which people will again be susceptible to garrison ideologies and global resource-grabbing. Jared Diamond, in his book *Collapse*, asks rhetorically, 'What were Easter Islanders saying as they cut down the last tree on their island?'[3] One possibility is that one group of islanders cut down the last tree of another group, rejoicing that their rivals no longer had an advantage. The capacity of political leaders and their constituents to pursue narrow factional benefits at the expense of the wider public good has no known limits. But recent history, as illustrated by the story of famines in this book, shows that enormous progress is achievable, and indeed there were precious achievements over the decades that should not casually be reversed.

Stopping Famine Crimes

I hope to have demonstrated that criminal actions of various kinds are an integral part in the creation of mass starvation. Most faminogenic actions are prohibited under existing provisions of international law, and those that are not expressly forbidden are clearly recognizable violations of norms of humane politics. Codifying and prosecuting famine crimes is at once beguilingly simple – because of the array of prohibitions already on the books – and frustratingly complicated because of the evidentiary difficulties of proving criminal culpability for starvation. This Gordian knot cannot simply be cut. Instead, we can take inspiration from the campaign to put gender and sex crimes at the top of the international moral and legal agenda for responding to armed conflicts and atrocities, and press for more political and legal attention to starvation crimes.

One place to start is the preservation of those humanitarian norms so slowly and painstakingly established over the last 70 years. By the turn of the millennium, a famine crime could be committed through an act of omission, such as blocking relief, failing to uphold the relevant laws of war or failing to provide international relief systems with the resources they need to operate. Over the years, authoritarian governments in countries such as Sudan fashioned many subtle instruments to hamstring, obstruct and distort humanitarian efforts, and in response the UN and major donors incrementally moved towards a position that the right to emergency relief should prevail over considerations of national sovereignty and should be weighed very heavily against claims of military necessity. Unfortunately, the irrevocable right of people to be free from the threat of starvation has not been formalized. More worryingly, the counter-humanitarian backsliding has not just been the work of extremist insurgents and belligerent authoritarians but has also been abetted by western governments in the name of counter-terrorism and, more recently, nationalism. Heedlessly cut humanitarian budgets may emerge as the next culprit.

Humanitarians tend to be advocates of change. Some of them are redirected revolutionaries, people who in a previous era would have directed their idealism into domestic politics. Today, humanitarians should seek first to consolidate the edifice that they have built over the last two generations, when – it seemed – history was on their side. The agenda of ending famines was prevailing, to the extent that the doctrine of 'no famine on our watch' was adopted by a Republican administration in Washington DC in the first decade of this millennium. The tide is turning. It is time for humanitarians to turn conservative, in the sense that they should recognize and applaud the huge benefits brought by the liberal-humanitarian world order. These institutions and norms should be cherished and not be lightly cast aside.

One mechanism that could help preserve the humanitarian order is a high-profile exercise in assessment. It is now standard that, in the wake of mass atrocity, there should be a process of truth telling and accountability. This would be appropriate for famine also. This is not the standard technical or programmatic evaluation of lessons learned but a full examination of causes, especially political causes. Following each declaration of famine, the UN should establish a commission of inquiry to investigate what happened and why, and call to account those whose crimes and errors caused the disaster.

Promoting humanitarian norms, institutions and resources will not in itself prevent the perpetration of famine crimes. Achieving that goal requires a more ambitious agenda: resuming the liberal project of promoting peace, resolving conflicts by political means including negotiation, affirming humane universal values and seeking common solutions to global problems. Part one of this is resolving existing armed conflicts, associated with the war on terror and the revived regional power rivalries that have come in its train. Part two is the collective management of global resources, to pre-empt the kinds of aggressive resource-grabs or punitive xenophobic measures that could be unleashed by authoritarian zero-sum economics.

Abolishing mass starvation is ultimately an ethical project. The paradigm of famine crimes might seem to imply two different tasks: the *political* task of preventing faminogenic actions and the *technical* (economic, public health, humanitarian) tasks of preventing people from dying in a famine that is already occurring. There are indeed both political and technocratic jobs to be done, and both elements can be credited with historic successes in reducing mass starvation. But the distinction is not quite so straightforward. Technical measures can prevent a crisis turning into a famine, but they must be activated by political decision. Most importantly, the core humanitarian norm that *all* people should be protected from starvation is central to both the political agenda of famine prevention and the ostensibly technical one of saving lives.

Over the seventy years following the end of the Second World War, the multilateral world order presided over an immense and under-celebrated achievement: the near-conquest of mass starvation. That was achieved in parallel with the eclipse of governmental attitudes that regard human life as without value. Despite the recent reverses, this achievement has not unravelled. The final end of great famines is still within our grasp. Mass starvation could be ended for good – if we decide that it is to be so.

Notes

Preface

1 Stephen O'Brien, 'The people of Yemen are being subjected to deprivation, disease and death as the world watches'. Statement to United Nations Security Council, 30 May 2017. http://www.unocha.org/story/extensive-resurgence-cholera-shows-strain-being-placed-upon-all-too-fragile-yemeni-system.
2 De Waal 2015.
3 H. R. McMaster and Gary D. Cohn, 'America first doesn't mean America alone; we are asking a lot of our allies and partners. But in return the US will once again be a true friend.' *Wall Street Journal*, 30 May 2017.
4 Stephen O'Brien, 'The people of Yemen are being subjected to deprivation, disease and death as the world watches.' Statement to United Nations Security Council, 30 May 2017. http://www.unocha.org/story/extensive-resurgence-cholera-shows-strain-being-placed-upon-all-too-fragile-yemeni-system.
5 For a disturbing example, see Adam Goldman and Eric Schmitt, 'Aid Coordinator in Yemen had Secret Job Overseeing US Commando Shipments', *New York Times*, 6 June 2017.
6 Nikki Haley, 'Remarks at a UN Security Council Briefing on the Humanitarian Situation in Syria', 27 April 2017. https://usun.state.gov/remarks/7813.
7 Nikki Haley, 'Remarks at a UN Security Council Open Debate on the Protection of Civilians and Medical Care in Armed Conflict,' 25 May 2017. https://usun.state.gov/remarks/7784.
8 Clarke and Dercon 2016, p. 16.
9 Graziosi 2009.

10 Sen 1981.
11 UNOCHA, 'Humanitarian assistance works and can pull people back from famine'. UN Humanitarian Chief, 21 June 2017. http://www.unocha.org/story/humanitarian-assistance-works-and-can-pull-people-back-famine-un-humanitarian-chief.

Chapter 1   An Unacknowledged Achievement

1   My book on this famine is De Waal 1989. It includes the results of a demographic survey that I organized for Save the Children Fund.
2   African Rights 1997.
3   David Keen 1994 wrote the finest account of this disaster.
4   Scroggins 2002, p. 124.
5   Rivers et al. 1976.
6   Among them Hassan Abdel Ati, Ahmed Karadawi, Dessalegn Rahmato, Mark Duffield, David Keen, Ray Bush, Barbara Hendrie, Joanna Macrae and myself.
7   Watts 1983.
8   Africa Watch 1990, 1991; Human Rights Watch 1992 (chapter on famine); African Rights 1997.
9   De Waal 2008.
10 See Magone, Neuman and Weissman 2012 for a fascinating discussion of how Médecins Sans Frontières deals with the dilemmas of humanitarian negotiations.
11 Tawney 1964.

Chapter 2   Famines as Atrocities

1   Lemkin 1944, pp. 87–8.
2   Lemkin 2009, p. 128.
3   Prime Minister Winston Churchill's broadcast to the world about the meeting with President Roosevelt. 24 August 1941.
4   I explore it in more detail in chapter 6.
5   Snyder 2010.
6   Collingham 2012.
7   See the Imaging Famine project, http://www.imaging-famine.org/
8   Sen 1981 p. 40 (footnote).
9   Devereux 2000; Howe and Devereux 2004.
10 Barrett 2010.
11 Young and Jaspars 2009, p. 8.
12 Lemkin 1944, p. 79
13 Conley-Zilkic 2016b, p. 4.
14 Guichaoua 2015.

15 Snyder 2015a.
16 Straus 2015.
17 Conley-Zilkic 2016b, p. 2.
18 http://auschwitz.org/en/history/punishments-and-executions/starvation
    -to-death
19 Keys et al. 1950.
20 Sen 1981, p. 40.
21 See also Edkins 2002.
22 Levi 1996 (1958), p. 90.
23 See chapter 7.
24 Barry 2004.
25 Edkins 2003, pp. 118–23.
26 Edkins 2003, p. 11.
27 Caffrey 2016.
28 Levi 1996 (1958), pp. 37, 76–7, and 74.
29 Levi 1996 (1958), p. 90.
30 Ó Gráda, 2015.
31 Sorokin 1975 (1922).
32 Sorokin 1975 (1922), p. xxxix.
33 Sorokin 1975 (1922), pp. 137 and 148.
34 Sorokin 1975 (1922), p. 137.
35 Levi 1996 (1958), p. 17.
36 Levi 1996 (1958), p. 15.
37 Laughlin 1974.
38 Firth 1959, p. 83.
39 See Edkins 2002.
40 Mark Levene, Dirk Moses, Ward Churchill are some notable examples.
41 Thomas de Waal 2015, pp. 35, 76.
42 Suny 2015, p. 330.
43 Kiernan 2003.
44 Howe 2007.
45 See chapter 9.
46 Keen 1994.
47 Magone, Neuman and Weissman 2012.
48 Power 2002.
49 Tooze 2014.

Chapter 3   Malthus's Zombie

1 Beck and Beck-Gernsheim 2002.
2 Malthus 1798.
3 Smith 1951; Mayhew 2014.
4 Lepenies 2013.
5 Townsend 1971 (1786).
6 Townsend 1971 (1786), p. 37.

7 Townsend 1971 (1786), p. 38.
8 Young 1792.
9 Young 1794, p. 49.
10 Young 1794, pp. 101–2.
11 See Malthus 1803.
12 Cited in Mayhew 2014, p. 105.
13 Mayhew 2014, chapter 5.
14 Malthus 1798, p. 35.
15 Watkins and Menken 1985.
16 Mayhew 2014, pp. 121–3.
17 Sen 1981.
18 Beckert 2015, pp. 75 and 87–8.
19 Caldwell 1998, p. 680.
20 Mayhew 2014, p. 174.
21 Smith 1951.
22 Ambirajan 1976.
23 Caldwell 1998, pp. 678–9.
24 Woodham-Smith 1962, pp. 375–6.
25 Mayhew 2014.
26 See Piketty 2014, pp. 5–6.
27 Ehrlich and Holdren 1971.
28 References for this paragraph are Ehrlich 1968, Cribb 2010 and Faris 2009.
29 Attenborough 2011. The direct quotations are from the video, at 18m36s, 14m50s and 8m36s respectively.
30 Attenborough in the *Daily Telegraph* 2013.
31 Diamond 2011, ch. 2.
32 Fraser 1911, p. 281.
33 This was noted by John Boyd-Orr, the first Director-General of the FAO; see de Castro 1952, p. ix.
34 De Castro 1952, p. 16.
35 Sen 1981, p. 1.
36 E.g. Bowbrick 1986.
37 Devereux 2001.
38 Dyson 1989.
39 De Waal 1989.
40 Ó Gráda 2015.
41 De Waal 1990a.
42 Currey 1978.
43 Rangasami 1985.
44 Ó Gráda 2015.
45 De Waal 1990a.
46 GHI 2015.
47 Neumayer and Plümper 2007.
48 Rivers 1982; MacIntyre 2002.
49 De Waal 1989, p. 181.
50 Dyson 1991a,b; Neumayer and Plümper 2007.

51 Plümper and Neumayer 2006.
52 Vaughan 1987.
53 Vaughan 1987, p. 119.
54 Sylvester 2013.

Chapter 4   A Short History of Modern Famines

1 Davis 2002.
2 Post 1977.
3 Devereux 2000.
4 De Waal 1989.
5 Compare the high estimates of Noland, Robinson and Tang 1999 with the lower estimates of Goodkind et al. 2011 and Spoorenberg and Schwekendiek 2012.
6 Ó Gráda 2015, pp. 174–5.
7 Roberts 2000; Roberts et al. 2001, 2003; Coghlan et al. 2006, 2007.
8 Human Security Report Project 2010.
9 In the absence of a reliable total figure, I have used the proportion of the excess deaths estimated by IRC for eastern DRC during 1998–2007, attributed to malnutrition. This gives a figure of 290,500.
10 Watkins and Menken 1985.
11 http://fletcher.tufts.edu/World-Peace-Foundation/Program/Research/Mass-Atrocities-Research-Program/Mass-Famine
12 The Oxford online bibliography entry on 'famine' is misclassified under 'African Studies' over the objections of its authors (Maxwell and Fitzpatrick 2012).
13 Levene 2005.
14 Churchill 1997; Thornton 2005.
15 Turnbull 1965 (1948); Curthoys 2008; Hinton et al. 2014.
16 Quoted in Riordan 2010, p. 169.
17 Beckert 2015, p. 171.
18 Piketty 2014; Beckert 2015.
19 Sources: Maddison 2003; Conference Board 2016 in conjunction with the Groningen Growth and Development Centre (University of Groningen, The Netherlands). Western Europe is taken to consist of what today are the states of Austria, Belgium, Denmark, Finland, France, Germany, Italy, Netherlands, Norway, Portugal, Spain, Sweden, Switzerland and the United Kingdom. The size of these economies is estimated in 1990 Geary Khamis dollars, that is, in a hypothetical currency where each unit of that currency has the same purchasing power as one dollar in the United States in 1990.
20 Mallory 1926.
21 Davis 2002.
22 The following two paragraphs are contributed by Aditya Sarkar.
23 Edgerton-Tarpley 2013.

24 Edgerton-Tarpley 2008; Li 2007; Davis 2002.
25 Fuller 2015.
26 Edgerton-Tarpley 2013.
27 De Castro 1952.
28 Acherson 1999 (1963), p. 9.
29 Callwell 1996 (1906), p. 40.
30 Collingham 2012. This total number does not appear in the catalogue of famines because its individual components could not separately be sourced. The famine toll in Poland and Belarus is therefore excluded.
31 Snyder 2012, p. 163.
32 Alexander 2017.
33 Collingham 2012, p. 153.
34 Lowe 2012.
35 Dikötter 2010.
36 De Waal 1989, pp. 26–8.
37 This figure was determined by calculating the mortality attributed to malnutrition for the eastern DRC in the surveys by the IRC from 2000–7.
38 Baram 2000.
39 Garfield 1999a, 1999b; Ali and Shah 2000. Garfield's median figure is 166,000; UNICEF (Ali and Shah) did not calculate their own estimated total but a median figure is 300,000.
40 Graham-Brown 1999, p. 318.
41 Gazdar 2007.
42 Human Rights Watch 1995, p. 11.

Chapter 5   Demography, Economics, Public Health

1   Dyson and Ó Gráda 2002.
2   Conway 1997; Patel 2013.
3   IFPRI 2002.
4   IFPRI 2002.
5   Perkins 1997, p. 258.
6   Ó Gráda 2005, p. 143.
7   Sen 1981.
8   Wiggins and Keats 2013; United Nations Department of Economic and Social Affairs 2011.
9   Swan, Hadley and Chichon 2010; Peeters and Maxwell 2011.
10 Maxwell and Majid 2016.
11 Ó Gráda 1997, 2005, 2009.
12 Ó Gráda 2005, p. 166.
13 Sen 1981.
14 Ravallion 1987.
15 De Waal 1997.
16 Devereux 1988.
17 Maharatna 2002.

18 De Castro 1952, p. 8.
19 Toole and Waldman 1988; Guha-Sapir and Degomme 2005.

Chapter 6   Politics, War, Genocide

1   Sen 1990.
2   Sen 2000.
3   De Waal 1997; Banik 2007.
4   Clarke and Dercon 2016, pp. 22, 26–7 and 43.
5   Drèze and Sen 1989, p. 214.
6   Neumayer and Plümper 2009.
7   Rubin 2011.
8   De Waal 1997.
9   Barrett and Maxwell 2005, pp. 201–2.
10 Devereux 1993, p. 175.
11 Osmani 1991, pp. 330–1.
12 Crow 1986, p. 21.
13 Shaikh et al. 1990, pp. 148–9.
14 African Rights 1997.
15 Banerjee et al. 2014.
16 Themner and Wallensteen 2014.
17 Human Security Report 2010.
18 Melander, Öberg, and Hall 2009, p. 523.
19 Valentino 2014, p. 100.
20 The Minorities at Risk project 1991–2004, quoted in Human Security Report Project 2010, p. 77.
21 Human Security Report Project 2010; Bellamy 2013.
22 Straus 2012, pp. 187–8.
23 E.g. Turnbull 1965 (1948); Churchill 1997; Moses 2008; Woolford 2009.
24 Snyder 2012.
25 T. de Waal 2015, p. 66.
26 Kévorkian 2011, p. 307.
27 Kévorkian 2011, pp. 633–6, 693.
28 Kévorkian 2011, p. 656–69.
29 Lemkin 2009.
30 Martin 2001, pp. 23–7; Boeck 2008; Snyder 2012, pp. 24–46.
31 Brauer 2002, p. 391.
32 Tooze 2014.
33 Mayhew 2014, pp. 179–81.
34 Snyder 2012, pp. 162–6.
35 International Military Tribunal 1947, p. 240.
36 Kay 2006a, p. 699.
37 Kay 2012, pp. 110–11.
38 Memo of 2 May, cited by Kay 2006a.
39 Tooze 2014, pp. 478–80.

40 Kay 2006a, p. 699.
41 Kay 2006a,b; Snyder 2012; Tooze 2014.
42 Collingham 2012, p. 190.
43 Snyder 2012, pp. 177–84.
44 Collingham 2012, p. 204.
45 Snyder 2012, p. 172.
46 Collingham 2012, pp. 225–6.
47 Lowe 2012, p. 117.
48 Dũng 1985.
49 Collingham 2012, p. 235.
50 Collingham 2012, pp. 292–303.
51 African Rights 1997.
52 Marcus 2003.
53 Marcus 2003, p. 247.
54 Marcus 2003, p. 247.
55 DeFalco 2014.
56 De Waal 2008.
57 Levi 1996 (1958), p. 173.
58 Conley-Zilkic 2016a; Conley-Zilkic and Hazlett forthcoming.

Chapter 7   The Humanitarian International

1 Duffield 2001.
2 Powell 2001.
3 OECD, Global Humanitarian Assistance Report, 2016.
4 Barrett and Maxwell 2005, pp. 7, 14.
5 Clarke and Dercon 2016, p. 16.
6 Carbonnier 2015, p. 65.
7 Carbonnier 2015, pp. 65–6.
8 Barrett and Maxwell 2005, p. 192.
9 Watenpaugh 2015.
10 Cabanes 2014.
11 De Waal 1997.
12 CRED 2013, pp. 23–4.
13 De Waal 1997, pp. 181–5.
14 UN Security Council resolution 794, adopted 3 December 1992.
15 African Rights 1993.
16 African Rights 1993.
17 Gill 2016.
18 Alnasrawi 2000; Gazdar 2007.
19 CBS News 1996.
20 Natsios 2001, p. 238.
21 Personal communication, March 2017.
22 Slim 2007.
23 Rieff 2002.

24 Black 1992.
25 Barnett 2011, p. 210.
26 Harcourt 1863, pp. 41 and 46.
27 Bentwich 1911.
28 United Nations 1948.
29 Allen 1989.
30 Speaking in the House of Commons, 23 January 1948. http://hansard.millbanksystems.com/commons/1948/jan/23/foreign-affairs#column_557
31 International Military Tribunal 1947, p. 43
32 International Military Tribunal 1947, p. 55.
33 International Military Tribunal 1947, p. 298.
34 United Nations War Crimes Commission 1949, p. 59.
35 United Nations War Crimes Commission 1949, p. 84.
36 Hyde 1945, vol. 3, pp. 1802–3.
37 United Nations War Crimes Commission 1949, p. 84.
38 Allen 1989, p. 34.
39 International Committee of the Red Cross 1977.
40 Marcus 2003, p. 269.
41 Schabas 2011, p. 115.
42 United Nations 2002b, pp. 240 and 242.
43 United Nations 2002a, p. 126.
44 Riordan 2010, p. 172.
45 Kearney 2013.
46 Cook 2012.
47 Urquhart 2006.
48 Kearney 2013, p. 279.
49 United Nations 2010, Article 8.2(c).
50 Dannenbaum 2017.
51 Rosset 2002.
52 Marcus 2003; Kearney 2013.
53 DeFalco 2011.
54 DeFalco 2011, p. 158.
55 Extraordinary Chambers in the Courts of Cambodia 2014, p. 579.
56 Howard-Hassmann 2016.
57 Short 2016.
58 Falk 1973.
59 Higgins 2010.
60 Nixon 2011.
61 Marcus 2003; Howard-Hassmann 2016.

Chapter 8 Ethiopia: No Longer the Land of Famine

1 De Waal 2016.
2 *The Guardian* published three pieces on this topic (Davison 2015; Munro and Wild 2016; Gromko 2016); the *New York Times* also published

a piece on how the drought could turn into famine (Fortin 2015); and Bloomberg published an article reviewing the successful famine prevention efforts (Little 2016).

3   See: http://www.nytimes.com/2016/05/09/opinion/is-the-era-of-great-famines-over.html
4   *Daily Telegraph* 2013.
5   Sources: UN Inter-agency Group for Child Mortality Estimation (UNICEF, WHO, World Bank, UN DESA Population Division), http://www.childmortality.org/; UN Inter-agency Group for Child Mortality Estimation; World Bank Open Data.
6   Moreland and Smith 2012.
7   Pankhurst 1985; Wolde Mariam 1986; Africa Watch 1991.
8   Wolde Mariam 1986; Pankhurst 1985.
9   United States Census Bureau, 'International Programs', https://www.census.gov/population/international/data/idb/region.php.
10   Africa Watch 1991, pp. 132–4.
11   Korn 1986, p. 137.
12   Africa Watch 1991, p. 199.
13   Some estimates are for a shrinkage of about half that value. See Abegaz 1999, p. 6.
14   World Bank Open Data, http://data.worldbank.org/.
15   Salama et al. 2001; Hammond and Maxwell 2002, Hagmann and Korf 2012.
16   De Waal, Tafesse and Carruth 2006.
17   World Bank Open Data.
18   Gebreegziabher et al. 2011.
19   Aragie 2013.
20   Tierney, Ummenhofer and deMenocal 2015.
21   Admassu et al. 2014.
22   You and Ringler 2010.
23   EEA 2008; FDRE 2011.
24   FDRE 2011; Kaur 2013.
25   FDRE 2002.
26   The Maddison Project 2013; Bolt and van Zanden 2014.
27   Lavers 2016.
28   Lavers 2016.
29   Cochrane and Tamiru 2016.
30   Seaman and Holt 1980.
31   Devereux 1988, p. 277.
32   De Waal 1990b.
33   Dercon 1995, p. 114.
34   FDRE 2016, pp. 81–2.
35   Tamru 2013, p. 9.
36   Jaleta and Gebremedhin 2012.
37   AKLDP 2016b.
38   FDRE 2002, at pp. 38, 12, 30 and 23.
39   McNeil 2016.

40   Jeffrey 2016.
41   Endeshaw 2017; FDRE and UNOCHA 2017.
42   AKLDP 2016a, b; WFP 2016b, 2016c; Dreschler and Soer 2016.
43   FDRE and UNOCHA 2017.
44   AKLDP 2016a, p. 11.
45   Hagmann and Korf 2012.

Chapter 9   The Famine that Isn't Coming

1   McGuire 2002, p. vii.
2   Devereux 2007.
3   GHI 2015.
4   CRED 2013.
5   CRED 2013.
6   CRED 2013, p. 12.
7   Geneva Declaration 2011.
8   Mazurana et al. 2014.
9   Carbonnier 2015, pp. 52–4.
10   United Nations Department of Economic and Social Affairs 2011; Ghosh 2010.
11   Headey and Fan 2010; Wiggins, Keats and Compton 2010; Wiggins and Keats 2013.
12   United Nations Department of Economic and Social Affairs 2011, p. 63.
13   Wiggins and Keats 2013, pp. 13–16.
14   Headey 2011; Sumner 2009.
15   Headey and Fan 2010, p. 9.
16   Baldos and Hertel 2016.
17   Headey and Fan 2010, p. 9.
18   Wiggins, Keats and Compton 2010.
19   Maxwell and Majid 2016.
20   Bellemare 2015.
21   Noman et al. 2012; OECD 2012.
22   Xiaoyang 2014.
23   OECD 2012, p. 24.
24   Devereux and Tiba 2007.
25   Rubin 2011, p. 99; Reza et al. 2008.
26   Clarke and Dercon 2016.
27   Dana 2013; World Bank 2014; Clarke and Dercon 2016, pp. 95–8.
28   Kaplan 1994.
29   Kaplan 1994, p. 3 on electronic version.
30   Diamond 2011, p. 313.
31   Richards 1996; Uvin 2001.
32   Garrett 1995.
33   Davis and Feshbach 1980; Eberstadt 1988.
34   Esty et al. 1995.

35 National Intelligence Council 2000; see also National Intelligence Council 2002.
36 National Intelligence Council 2008.
37 See De Waal 2006, 2010.
38 Whiteside and de Waal 2003.
39 De Waal 2007a.
40 Richards 2016; Elver 2014.
41 FAO 2016.
42 FAO 2016, pp. 22–3.
43 FAO 2016, p. 23
44 Trenberth et al. 2014.
45 Walsh 2014.
46 Dong and Sutton 2015.
47 CarbonBrief 2015.
48 FAO 2016, p. 34.
49 FAO 2016, pp. xi–xii.
50 FAO 2016, pp. 8 and 9.
51 Biello 2009.
52 Though the Guinness World Records website includes it: http://www.guinnessworldrecords.com/world-records/first-climate-change-war
53 Ki-moon 2007a.
54 Ki-moon 2007b.
55 Faris 2007; this article was the basis for his book Faris 2009.
56 De Waal 2004.
57 Dong and Sutton 2015.
58 Flint and de Waal 2008.
59 Salih 1999.
60 De Châtel 2014.
61 Maystadt and Ecker 2014; Maystadt, Calderone, and You 2014.
62 Buhaug et al. 2015.
63 Islam and Susskind 2012.
64 Shah 2008.
65 Snyder 2012.
66 Snyder 2015a.
67 Snyder 2015b.
68 Snyder 2015a, p. 324.
69 Snyder 2015a, p. 325.

Chapter 10   The New Atrocity Famines

1 FEWSNET 2017c.
2 Stephen O'Brien, Under-Secretary-General for Humanitarian Affairs and Emergency Relief Coordinator, 'Statement to the Security Council on Missions to Yemen, South Sudan, Somalia and Kenya and an Update on the Oslo Conference on Nigeria and the Lake Chad Region', United

Nations Security Council, 10 March 2017, https://docs.unocha.org/sites/
dms/Documents/ERC_USG_Stephen_OBrien_Statement_to_the_SecCo_
on_Missions_to_Yemen_South_Sudan_Somalia_and_Kenya_and_update_
on_Oslo.pdf
3 Grein et al. 2003.
4 FAO and WFP 2016.
5 Richards 1983, p. 44.
6 Howe and Devereux 2004.
7 Integrated Food Security Phase Classification, http://www.ipcinfo.org/
8 IPC 2012, p. 32.
9 IPC 2012, p. 29.
10 This would not be useful for historical comparisons as general mortality
levels have reduced so substantially. See Ó Gráda 2015.
11 De Waal 2007b.
12 General Accountability Office 2006.
13 Flint and de Waal 2008.
14 Egeland 2004, p. 3.
15 United Nations Security Council 2004; United Nations OCHA/IRIN 2004.
16 Mazurana et al. 2014, p. 31.
17 World Health Organization 2005.
18 Branch 2011, p. 91.
19 Schomerus 2015.
20 Maxwell and Majid 2016.
21 Orozco and Yansura 2012.
22 Chonka 2016.
23 Checchi and Courtland Robinson 2013.
24 Etienne Peterschmitt, FAO deputy representative and emergency
response team leader in Yemen, quoted in: Ben Norton, ' "A forgotten crisis": Mass starvation in Yemen as U.S.-backed Saudi war &
blockade push millions to brink of famine', *Salon*, 29 January 2016,
http://www.salon.com/2016/01/29/a_forgotten_crisis_mass_starvation_in_
yemen_as_u_s_backed_saudi_war_blockade_push_millions_to_brink_of_
famine/
25 UN News Centre, 'Central Yemeni city of Taiz under virtual siege,
200,000 need water, food – UN relief chief', 24 November 2015, http://
www.un.org/apps/news/story.asp?NewsID=52644#.WAwLca47noV
26 WFP 2016a.
27 *Yemen Times* 2015.
28 OCHA 2015b.
29 O'Brien 2017.
30 Abdel Kouddous 2016.
31 Sengupta 2015.
32 OCHA 2016c.
33 Borger 2015.
34 OCHA 2016c.
35 FEWSNET 2017a.
36 FEWSNET 2017a.

37 O'Brien 2017.
38 OCHA 2015a.
39 Amnesty International 2015.
40 Amnesty International 2014.
41 Amnesty International 2016.
42 Ki-moon 2016.
43 Melvin 2016.
44 Syrian Centre for Policy Research 2016a, p. 47.
45 OCHA 2015a; O'Brien 2017.
46 World Bank 2016.
47 De Châtel 2014.
48 Syrian Centre for Policy Research 2016a.
49 Yourish, Lai and Watkins 2015.
50 Syrian Centre for Policy Research 2016b, p. 61.
51 Launspach 2016; Sue Lautze quoted in Kristof 2016.
52 De Waal 2012.
53 De Waal 2014.
54 OCHA 2016a.
55 FEWSNET 2017b.
56 Watts 1983.
57 OCHA 2016b; International Rescue Committee 2016.
58 FEWSNET 2016.
59 PS21 2015.
60 PHPCR 2012.
61 Gill 2016.
62 Jones and Libicki 2008; Powell 2014.
63 International Crisis Group 2010.

Chapter 11   Mass Starvation in the Future

1 Walker et al. 2009.
2 See Lappé and Collins 2015 for a good example.
3 Diamond 2011, p. 147.

References

Abdel Kouddous, Sharif. 2016. 'America has Blood on Its Hands: Yemen is Now the World's Worst Humanitarian Crisis'. *Salon*, 18 January, at: http://www.salon.com/2016/01/18/yemen_is_now_the_worlds_worst_humanitarian_crisis_partner/

Abegaz, Berhanu. 1999. 'Aid and Reform in Ethiopia'. *World Bank Working Paper*, at: http://documents.worldbank.org/curated/en/716401468029717101/pdf/357250ET0Aid010reform0ethiopia2.pdf.

Acherson, Neal. 1999 (1963). *The King Incorporated: Leopold the Second and the Congo*. Cambridge: Granta.

Admassu, Habtamu, Getinet, Mezgebu, Thomas, Timothy et al. 2014. 'East African Agriculture and Climate Change: A Comprehensive Analysis – Ethiopia,' Washington, DC: International Food Policy Research Institute (IFPRI).

Afkhami, Amir. 2003. 'Compromised Constitutions: The Iranian Experience with the 1918 Influenza Pandemic'. *Bulletin of the History of Medicine* 77(2): 367–92.

Africa Watch. 1990. *'Denying the Honor of Living': Sudan, A Human Rights Disaster*. New York and London: Human Rights Watch.

Africa Watch. 1991. *Evil Days: Thirty Years of War and Famine in Ethiopia*. New York and London: Human Rights Watch.

African Rights. 1993. *Somalia: Human Rights Violations by the United Nations*. London: African Rights.

African Rights. 1997. *Food and Power in Sudan: A Critique of Humanitarianism*. London: African Rights.

AKLDP (Agriculture Knowledge, Learning, Documentation and Policy Project). 2016a. 'El Niño in Ethiopia, 2015–2016: A Real-Time Review of Impacts and Responses'. AKLDP, USAID/Ethiopia, Addis Ababa, March.

AKLDP (Agriculture Knowledge, Learning, Documentation and Policy project). 2016b. 'Food Security in Ethiopia in 2016: Analysing crop production and market function after the main Meher agricultural season'. AKLDP, USAID/Ethiopia, Addis Ababa, April.

Alamgir, Mohiuddin. 1980. *Famine in South Asia: Political Economy of Mass Starvation*. Cambridge: Oelgeschlager, Gunn and Hain.

Alexander, Colin. 2017. *The Raj and World War II: The Indian Civil Service, Broadcasting and Famine*. Oxford: Oxford University Press.

Ali, Mohamed M. and Shah, Iqbal H. 2000. 'Sanctions and Childhood Mortality in Iraq'. *The Lancet* 355: 1851–7.

Allen, Charles A. 1989. 'Civilian Starvation and Relief during Armed Conflict: The Modern Humanitarian Law'. *Georgia Journal of International and Comparative Law* 19(1): 1–85.

Alnasrawi, Abbas. 2000. 'Iraq: Economic Embargo and Predatory Rule', in E. Wayne Nafziger, Frances Stewart and Raimo Väyrynen (eds), *War, Hunger and Displacement: The Origins of Humanitarian Emergencies, Volume 2: Case Studies*. Oxford: Oxford University Press, pp. 89–118.

Ambirajan, S. 1976. 'Malthusian Population Theory and Indian Famine Policy in the Nineteenth Century'. *Population Studies* 30(1): 5–14.

Amnesty International. 2014. *Syria: Squeezing the Life out of Yarmouk: War Crimes against Besieged Civilians*. London: Amnesty International.

Amnesty International. 2015. *'Left to Die under Siege': War Crimes and Human Rights Abuses in Eastern Ghouta, Syria*. London: Amnesty International.

Amnesty International. 2016. ' "In Madaya you see walking skeletons": Harrowing accounts of life under siege in Syria', at: https://www.amnesty.org/en/press-releases/2016/01/harrowing-accounts-of-life-under-siege-in-syria/.

Antonius, George. 1946. *The Arab Awakening: The Story of the Arab National Movement*. New York: Capricorn Books.

Aragie, Emerta Asaminew. 2013. 'Climate Change, Growth and Poverty in Ethiopia'. Austin, TX: Robert S. Strauss Center for International Security and Law, Working Paper No 3, at: https://www.strausscenter.org/research-reports

Ashton, Basil, Hill, Kenneth, Piazza, Alan and Zeitz, Robin. 1984. 'Famine in China, 1958–61'. *Population and Development Review* 10(4): 613–45.

Attenborough, Sir David. 2011. 'People and Planet'. London: Royal Society of Arts, President's Lecture, at: https://www.populationmatters.org/attenborough-talk/.

Baldos, Uris Lantz and Hertel, Thomas 2016. 'Debunking the "New Normal": Why World Food Prices are Expected to Resume their Long Run Downward Trend'. *Global Food Security* 8: 27–38.

Banerjee, O., Darbas, T., Brown, P. R. and Roth, C. H. 2014. 'Historical Divergence in Public Management of Foodgrain Systems in India and Bangladesh: Opportunities to Enhance Food Security'. *Global Food Security-Agriculture Policy Economics and Environment* 3(3–4): 159–66.

Banik, Dan. 2007. *Starvation and India's Democracy*. London: Routledge.

Baram, Amatzia, 2000. 'The Effects of Iraq Sanctions: Statistical Pitfalls and Responsibilities'. *Middle East Journal* 54: 194–223.

Barnett, Michael. 2011. *Empire of Humanity: A History of Humanitarianism*. Ithaca, NY and London: Cornell University Press.

Barrett, Christopher. 2010. 'Measuring Food Insecurity'. *Science* 327/5967: 825–8.

Barrett, Christopher and Maxwell, Daniel. 2005. *Food Aid after Fifty Years: Recasting Its Role*. London: Routledge.

Barry, John M. 2004. *The Great Influenza: The Epic Story of the Deadliest Plague in History*. New York: Viking Penguin.

Beck, Ulrich and Beck-Gernsheim, Elisabeth. 2002. *Individualization: Institutionalized Individualism and Its Social and Political Consequences*. London: SAGE.

Becker, Jasper. 1996. *Hungry Ghosts: Mao's Secret Famine*. New York: The Free Press.

Beckert, Sven. 2015. *Empire of Cotton: A Global History*. New York: Vintage Books,

Bellamy, Alex. 2013. 'The Other Asian Miracle? The Decline of Atrocities in East Asia'. *Peace & Security* 26(1): 1–19.

Bellemare, Marc. 2015. 'Rising Food Prices, Food Price Volatility, and Social Unrest'. *American Journal of Agricultural Economics* 97(1): 1–21.

Bentwich, Norman. 1911. *The Declaration of London with an Introduction and Notes and Appendices*. London: Effingham Wilson.

Biello, David. 2009. 'Can Climate Change Cause Conflict? Recent History Suggests So'. *Scientific American*, 23 November, at: http://www.scientificamerican.com/article/can-climate-change-cause-conflict/

Black, Maggie. 1992. *A Cause for Our Times: Oxfam, the First 50 Years*. Oxford: Oxfam and Oxford University Press.

Boeck, Brian. 2008. 'Complicating the National Interpretation of the Famine: Reexamining the Case of Kuban'. *Harvard Ukrainian Studies* 30(1/4): 31–48.

Bolt, Jutta and van Zanden, Jan Luiten. 2014. 'The Maddison Project: Collaborative Research on Historical National Accounts'. *The Economic History Review* 67(3): 627–51.

Borger, Julian. 2015. 'Saudi-Led Naval Blockade Leaves 20 m Yemenis Facing Humanitarian Disaster'. *The Guardian*, 5 June, at: https://www.theguardian.com/world/2015/jun/05/saudi-led-naval-blockade-worsens-yemen-humanitarian-disaster

Bowbrick, Peter. 1986. 'The Causes of Famine: A Refutation of Professor Sen's Theory'. *Food Policy* 11: 105–24.

Branch, Adam. 2011. *Displacing Human Rights: War and Intervention in Northern Uganda*. Oxford: Oxford University Press.

Brauer, Birgit. 2002. 'Chechens and the Survival of their Cultural Identity in Exile'. *Journal of Genocide Research* 4(3): 387–400.

Buhaug, H., Nordkvelle, J., Bernauer, T. et al. 2015. 'One Effect to Rule Them All? A Comment on Climate and Conflict'. *Climatic Change* 127(3–4): 391–7.

Burr, Millard. 1998. *Quantifying Genocide in Southern Sudan and the Nuba Mountains*. Washington, DC: Committee of Refugees.

Cabanes, Bruno. 2014. *The Great War and the Origins of Humanitarianism, 1918–1924*. Cambridge, UK: Cambridge University Press.

Caffrey, Jason. 2016. 'Shostakovich's Symphony Played by a Starving Orchestra'. *BBC Magazine*, 2 January, http://www.bbc.com/news/magazine-34292312

Caldwell, John. 1998. 'Malthus and the Less Developed World: The Pivotal Role of India'. *Population and Development Review* 24(4): 675–98.

Callwell, Colonel C. E. 1996 (1906). *Small Wars: Their Principle and Practice*, 3rd edn. Lincoln: Bison Books.

CarbonBrief. 2015. 'Factcheck: Is Climate Change Helping Africa?' 3 June, at: http://www.carbonbrief.org/factcheck-is-climate-change-helping-africa

Carbonnier, Gilles. 2015. *Humanitarian Economics: War, Disaster and the Global Aid Market*. New York: Oxford University Press.

Carver, Michael. 2000. *The National Army Museum Book of the Boer War*. London: Pan Macmillan.

CBS News. 1996. 'Punishing Saddam'. *Sixty Minutes*, 12 May, https://www.youtube.com/watch?v=R0WDCYcUJ4o

Checchi, Francesco and Courtland Robinson, W. 2013. 'Mortality and Populations of Southern and Central Somalia Affected by Severe Food Insecurity and Famine during 2010–12.' Washington, DC: FewsNet, at: http://reliefweb.int/sites/reliefweb.int/files/resources/Somalia_Mortality_Estimates_Final_Report_1May2013.pdf.

Chonka, Peter. 2016. 'Spies, Stonework, and the Stuq: Somali Nationalism and the Narrative Politics of Pro-Harakat Al Shabaab Al Mujaahidiin Online Propaganda'. *Journal of Eastern African Studies* 10(2): 247–65.

Churchill, Ward. 1997. *A Little Matter of Genocide: Holocaust and Denial in the Americas 1492–Present*. San Francisco: City Lights.

Clarke, Daniel and Dercon, Stefan. 2016. *Dull Disasters? How Planning Ahead Will Make a Difference*. Oxford: Oxford University Press.

Cochrane, Logan and Tamiru, Y. 2016. 'Ethiopia's Productive Safety Net Programme: Power, Politics and Practice'. *Journal of International Development* 28: 649–65.

Coghlan, Benjamin, Brennan, Richard, Ngoy, Pascal et al. 2006. 'Mortality in the Democratic Republic of Congo: A Nationwide Survey'. *The Lancet*, 367: 44–51.

Coghlan, Benjamin, Ngoy, Pascal, Mulumba, Flavien et al. 2007. *Mortality in the Democratic Republic of Congo: An Ongoing Crisis*. New York: International Rescue Committee.

Cohen, Paul A. 1997. *History in Three Keys: The Boxers as Event, Experience and Myth*. New York: Columbia University Press.

Collingham, Lizzie. 2012. *The Taste of War: World War II and the Battle for Food*. New York: Penguin.

Conference Board. 2016. *The Conference Board Total Economy Database*™, May, at: http://www.conference-board.org/data/economydatabase/.

Conley-Zilkic, Bridget (ed.). 2016a. *How Mass Atrocities End*. Cambridge: Cambridge University Press.

Conley-Zilkic, Bridget. 2016b. 'Introduction', in Bridget Conley-Zilkic (ed.), *How Mass Atrocities End*. Cambridge: Cambridge University Press.

Conway, Gordon. 1997. *The Doubly Green Revolution: Food for All in the Twenty-first Century*. London and New York: Penguin Books.

Cook, Jonathan. 2012. 'Israel's Starvation Diet for Gaza'. *The Electronic Intifada*, 24 October, at: http://electronicintifada.net/content/israels-starvation-diet-gaza/11810.

CRED (Centre for Research on the Epidemiology of Disasters). 2013. *People Affected by Conflict 2013: Humanitarian Needs in Numbers*. Louvain, Belgium: CRED.

Cribb, Julian, 2010. *The Coming Famine: The Global Food Crisis and What We Can Do to Avoid It*. Berkeley, CA: University of California Press.

Crow, Ben. 1986. 'US Policies in Bangladesh: The Making and the Breaking of Famine?' *The Open University, Development Policy and Practice, Working Paper No. 4*, Milton Keynes: Open University.

Cunniff, Roger. 1970. 'The Great Drought: Northeast Brazil, 1887–1880'. PhD dissertation, University of Texas, Austin.

Currey, Bruce. 1978. 'The Famine Syndrome: Its Definition for Relief and Rehabilitation in Bangladesh'. *Ecology of Food and Nutrition* 7: 87–98.

Curthoys, Ann. 2008. 'Genocide in Tasmania: The History of an Idea', in Dirk Moses (ed.), *Empire, Colony, Genocide: Conquest, Occupation, and Subaltern Resistance in World History*. New York: Berghahn Books.

Daily Telegraph. 2013. 'Sir David Attenborough: If We Don't Control Population, the Natural World Will', 18 September, at: http://www.telegraph.co.uk/culture/tvandradio/10316271/Sir-David-Attenborough-If-we-do-not-control-population-the-natural-world-will.html

Dana, Julie. 2013. 'Marked-based Approaches for Governments of Food-Importing Countries to Manage Food Security Risks'. *Global Food Security* 2(3): 182–7.

Dannenbaum, Tom. 2017. 'Why Have We Criminalized Aggressive War?' *Yale Law Journal* 126(5): 1242–1318.

Davis, Christopher and Feshbach, Murray. 1980. 'Rising Soviet Infant Mortality'. *INTERCOM* 8(17): 12–14.

Davis, Mike. 2002. *Late Victorian Holocausts: El Niño Famines and the Making of the Third World*. London: Verso.

Davison, William. 2015. 'Yes, Ethiopia has Problems – but This Drought Is No 1984 Rerun'. *The Guardian*, 11 November, at: https://www.theguardian.com/commentisfree/2015/nov/11/ethiopia-drought-1984-economic-growth-safety-net

De Castro, Josué. 1952. *The Geography of Hunger*. Boston: Little, Brown and Co.

De Châtel, Francesca. 2014. 'The Role of Drought and Climate Change in the Syrian Uprising: Untangling the Triggers of the Revolution'. *Middle Eastern Studies* 50(4): 521–35.

DeFalco, Randle C. 2011. 'Accounting for Famine at the Extraordinary Chambers in the Courts of Cambodia: The Crimes against Humanity of Extermination, Inhumane Acts and Persecution'. *The International Journal of Transitional Justice* 5: 142–58.

DeFalco, Randle C. 2014. 'Justice and Starvation in Cambodia: The Khmer Rouge Famine'. *Cambodia Law and Policy Journal* 2: 45–84.

Dercon, Stefan. 1995. 'On Market Integration and Liberalization: Method and Application to Ethiopia'. *Journal of Development Studies* 32(1): 112–43.

De Waal, Alex. 1989. *Famine that Kills: Darfur, Sudan 1984–1985*. Oxford: Clarendon Press.

De Waal, Alex. 1990a. 'A Reassessment of Entitlement Theory in the Light of Recent Famines in Africa'. *Development and Change* 21: 469–90.

De Waal, Alex. 1990b. 'Tigray: Grain Markets and Internal Purchase'. Report for OXFAM, February.

De Waal, Alex. 1997. *Famine Crimes: Politics and the Disaster Relief Industry in Africa*. London: James Currey.

De Waal, Alex. 2004. 'Counterinsurgency on the Cheap'. *London Review of Books* 26(15) at: http://www.lrb.co.uk/v26/n15/alex-de-waal/counter-insurgency-on-the-cheap.

De Waal, Alex. 2006. *AIDS and Power: Why There is No Political Crisis – Yet*. London: Zed Books.

De Waal, Alex. 2007a. 'AIDS, Hunger and Destitution: Theory and Evidence for the "New Variant Famines" Hypothesis in Africa', in Stephen Devereux (ed.), *The New Famines: Why Famines Persist in an Era of Globalization*. London: Routledge.

De Waal, Alex. 2007b. 'Reflections on the Difficulties of Defining Darfur's Crisis as Genocide'. *Harvard Journal of Human Rights* 20: 25–33.

De Waal, Alex. 2008. 'On Famine Crimes and Tragedies'. *The Lancet* 372(9649): 1538–9.

De Waal, Alex. 2010. 'Reframing Governance, Security and Conflict in the Light of HIV/AIDS'. *Social Science and Medicine* 70(1): 114–20.

De Waal, Alex. 2012. 'South Sudan's Doomsday Machine'. *New York Times*, 25 January, at: http://www.nytimes.com/2012/01/25/opinion/south-sudans-doomsday-machine.html.

De Waal, Alex. 2014. 'When Kleptocracy Becomes Insolvent: The Brute Causes of the Civil War in South Sudan'. *African Affairs* 113(452): 347–69.

De Waal, Alex. 2015. *The Real Politics of the Horn of Africa: Money, War and the Business of Power*. Cambridge: Polity.

De Waal, Alex. 2016. 'Is the Era of Great Famines Over?' *New York Times*, 8 May, at: http://www.nytimes.com/2016/05/09/opinion/is-the-era-of-great-famines-over.html.

De Waal, Alex and Omaar, Rakiya. 1993. *Somalia Operation Restore Hope: A Preliminary Assessment*. London: African Rights.

De Waal, Alex, Tafesse, Alemayehu S. and Carruth, Lauren. 2006. 'Child Survival during the 2002–2003 Drought in Ethiopia'. *Global Public Health* 1(2): 125–32.

De Waal, Thomas. 2015. *Great Catastrophe: Armenians and Turks in the Shadow of Genocide*. Oxford: Oxford University Press.

Devereux, Stephen. 1988. 'Entitlements, Availability and Famine: A Revisionist View of Wollo, 1972–74'. *Food Policy* 3: 270–82.

Devereux, Stephen. 1993. *Theories of Famine*. New York: Harvester Wheatsheaf.

Devereux, Stephen. 2000. 'Famine in the Twentieth Century'. University of Sussex, IDS Working Paper 105.

Devereux, Stephen. 2001. 'Sen's Entitlement Approach: Critiques and Counter-Critiques'. *Oxford Development Studies* 29(3): 245–63.

Devereux, Stephen. 2007. 'Introduction: From "Old Famines" to "New Famines"', in Stephen Devereux (ed.), *The New Famines: Why Famines Persist in an Era of Globalization*. London: Routledge.

Devereux, Stephen and Tiba, Zoltan. 2007. 'Malawi's First Famine, 2001–02,' in Stephen Devereux (ed.), *The New Famines: Why Famines Persist in an Era of Globalization*. London: Routledge.

Diamond, Jared. 2011. *Collapse: How Societies Choose to Fail or Succeed*, rev. edn. London: Penguin.

Dikötter, Frank. 2010. *Mao's Great Famine: The History of China's Most Devastating Catastrophe, 1958–1962*. New York: Walker & Company.

Dong, Buwen and Sutton, Rowan. 2015. 'Dominant Role of Greenhouse-Gas Forcing in the Recovery of Sahelian Rainfall'. *Nature Climate Change* 5: 757–60.

Dreschler, Mareile and Soer, Wolter. 2016. 'Early Warning, Early Action: The Use of Predictive Tools in Drought Response through Ethiopia's Productive Safety Net Programme'. *World Bank Policy Research Working Paper* 7716, at: https://papers.ssrn.com/sol3/papers.cfm?abstract_id=2811365.

Drèze, Jean, and Sen, Amartya. 1989. *Hunger and Public Action*. Oxford: Clarendon Press.

Duffield, Mark. 2001. *Global Governance and the New Wars: The Merging of Development and Security*. London: Zed Books.

Dũng, Bùi Minh. 1985. 'Japan's Role in the Vietnamese Starvation of 1944–45'. *Modern Asian Studies* 29(3): 573–618.

Dyson, Tim, 1989. *India's Historical Demography: Studies in Famine, Disease and Society*. London: SOAS.

Dyson, Tim. 1991a. 'On the Demography of South Asian Famines, Part 1'. *Population Studies* 45(1): 5–25.

Dyson, Tim. 1991b. 'On the Demography of South Asian Famines, Part 2'. *Population Studies* 45(2): 279–97.

Dyson, Tim and Maharatna, Arup. 1991. 'Excess Mortality during the Bengal Famine: A Re-evaluation'. *Indian Economic & Social History Review* 28: 281–97.

Dyson, Tim and Ó Gráda, Cormac (eds). 2002. *Famine Demography: Perspectives from the Past and Present*. Oxford: Oxford University Press.

Eberstadt, Nicholas. 1988. *The Poverty of Communism*. New York: Transaction.

Edgerton-Tarpley, Kathryn. 2008. *Tears from Iron: Cultural Responses to Famine in Nineteenth-Century China*. Berkeley: University of California Press.

Edgerton-Tarpley, Kathryn. 2013. 'Tough Choices: Grappling with Famine in Qing China, the British Empire and Beyond,' *Journal of World History* 24(1): 135–76.

Edkins, Jenny. 2002. 'Mass Starvations and the Limits of Famine Theorising'. *IDS Bulletin* 33(4): 12–18.

Edkins, Jenny. 2003. *Trauma and the Memory of Politics*. Cambridge: Cambridge University Press.

Edwards, Dwight W. (ed.) 1922. *The North China Famine of 1920–21 with Special Reference to the West Chihli Area: Being the Report of the Peking United International Famine Relief Committee*. Beijing: Commercial Press Works.

EEA (Ethiopian Economic Association). 2008. 'Climate Change and Development Adaptation Measures'. *Economic Focus* 11(1): Addis Ababa.

Egeland, Jan. 2004. 'Foreword', in United Nations OCHA/IRIN, *'When the Sun Sets, We Start to Worry ...' An Account of Life in Northern Uganda*. New York: United Nations, 5 January.

Ehrlich, Paul. 1968. *The Population Bomb: Population Control or the Race to Oblivion?* New York: Ballantine.

Ehrlich, Paul R. and Holdren, John P. 1971. 'Impact of Population Growth'. *Science* 171: 1212–17.

Elver, Hilal. 2014. 'West Africa on the Brink of a Major Food Crisis as Ebola Threatens Food Security, Warns UN Expert'. UN Commissioner for Human Rights, 11 November, http://www.ohchr.org/EN/NewsEvents/Pages/DisplayNews.aspx?NewsID=15276&LangID=E

Endeshaw, Dawit. 2017. 'Success as Ethiopia Downsizes Drought Figures'. *Fortune* (Addis Ababa), 24 January, http://addisfortune.net/articles/success-as-ethiopia-downsizes-drought-figures/

Esherick, Paul. 1987. *The Origins of the Boxer Uprising*. Berkeley, CA and London, UK: University of California Press.

Esty, Daniel, Goldstone, Jack A., Gurr, Ted et al. 1995. *State Failure Task Force Report*. Washington, DC.

Extraordinary Chambers in the Courts of Cambodia. 2014. 'Case 002/01 Judgement'. Pnom Penh, Kingdom of Cambodia, ECCC, 7 August.

Falk, Richard A. 1973. 'Environmental Warfare and Ecocide – Facts, Appraisal, and Proposals'. *Bulletin of Peace Proposals* 4: 80–107.

FAO. 2016. 'The State of Food and Agriculture: Climate Change, Agriculture and Food Security'. Rome: FAO, at: http://www.fao.org/3/a-i6030e.pdf.

FAO and WFP. 2016. 'Monitoring Food Security in Countries with Conflict Situations: A Joint FAO/WFP Update for the United Nations Security Council (July 2016)'. Rome, FAO and WFP, at: http://www.fao.org/3/a-c0335e.pdf

Faris, Stephan. 2007. 'The Real Roots of Darfur'. *Atlantic Monthly*, April, at: http://www.theatlantic.com/magazine/archive/2007/04/the-real-roots-of-darfur/305701/.

Faris, Stephan. 2009. *Forecast: The Consequences of Climate Change, from the Amazon to the Arctic, from Darfur to Napa Valley*. New York: Holt.

Fawaz, Leila. 2014. *A Land of Aching Hearts: The Middle East in the Great War*. Cambridge, MA: Harvard University Press.

FDRE (Federal Democratic Republic of Ethiopia). 2002. 'Foreign Affairs and National Security Policy and Strategy'. Addis Ababa: Ministry of Information, November.

FDRE (Federal Democratic Republic of Ethiopia). 2011. 'Ethiopia's Climate-Resilient Green Economy Strategy: The Path to Sustainable Development'. Addis Ababa: Inter-Ministerial Committee.

FDRE (Federal Democratic Republic of Ethiopia). 2016. *The Successful Path of Ethiopia: Challenges and Opportunities*. Addis Ababa: Communications Affairs Office, May.

FDRE (Federal Democratic Republic of Ethiopia) and UNOCHA. 2017. *Ethiopia: Humanitarian Requirements Document 2017*. Addis Ababa: UNOCHA.

FEWSNET (Famine Early Warning Systems Network). 2016. 'Alert: A Famine Likely Occurred in Bama LGA and may be Ongoing in Inaccessible Areas of

Borno State,' 13 December, http://www.fews.net/sites/default/files/documents/
reports/Nigeria%20Borno%20Alert_20161213_final.pdf

FEWSNET. 2017a. 'Alert: Improved Humanitarian Access and Trade Support
Needed to Limit Famine Risk in Yemen'. 4 January, http://www.fews.net/
east-africa/yemen/alert/january-4-2017

FEWSNET. 2017b. 'Alert: Famine (IPC Phase 5) Possible in South Sudan
during 2017'. 18 January, http://www.fews.net/east-africa/south-sudan/alert/
january-18-2017

FEWSNET. 2017c. 'Alert: Emergency Food Assistance Needs Unprecedented
as Famine Threatens Four Countries'. 25 January, http://www.fews.net/
global/alert/january-25-2017

Firth, Raymond. 1959. *Social Change in Tikopia*. London: Allen and Unwin.

Flint, Julie and de Waal, Alex. 2008. *Darfur: A New History of a Long War*.
London: Zed Books.

Foran, John. 1989. 'The Concept of Dependent Development as a Key to the
Political Economy of Qajar Iran (1800–1925)'. *Iranian Studies* 22(2/3):
5–56.

Fortin, Jacey. 2015. 'Ethiopia, a Nation of Farmers, Strains under Severe Drought'.
The *New York Times*, 18 October, at: http://www.nytimes.com/2015/10/19/
world/africa/ethiopia-a-nation-of-farmers-strains-under-severe-drought.html

Fraser, Lovat. 1911. *India under Curzon and After*. London: Heinemann.

Fuller, Pierre. 2013. 'North China Famine Revisited: Unsung Native
Relief in the Warlord Era, 1920–1921'. *Modern Asian Studies* 47(3):
820–50.

Fuller, Pierre. 2015. 'Changing Disaster Relief Regimes in China: An Analysis
using Four Famines between 1876 and 1962'. *Disasters* 39(S2): S146–S165.

Ganson, Nicholas. 2009. *The Soviet Famine of 1946–47 in Global and
Historical Perspective*. London: Palgrave Macmillan.

Garfield, Richard. 1999a. 'Morbidity and Mortality among Iraqi Children
from 1990 to 1998: Assessing the Impact of Economic Sanctions'. Goshen,
Indiana: Institute for International Peace Studies, University of Notre Dame
and the Fourth Freedom Forum.

Garfield, Richard. 1999b. 'The Impact of Economic Sanctions on Health and
Wellbeing'. London, Overseas Development Institute, Relief and Rehabilitation Network Paper No. 31.

Garnaut, Anthony. 2013. 'A Quantitative Description of the Henan Famine
of 1942'. *Modern Asian Studies* 47(6): 2007–45.

Garrett, Laurie. 1995. *The Coming Plague: Newly Emerging Diseases in a
World Out of Balance*. New York: Farrar, Straus and Giroux.

Gazdar, Haris. 2007. 'Pre-Modern, Modern and Post-Modern Famine in Iraq,
1990–2003,' in Stephen Devereux (ed.), *The New Famines: Why Famines
Persist in an Era of Globalization*. London: Routledge.

Gebreegziabher, Zenebe, Stage, Jesper, Mekonnen, Alemu and Alemu, Atlaw.
2011. 'Climate Change and the Ethiopian Economy: A Computable General
Equilibrium Analysis'. Addis Ababa, Environment for Development Discussion Paper Series, October, EfD DP 11-09, at: http://www.rff.org/files/
sharepoint/WorkImages/Download/EfD-DP-11-09.pdf.

General Accountability Office. 2006. 'Darfur Crisis: Death estimates demonstrate severity of crisis, but their accuracy and credibility could be enhanced,' Washington, DC: US GAO, Report GAO-07-24, November.

Geneva Declaration. 2011. *Global Burden of Armed Violence 2011: Lethal Encounters*. Cambridge: Cambridge University Press.

GHI (Global Hunger Index). 2015. *GHI 2015: Armed Conflict and the Challenge of Hunger*. Washington, DC: IFPRI and Dublin: Concern Worldwide and Bonn: Welthungerhilfe.

Ghosh, Jayati. 2010. 'The Unnatural Coupling: Food and Global Finance'. *Journal of Agrarian Change* 10(1): 72–86.

Gilbert, Martin. 1994. *The First World War: A Complete History*. New York: Henry Holt.

Gill, Peter. 2016. *Today We Drop Bombs, Tomorrow We Build Bridges: How Foreign Aid Became a Casualty of War*. London: Hurst.

Global Humanitarian Assistance. 2016. *Global Humanitarian Assistance Report 2016*, at: http://www.globalhumanitarianassistance.org/report/gha2016/.

Goodkind, D., West, L. and Johnson, P. 2011. 'A Reassessment of Mortality in North Korea, 1993–2008.' Paper presented at the annual meeting of the Population Association of America, Washington, DC, at: http://paa2011.princeton.edu/papers/111030.

Government Accountability Office. 2006. *Darfur Crisis: Death Estimates Demonstrate Severity of Crisis, but Their Accuracy and Credibility Could be Enhanced*, US GAO, Report GAO-07-24. Washington, DC.

Graham-Brown, Sarah. 1999. *Sanctioning Saddam: The Politics of Intervention in Iraq*. London: I B Tauris.

Graziosi, Andrea. 2009. *Stalinism, Collectivization and the Great Famine*. Cambridge, MA: Ukrainian Studies Fund.

Grein, Thomas, Checchi, Francesco, Escriba, Joseph et al. 2003. 'Mortality among Displaced Former UNITA Members and their Families in Angola: A Retrospective Cluster Survey'. *British Medical Journal* 327(7416): 650.

Gromko, Duncan. 2016. 'Ethiopia's Farmers Fight Devastating Drought with Land Restoration'. *The Guardian*, May 2, at: https://www.theguardian.com/sustainable-business/2016/may/02/ethiopia-famine-drought-land-restoration.

Guha-Sapir, Debarati and Degomme, Olivier. 2005. 'Darfur: Counting the Deaths: Mortality Estimates from Multiple Survey Data'. Louvain: Center for Research in the Epidemiology of Disasters.

Guichaoua, André. 2015. *From War to Genocide: Criminal Politics in Rwanda 1990–1994*. Madison, WI: University of Wisconsin Press.

Gunn, Geoffrey. 2011. 'The Great Vietnamese Famine of 1944–45 Revisited'. *The Asia-Pacific Journal* 9/5(4), 31 January, at: http://japanfocus.org/-Geoffrey-Gunn/3483

Hagmann, Tobias and Korf, Benedict. 2012. 'Agamben in the Ogaden: Violence and Sovereignty in the Ethiopian–Somali Frontier'. *Political Geography* 31(4): 205–14.

Hammond, Laura and Maxwell, Daniel. 2002. 'The Ethiopian Crisis of 1999–2000: Lessons Learned, Questions Unanswered'. *Disasters* 26(3): 262–79.

Hansch, S., Lillibridge, S., Egeland, G. et al. 1994. 'Lives Lost, Lives Saved: Excess Mortality and the Impact of Health Intervention in the Somali Emergency'. Washington, DC: Refugee Policy Group.

Harcourt, William V. 1863. 'A Letter on the Perils of Intervention'. *Letters of Historicus on Some Questions of International Law*. London: Macmillan.

Headey, Derek. 2011. 'Was the Global Food Crisis Really a Crisis? Simulations versus Self-Reporting'. Washington, DC: International Food Policy Research Institute, Discussion Paper 01087, May.

Headey, Derek and Fan, Shenggen. 2010. 'Reflections on the Global Food Crisis: How Did It Happen? How Has It Hurt? And How Can We Prevent the Next One?' Washington, DC, International Food Policy Research Institute, Research Monograph 165.

Higgins, Polly. 2010. *Eradicating Ecocide: Laws and Governance to Prevent the Destruction of our Planet*. London: Shepheard-Walwyn.

Hinton, Alexander Laban, Woolford, Andrew and Benvenuto, Jeff. 2014. *Colonial Genocide in Indigenous North America*. Durham, NC: Duke University Press.

Hochschild, Adam. 1998. *King Leopold's Ghost: A Story of Greed, Terror and Heroism in Colonial Africa*. New York: Mariner.

Hovannisian, Richard. 1971. *The Republic of Armenia, Volume I: The First Year, 1918–1919*. Berkeley: University of California Press.

Howard-Hassmann, Rhoda. 2016. *State Food Crimes*. Cambridge: Cambridge University Press.

Howe, Paul, 2007. 'Priority Regimes and Famine', in Stephen Devereux (ed.), *The New Famines: Why Famines Persist in an Era of Globalization*. London: Routledge.

Howe, Paul and Devereux, Stephen. 2004. 'Famine Intensity and Magnitude Scales: A Proposal for an Instrumental Definition of Famine'. *Disasters* 28(1): 353–72.

Human Rights Watch. 1992. *Indivisible Human Rights: The Relationship of Political and Civil Rights to Survival, Subsistence and Poverty*. New York: Human Rights Watch.

Human Rights Watch. 1995. 'The Fall of Srebrenica and the Failure of UN Peacekeeping'. New York: Human Rights Watch.

Human Security Report Project. 2010. *Human Security Report 2009/2010: The Causes of Peace and the Shrinking Costs of War*. New York: Oxford University Press.

Hyde, Charles. 1945. *International Law Chiefly as Interpreted and Applied by the United States*, 2nd rev. edn, 3 vols. Boston, MA: Little, Brown and Co.

IFPRI. 2002. 'Green Revolution: Blessing or Curse?' at: http://www.ifpri.org/publication/green-revolution.

Iliffe, John. 1979. *A Modern History of Tanganyika*. Cambridge: Cambridge University Press.

Integrated Food Security Phase Classification. 2012. 'Technical Manual Version 2.0: Evidence and Standards for Better Food Security Decisions', at: http://www.fews.net/sites/default/files/uploads/IPC-Manual-2-Interactive.pdf.

International Committee of the Red Cross. 1977. 'Protocols Additional to the Geneva Conventions of 12 August 1949'. Geneva: ICRC.

International Crisis Group. 2010. *War Crimes in Sri Lanka*. ICG Asia Report No. 191, Brussels: ICG.

International Military Tribunal. 1947. *Trial of the Major War Criminals before the International Military Tribunal*. Nuremberg.

International Rescue Committee. 2016. 'Nigeria: Risk of Man-Made Famine Threatens Millions'. IRC press release, 15 September, at: https://www.rescue.org/press-release/nigeria-risk-man-made-famine-threatens-millions

IPC. 2012. 'Integrated Food Security Phase Classification, Technical Manual Version 2.0.: Evidence and Standards for Better Food Security Decisions'. Rome: FAO.

Islam, Shawfiq and Susskind, Lawrence. 2012. *Water Diplomacy: A Negotiated Approach to Managing Complex Water Networks*. London: Routledge.

Jaleta, Moti and Gebremedhin, Berhanu. 2012. 'Price Co-integration Analyses of Food Crop Markets: The Case of Wheat and *Teff* Commodities in Northern Ethiopia'. *African Journal of Agricultural Research* 7(25): 3643–52.

Jeffrey, James. 2016. 'Ethiopia's Drought Response: Success or Anguish?' *African Business*, April 22, at: http://africanbusinessmagazine.com/sectors/infrastructure/ethiopias-drought-response-success-anguish/

Jones, Seth and Libicki, Martin. 2008. *How Terrorists Groups End: Lessons for Countering al Qa'ida*. Washington, DC: RAND Corporation.

Kaplan, Robert. 1994. 'The Coming Anarchy: How Scarcity, Crime, Overpopulation, Tribalism, and Disease are Rapidly Destroying the Social Fabric of Our Planet'. *Atlantic Monthly* (February).

Kaur, Nanki. 2013. 'Ethiopia: Can it Adapt to Climate Change and Build a Green Economy?' London: International Institute for Environment and Development, blog 25 March, http://www.iied.org/ethiopia-can-it-adapt-climate-change-build-green-economy

Kay, Alex. 2006a. 'Germany's Staatssekretäre, Mass Starvation and the Meeting of 2 May 1941'. *Journal of Contemporary History* 41(4): 685–700.

Kay, Alex. 2006b. *Exploitation, Resettlement, Mass Murder: Political and Economic Planning for German Occupation Policy in the Soviet Union, 1940–1941*. New York and Oxford: Berghahn Books.

Kay, Alex. 2012. ' "The Purpose of the Russian Campaign is the Decimation of the Slavic Population by Thirty Million": The Radicalization of German Food Policy in Early 1941', in Alex Kay, Jeff Rutherford, David Stahel (eds), *Nazi Policy on the Eastern Front, 1941*. Rochester: University of Rochester Press.

Kearney, Diana. 2013. 'Food Deprivations as Crimes against Humanity'. *NYU Journal of International Law and Politics* 46: 253–89.

Keen, David. 1994. *The Benefits of Famine: A Political Economy of Famine and Relief in Southwestern Sudan, 1983–1989*, Princeton, NJ: Princeton University Press.

Kévorkian, Raymond. 2011. *The Armenian Genocide: A Complete History*. London: I B Tauris.

Keys, Ancel, Brozek, Josef, Henschel, Austin et al. 1950. *The Biology of Human Starvation*, Vols I–II. Minneapolis, MN: University of Minnesota Press.

Kiernan, Ben. 2003. 'The Demography of Genocide in Southeast Asia: The Death Tolls in Cambodia, 1975–79 and East Timor, 1975–80'. *Critical Asian Studies* 35(4): 585–97.

Kiernan, Ben. 2008. *The Pol Pot Regime: Race, Power, and Genocide in Cambodia Under the Khmer Rouge, 1975–79*, 3rd edn. New Haven, CT: Yale University Press.

Ki-moon, Ban. 2007a. 'A Climate Culprit for Darfur'. *Washington Post*, 15 June, at: http://www.washingtonpost.com/wp-dyn/content/article/2007/06/15/AR2007061501857.html

Ki-moon, Ban. 2007b. 'What I Saw in Darfur'. *Washington Post*, 14 September, http://www.washingtonpost.com/wp-dyn/content/article/2007/09/13/AR2007091301680.html

Ki-moon, Ban. 2016. 'Full Transcript of Secretary-General's Press Encounter following Briefing to the General Assembly on his Priorities for 2016'. United Nations, 14 January, at: https://www.un.org/sg/en/content/sg/press-encounter/2016-01-14/full-transcript-secretary-generals-press-encounter-following

Korn, David A. 1986. *Ethiopia, the United States and the Soviet Union*, Carbondale, IL: Southern Illinois University Press.

Kristof, Nicholas. 2016. 'Are as Many Civilians Dying in South Sudan as in Syria?' *New York Times*, 11 March, at http://kristof.blogs.nytimes.com/2016/03/11/are-as-many-civilians-dying-in-south-sudan-as-in-syria/#more-13682.

Kte'pi, Bill. 2011. 'Chinese Famine (1907)', in K. Bradley Penuel and Matt Statler (eds), *Encyclopedia of Disaster Relief*. Thousand Oaks, CA: SAGE, pp. 70–2.

Lappé, Frances Moor and Collins, Joseph. 2015. *World Hunger: Ten Myths*. New York, Grove Press and Oakland: Food First Books.

Laughlin, Charles D. 1974. 'Deprivation and Reciprocity'. *Man* 9: 380–96.

Launspach, Fleur. 2016. 'UN: Tens of Thousands Killed in South Sudan War'. *Al Jazeera*, 3 March, at: http://www.aljazeera.com/news/2016/03/tens-thousands-killed-south-sudan-war-160303054110110.html.

Lavers, Tom. 2016. Social Protection in an Aspiring "Developmental State: The Political Drivers of Ethiopia's PSNP"'. ESID Working Paper No. 73. Manchester: Effective States and Inclusive Development Research Centre, The University of Manchester: https://ssrn.com/abstract=2893133 or http://dx.doi.org/10.2139/ssrn.2893133

Leitenberg, Milton. 2006. 'Deaths in Wars and Conflicts in the 20th Century'. Cornell University Peace Studies Program, at http://drum.lib.umd.edu/bitstream/handle/1903/7964/deathswarsconflictsjune52006.pdf?sequence=1

Lemkin, Raphael. 1944. *Axis Rule in Occupied Europe*. Washington, DC: Carnegie Endowment for International Peace.

Lemkin, Raphael. 2009. 'Soviet Genocide in Ukraine,' cited in Roman Serbyn, 'Lemkin on the Ukrainian Genocide'. *Journal of International Criminal Justice* 7: 123–30. https://academic.oup.com/jicj/article-abstract/7/1/123/884857/Lemkin-on-Genocide-of-Nations?redirectedFrom=fulltext

Lepenies, Philipp. 2013. 'Of Goats and Dogs: Joseph Townsend and the Idealisation of Markets – A Decisive Episode in the History of Economics'. *Cambridge Journal of Economics* 38: 447–57.

Levene, Mark. 2005. *Genocide in the Age of the Nation State, Vol. 2: The Rise of the West and the Coming of Genocide*. London: I B Tauris.

Levi, Primo. 1996 (1958). *Survival in Auschwitz*, trans. Stuart Woolf. New York: Touchstone.

Li, Lillian M. 2007. *Fighting Famine in North China: State, Market and Environmental Decline, 1690s–1990s*. Stanford: Stanford University Press.

Little, Amanda. 2016. 'The Ethiopian Guide to Famine Prevention'. *Bloomberg Businessweek*, 22 December: https://www.bloomberg.com/news/features/2016-12-22/ethiopian-guide-to-famine-prevention

Lowe, Keith. 2012. *Savage Continent: Europe in the Aftermath of World War II*. London: Picador.

Lowe, Norman. 2002. *Mastering Twentieth-Century Russian History*. London: Palgrave.

Macintyre, Kate. 2002. 'Famine and the Female Mortality Advantage', in Tim Dyson and Cormac Ó Gráda (eds), *Famine Demography: Perspectives from the Past and Present*. Oxford: Oxford University Press, pp. 240–60.

Maddison, Angus. 2003. *The World Economy: Historical Statistics*. Paris: OECD.

The Maddison Project. 2013. At: http://www.ggdc.net/maddison/maddison-project/home.htm.

Magone, Clair, Neuman, Michael and Weissman, Fabrice. 2012. *Humanitarian Negotiations Revealed: The MSF Experience*. London: Hurst.

Maharatna, Arup. 2002. 'Famines and Epidemics: An Indian Historical Perspective', in Tim Dyson and Cormac Ó Gráda (eds), *Famine Demography: Perspectives from the Past and Present*. Oxford: Oxford University Press, pp. 113–41.

Mallory, Walter Hampton. 1926. *China: Land of Famine*, Special Publication No. 6. New York: American Geographical Society.

Malthus, Thomas R. 1798. *An Essay on the Principle of Population, as it Affects the Future Improvement of Society with Remarks on the Speculations of Mr. Godwin, M. Condorcet, and Other Writers*. London: J. Johnson.

Malthus, Thomas R. 1803. *An Essay on the Principle of Population; or, a view of its past and present effects on human happiness, with an inquiry into our prospects respecting the future removal or mitigation of the evils which it occasions. A new edition, very much enlarged*. London: J. Johnson.

Marcus, David. 2003. 'Famine Crimes in International Law'. *The American Journal of International Law* 97(2 : 245–81.

Martin, Terry. 2001. *The Affirmative Action Empire: Nations and Nationalism in the Soviet Union, 1923–1939*. Ithaca: Cornell University Press,

Maxwell, Daniel and Fitzpatrick, Merry. 2012. 'Famine'. Oxford University Press, *Oxford Bibliographies Online*, http://oxfordbibliographiesonline.com/view/document/obo-9780199846733/obo-9780199846733-0083.xml

Maxwell, Daniel and Majid, Nisar. 2016. *Famine in Somalia: Competing Imperatives, Collective Failures, 2011–12.* London: Hurst.

Mayhew, Robert J. 2014. *Malthus.* Cambridge, MA: Harvard University Press.

Maystadt, Jean-François and Ecker, Olivier. 2014. 'Extreme Weather and Civil War: Does Drought Fuel Conflict in Somalia through Livestock Price Shocks?' *American Journal of Agricultural Economics* 96(4): 1157–82.

Maystadt, Jean-François, Calderone, Margherita and You, Liangzhi. 2014. 'Local Warming and Violent Conflict in North and South Sudan'. *Journal of Economic Geography* 15(3): 649–71.

Mazower, Mark. 1993. *Inside Hitler's Greece: The Experience of Occupation, 1941–44.* New Haven: Yale University Press.

Mazurana, Dyan, Marshak, Anastasia, Opio, Jimmy Hilton et al. 2014. 'The Impact of Serious Crimes during the War on Households Today in Northern Uganda'. Briefing Paper 5, London: Overseas Development Institute, Secure Livelihoods Research Consortium.

McNeil, Taylor. 2016. 'Staving off Famine in Ethiopia', *Phys Org*, June 10. http://phys.org/news/2016-06-staving-famine-ethiopia.html.

McGuire, Bill. 2002. *A Guide to the End of the World: Everything You Never Wanted to Know.* Oxford: Oxford University Press.

Medley, Michael. 2010. 'Humanitarian Parsimony in Sudan: The Bahr al Ghazal Famine of 1998'. Unpublished PhD Thesis. University of Bristol.

Melander, Erik, Öberg, Magnus and Hall, Jonathon. 2009. 'Are "New Wars" More Atrocious? Battle Severity, Civilians Killed and Forced Migration Before and After the End of the Cold War'. *European Journal of International Relations* 15(3): 505–36.

Melvin, Don. 2016. 'Amnesty: Famine in Syrian City of Madaya "the Tip of an Iceberg"'. CNN, 9 January, at: http://www.cnn.com/2016/01/09/middleeast/syria-madaya-starvation/.

Milanovic, Branko. 2016. *Global Inequality: A New Approach for the Age of Globalization.* Cambridge, MA: Harvard University Press.

Moreland, Scott and Smith, Ellen. 2012. 'Modelling Climate Change, Food Security and Population: Pilot Testing the Model in Ethiopia'. New Orleans: Tulane University, Futures Group.

Morgenthau, Henry. 1918. *Ambassador Morgenthau's Story.* New York: Doubleday.

Moses, Dirk A. (ed.). 2008. *Empire, Colony, Genocide: Conquest, Occupation, and Subaltern Resistance in World History.* New York: Berghahn Books.

Munro, Tate and Wild, Lorenz. 2016. 'As Drought Hits Ethiopia Again, Food Aid Risks Breaking Resilience'. *The Guardian*, March 10, at: https://www.theguardian.com/global-development-professionals-network/2016/mar/10/drought-ethiopia-food-aid-resilience.

Muscolino, Micah. 2015. *The Ecology of War in China: Henan Province, the Yellow River, and Beyond, 1938–1950.* Cambridge: Cambridge University Press.

National Intelligence Council. 2000. 'The Global Infectious Disease Threat and its Implications for the United States'. Washington, DC, NIC, NIE. 99–17D, January.

National Intelligence Council. 2002. 'The Next Wave of HIV/AIDS: Nigeria, Ethiopia, Russia, India and China'. Washington, DC: ICA. 2002–04D, September.

National Intelligence Council. 2008. 'Strategic Implications of Gobal Health'. Washington, DC, ICA, 2008-10D, December.

Natsios, Andrew. 2001. *The Great North Korean Famine: Famine, Politics, and Foreign Policy*. Washington, DC: US Institute of Peace.

Neumayer, Eric and Plümper, Thomas. 2007. 'The Gendered Nature of Natural Disasters: The Impact of Catastrophic Events on the Gender Gap in Life Expectancy, 1981–2002'. *Annals of the Association of American Geographers* 97(3): 551–66.

Neumayer, Eric and Plümper, Thomas. 2009. 'Famine Mortality, Rational Political Inactivity, and Food Aid'. *World Development* 37(1): 50–61.

Nixon, Rob. 2011. *Slow Violence and the Environmentalism of the Poor*. Cambridge, MA: Harvard University Press.

Noland, Marcus, Robinson, Sherman and Tang, Tao. 1999. 'Famine in North Korea: Causes and Cures'. *Peterson Institute for International Economics Working Paper No. 2*, at: https://piie.com/publications/wp/99-2.pdf.

Noman, Akbar, Botchwey, Kwesi, Stein, Howard and Stiglitz, Joseph E. (eds). 2012. *Good Growth and Governance in Africa: Rethinking Development Strategies*. Oxford: Oxford University Press.

O'Brien, Stephen. 2017. 'Under-Secretary-General for Humanitarian Affairs and Emergency Relief Coordinator, Statement to the Security Council on Missions to Yemen, South Sudan, Somalia and Kenya and an Update on the Oslo Conference on Nigeria and the Lake Chad Region,' United Nations Security Council, 10 March 2017, https://docs.unocha.org/sites/dms/Documents/ERC_USG_Stephen_OBrien_Statement_to_the_SecCo_on_Missions_to_Yemen_South_Sudan_Somalia_and_Kenya_and_update_on_Oslo.pdf

OCHA. 2015a. 'Humanitarian Needs Overview 2016: Syrian Arab Republic'. New York, October, at: http://reliefweb.int/report/syrian-arab-republic/2016-humanitarian-needs-overview-syrian-arab-republic.

OCHA. 2015b. 'Yemen: Humanitarian Needs Overview'. November, at: http://reliefweb.int/sites/reliefweb.int/files/resources/2016_HNO_English_%20FINAL.pdf

OCHA. 2016a. 'Crisis Impacts on Households in Unity State, South Sudan, 2014–2015: Initial Results of a Survey'. Juba: Office of the Deputy Humanitarian Coordinator for South Sudan, January.

OCHA. 2016b. 'Lake Chad Basin: Crisis Update No. 7', 6 September, at: http://reliefweb.int/report/nigeria/lake-chad-basin-crisis-update-7.

OCHA. 2016c. 'Yemen: Crisis overview 2016', October, at: http://www.unocha.org/yemen/crisis-overview

OECD. 2012. *Think Global, Act Global: Confronting Global Factors that Influence Conflict and Fragility*. September. Paris, OECD International Network on Conflict and Fragility.

OECD. 2016. Query Wizard for International Development Statistics (QWIDS). At: http://stats.oecd.org/qwids.

Ó Gráda, Cormac. 1997. 'Markets and Famines: A Simple Test with Indian Data'. *Economics Letters* 57: 241–4.

Ó Gráda, Cormac. 2005. 'Markets and Famines in Pre-industrial Europe'. *Journal of Interdisciplinary History* 26(2): 143–66.

Ó Gráda, Cormac. 2008. 'The Ripple that Drowns? Twentieth-Century Famines in China and India as Economic History'. *The Economic History Review* 61: 5–37.

Ó Gráda, Cormac. 2009. *Famine: A Short History*. Princeton, NJ: Princeton University Press.

Ó Gráda, Cormac. 2015. *Eating People is Wrong and Other Essays on Famine, Its Past, Present and Future*. Princeton: Princeton University Press.

Okazaki, Shoko, 1986. 'The Great Persian Famine of 1870–71'. *Bulletin of the School of Oriental and African Studies* 49(1): 183–92.

Orozco, Manuel and Yansura, Julia. 2012. *Keeping the Lifeline Open: Remittances and Markets in Somalia*. Boston, MA: Oxfam America.

Osmani, S. R. 1991. 'The Food Problems of Bangladesh', in Jean Drèze and Amartya Sen (eds), *The Political Economy of Hunger, Vol. 3: Endemic Hunger*. Oxford: Clarendon Press.

Paice, Edward. 2007. *Tip and Run: The Untold Tragedy of the Great War in Africa*. London: Phoenix.

Pankhurst, Richard. 1968. *Economic History of Ethiopia*. Addis Ababa: Haile Selassie I University Press.

Pankhurst, Richard. 1985. *The History of Famine and Epidemics in Ethiopia Prior to the Twentieth Century*. Addis Ababa: Relief and Rehabilitation Commission.

Patel, Raj. 2013. 'The Long Green Revolution'. *The Journal of Peasant Studies* 40(1): 1–63.

Patenaude, Bertrand M. 2002. *The Big Show in Bololand: The American Relief Expedition to Soviet Russia in the Famine of 1921*. Stanford: Stanford University Press.

Peeters, Loek, and Maxwell, Daniel. 2011. 'Characteristics and Strategies Favouring Sustained Food Access during Guinea's Food-Price Crisis'. *Development in Practice* 21 (4–5): 613–28.

Peng, Xizhe. 1987. 'Demographic Consequences of the Great Leap Forward in China's Provinces'. *Population and Development Review* 13(4): 639–70.

Perkins, John H. 1997. *Geopolitics and the Green Revolution: Wheat, Genes and the Cold War*. Oxford: Oxford University Press.

PHPCR (Program on Humanitarian Policy and Conflict Research). 2012. 'Countering Terror in Humanitarian Crises: Challenges of Delivering Aid to Somalia'. Harvard University, PHPCR, at: http://hhi.harvard.edu/publications/countering-terror-humanitarian-crises-challenges-delivering-aid-somalia.

Piketty, Thomas. 2014. *Capital in the Twenty-First Century*. Cambridge, MA: Belknap.

Plümper, Thomas and Neumayer, Eric. 2006. 'The Unequal Burden of War: The Effect of Armed Conflict on the Gender Gap in Life Expectancy'. *International Organization* 60: 723–54.

Post, John. 1977. *The Last Great Subsistence Crisis in the Western World*. Baltimore, MD: Johns Hopkins University Press.

Powell, Jonathan. 2014. *Talking to Terrorists: How to End Armed Conflicts*. London: The Bodley Head.

Powell, Colin. 2001. 'September 11, 2001: Attack on America: Secretary Colin L. Powell Remarks to the National Foreign Policy Conference for Leaders of Nongovernmental Organizations'. 26 October, at: http://avalon.law.yale.edu/sept11/powell_brief31.asp.

Power, Samantha. 2002. *'A Problem from Hell': America and the Age of Genocide*. New York: Basic Books.

PS21 (Project of the Study of the 21st Century) 2015. 'Death Toll in 2014's Bloodiest Wars Sharply Up on Previous Year', at: https://projects21.org/2015/03/17/death-toll-in-2014s-bloodiest-wars-sharply-up-on-previous-year/

Rangasami, Amrita. 1985. 'Failure of Exchange Entitlements Theory: A Response'. *Economic and Political Weekly* 20(42): 1797–1801.

Ravallion, Martin. 1987. *Markets and Famines*. Oxford: Clarendon Press.

Reza, Avid, Tomczyk, Basia, Aguayo, Victor M. et al. 2008. 'Retrospective Determination of Whether Famine Existed in Niger, 2005: Two Stage Cluster Survey'. *British Medical Journal* 337(7675): 915–18.

Richards, Paul. 1983. 'Ecological Change and the Politics of Land Use'. *African Studies Review* 26: 1–72.

Richards, Paul. 1996. *Fighting for the Rainforest: War, Youth and Resources in Sierra Leone*. London: James Currey.

Richards, Paul, 2016. *Ebola: How a People's Science Helped End an Epidemic*. London: Zed Books.

Rieff, David. 2002. *A Bed for the Night: Humanitarianism in Crisis*. New York: Simon and Schuster.

Riordan, K. J. 2010. 'Shelling, Sniping and Starvation: the Law of Armed Conflict and the Lessons of the Siege of Sarajevo'. *Victoria University Wellington Law Review* 41: 149–78.

Rivers, John. 1982. 'Women and Children Last: An Essay on Sex Discrimination in Disasters'. *Disasters* 6(4): 256–67.

Rivers, John, Holt, Julius, Seaman, John and Bowden, Mark. 1976. 'Lessons for Epidemiology from the Ethiopian Famines'. *Annales Société Belge de Médecine Tropicale* 56: 345–57.

Robbins, Richard Gardiner. 1970. 'The Russian Famine of 1891–1892 and the Relief Policy of the Imperial Government'. PhD dissertation, Columbia University.

Roberts, Les. 2000. *Mortality in Eastern DRC: Results from Five Mortality Surveys*. New York: International Rescue Committee.

Roberts, Les, Hale, Charles, Belyakdoumi, Fethi et al. 2001. *Mortality in Eastern Democratic Republic of Congo: Results from Eleven Mortality Surveys*. New York: International Rescue Committee.

Roberts, Les, Ngoy, Pascal, Mone, Colleen et al. 2003. *Mortality in the Democratic Republic of Congo: Results from a Nationwide Survey*. New York: International Rescue Committee.

Rosset, Peter. 2002. 'US Opposes Right to Food at World Summit'. *World Editorial and International Law*, 30 June, http://www.iatp.org/news/us-opposes-right-to-food-at-world-summit

Rubin, Olivier. 2011. *Democracy and Famine*. London: Routledge.

Salama, Peter, Assefa, Fitsum, Talley, Leisel et al. 2001. 'Malnutrition, Measles, Mortality, and the Humanitarian Response during a Famine in Ethiopia'. *Journal of the American Medical Association* 58: 563–71.

Salih, M. A. Mohamed. 1999. *Environmental Politics and Liberation in Contemporary Africa*. Amsterdam: Kluwer.

Schabas, William. 2011. *An Introduction to the International Criminal Court*, 4th edn. New York: Cambridge University Press.

Schilcher, Linda. 1992. 'The Famine of 1915–1918 in Greater Syria', in J. P. Spagnolo (ed.), *Problems of the Modern Middle East in Historical Perspective: Essays in Honour of Albert Hourani*. Reading: Ithaca Press.

Schomerus, Mareike. 2015, ' "Make Him Famous": The Single Conflict Narrative of Kony and *Kony2012*', in Alex de Waal (ed.), *Advocacy in Conflict: Critical Perspectives on Transnational Activism*. London: Zed.

Schove, D. J. 1977. "African Droughts and the Spectrum of Time," in D. Dalby, R. J. Harrison-Church and F. Bezzaz (eds), *Drought in Africa 2*. African Environment Special Report No. 6, London: International African Institute.

Scroggins, Deborah. 2002. *Emma's War: Love, Betrayal and Death in the Sudan*. New York: Vintage.

Seaman, John and Holt, Julius. 1980. 'Markets and Famines in the Third World'. *Disasters* 4(3): 283–97.

Sen, Amartya. 1981. *Poverty and Famines: An Essay on Entitlement and Deprivation*. Oxford: Clarendon Press.

Sen, Amartya. 1990. 'Individual Freedom as a Social Commitment', *New York Review of Books*, 14 June, at: http://www.nybooks.com/articles/1990/06/14/individual-freedom-as-a-social-commitment/

Sen, Amartya. 2000. *Development as Freedom*. Oxford: Clarendon Press.

Sengupta, Somini. 2015. 'UN Security Council Bans Sales of Arms to Houthi Fighters in Yemen'. *New York Times*, 14 April, at: http://www.nytimes.com/2015/04/15/world/middleeast/yemen-houthis-saudi-airstrikes-arms-embargo.html.

Shah, Anup. 2008. 'World Food Crisis 2008'. *Global Issues*, 10 August, http://www.globalissues.org/article/758/global-food-crisis-2008

Shaikh, Kashem, Wojtynaik, Bogdan, Mostafa, G. and Khan, M. U. 1990. 'Pattern of Diarrhoeal Deaths during 1966–1987 in a Demographic Surveillance Area in Rural Bangladesh'. *Journal of Diarrhoeal Diseases Research* 8(4): 147–54.

Short, Damien. 2016. *Redefining Genocide: Settler Colonialism, Social Death and Ecocide*. London: Zed Books.

Slim, Hugo. 2007. *Killing Civilians: Method, Madness and Morality in War*. London: Hurst.

Smith, Kenneth. 1951. *The Malthusian Controversy*. London: Routledge.

Smith, Lynn. 1946. *Brazil: People and Institutions*. Baton Rouge, LA: Louisiana University Press.

Snyder, Timothy. 2010. 'The Reich's Forgotten Atrocity'. *The Guardian*, 21 October, https://www.theguardian.com/commentisfree/cifamerica/2010/oct/21/secondworldwar-russia

Snyder, Timothy. 2012. *Bloodlands: Europe between Hitler and Stalin*. New York: Basic Books.

Snyder, Timothy. 2015a. *Black Earth: The Holocaust as History and Warning*. New York: Basic Books.

Snyder, Timothy. 2015b. 'The Next Genocide'. *New York Times*, 13 September, at: www.nytimes.com/2015/09/13/opinion/sunday/the-next-genocide.html

Sorokin, Pitrim. 1975 (1922). *Hunger as a Factor in Human Affairs*. Gainesville, FL: University of Florida Press.

Spoorenberg, Thomas and Schwekendiek, Daniel. 2012. 'Demographic Changes in North Korea: 1993–2008'. *Population and Development Review* 38(1): 133–58.

Straus, Scott. 2012. 'Wars Do End! Changing Patterns of Political Violence in Sub-Saharan Africa'. *African Affairs* 11(443): 179–201.

Straus, Scott. 2015. *Making and Unmaking Nations: War, Leadership, and Genocide in Modern Africa*. Ithaca: Cornell University Press.

Sumner, Daniel. 2009. 'Recent Commodity Price Movements in Historical Perspective'. *American Journal of Agricultural Economics* 91(5): 1250–6.

Suny, Ronald Grigor. 2015. *'They Can Live in the Desert but Nowhere Else': A History of the Armenian Genocide*. Princeton: Princeton University Press.

Swan, Samuel, Hadley, Sierd and Cichon, Bernardette. 2010. 'Crisis behind Closed Doors: Global Food Crisis and Local Hunger'. *Journal of Agrarian Change* 10(1): 107–18.

Sylvester, Christine. 2013. *War as Experience: Contributions from International Relations and Feminist Analysis*. London: Routledge.

Syrian Centre for Policy Research. 2016a. *Syria: Confronting Fragmentation: Impact of Syrian Crisis Report*. February. Beirut: Syrian Centre for Policy Research.

Syrian Centre for Policy Research. 2016b. *Forced Dispersion: A Demographic Report on Human Status in Syria*. December. Beirut: Syrian Centre for Policy Research.

Tamru, Seneshaw. 2013. 'Spatial Integration of Cereal Markets in Ethiopia'. *Ethiopia Strategy Support Program Working Paper 56*. Addis Ababa, Ethiopian Development Research Institute and Washington DC, International Food Policy Research Institute.

Tawney, Richard H. 1964. *Land and Labour in China*. New York: Octagon Books.

Themner, Lotte and Wallensteen, Peter. 2014. 'Armed Conflicts, 1946–2013'. *Journal of Peace Research* 51(4): 541–54.

Thornton, Russell. 2005. 'Native American Demographic and Tribal Survival into the Twenty-first Century'. *American Studies* 46(3): 23–38.

Tierney, Jessica, Ummenhofer, Caroline and deMenocal, Peter. 2015. 'Past and Future Rainfall in the Horn of Africa'. *Science Advances* 1(9), at http://advances.sciencemag.org/content/1/9/e1500682.full.

Toole, Michael J. and Waldman, Ronald J. 1988. 'An Analysis of Mortality Trends among Refugee Populations in Somalia, Sudan and Thailand'. *Bulletin of the World Health Organization* 66(2): 237–47.

Tooze, Adam. 2014. 'The Sense of a Vacuum: A Response.' *Historical Materialism* 22(3–4): 351–70.

Townsend, Joseph. 1971 (1786). *A Dissertation on the Poor Laws, by a Well-Wisher to Mankind*. Berkeley: University of California Press.

Trenberth, Kevin, Dai, Aiguo, van der Schrier, Gerard et al. 2014. 'Global Warming and Changes in Drought'. *Global Climate Change* 4: 17–22.

Turnbull, Clive. 1965 (1948). *Black War: The Extermination of the Tasmanian Aborigines*. Melbourne: Cheshire-Lansdowne.

United Nations. 1948. 'Convention on the Prevention and Punishment of the Crime of Genocide'. Adopted by the General Assembly of the United Nations, 9 December.

United Nations. 2002a. 'United Nations Diplomatic Conference of Plenipotentiaries on the Establishment of an International Criminal Court, Rome, 15 June–17 July 1998, Official Records: Volume II: Summary Records of the Plenary Meetings and of the Meetings of the Committee of the Whole'. New York: United Nations.

United Nations. 2002b. 'United Nations Diplomatic Conference of Plenipotentiaries on the Establishment of an International Criminal Court, Rome, 15 June–17 July 1998, Official Records: Volume III: Reports and Other Documents'. New York: United Nations.

United Nations. 2010. 'Resolution RC/Res.6 of the Review Conference of the Rome Statute'. New York: United Nations.

United Nations Department of Economic and Social Affairs. 2011. *The Global Social Crisis: Report on the World Social Situation 2011*. New York: United Nations, ST/ESA/334.

United Nations OCHA/IRIN. 2004. *'When the Sun Sets, We Start to Worry …' An Account of Life in Northern Uganda*. New York: United Nations (5 January).

United Nations Security Council. 2004. 'Report of the Representative of the Secretary-General on Internally Displaced Persons: Mission to Uganda' (3 March). UN Doc E/CN.4/2004/77/Add.1, 12.

United Nations War Crimes Commission. 1949. *Law Reports of Trials of War Criminals. Volume XII: The German High Command Trial*. London: HMSO.

United States Holocaust Memorial Museum. nd. 'Warsaw'. Holocaust Encyclopedia, at https://www.ushmm.org/wlc/en/article.php?ModuleId=10005069.

Urquhart, Conal. 2006. 'Gaza on Brink of Implosion as Aid Cut-Off Starts to Bite'. *The Guardian*, 15 April, at: http://www.theguardian.com/world/2006/apr/16/israel.

Uvin, Peter. 2001. 'Reading the Rwandan Genocide'. *International Studies Review* 3(3): 75–99.

Valentino, Benjamin. 2014. 'Why We Kill: The Political Science of Political Violence against Civilians'. *Annual Review of Political Science* 17: 89–103.

Van der Eng, Pierre. 2008. *Food Supply in Java during War and Decolonisation 1940–1950*. Munich Personal RePEc Archive Paper No. 8852, at: http://mpra.ub.uni-muenchen.de/8852/.

Van Klinken, Gerry. 2012. *Death by Deprivation in East Timor 1975–1980*. World Peace Foundation, at: https://sites.tufts.edu/reinventingpeace/2012/04/17/death-by-deprivation-in-east-timor-1975-1980/.

Vaughan, Megan, 1987. *The Story of an African Famine: Gender and Famine in Twentieth-Century Malawi*. Cambridge: Cambridge University Press.

Vincent, C. Paul. 1985. *The Politics of Hunger: The Allied Blockade of Germany, 1915–1919*. Athens, OH: Ohio University Press.

Walker, Brian, Barrett, Scott, Polasky, Stephen et al. 2009. 'Looming Global Scale Failures and Missing Institutions'. *Science* 325(5946): 1345–6.

Walsh, Bryan. 2014. 'Climate Change Could Cause the Next Great Famine'. *Time*, 17 March, at: http://time.com/27201/climate-change-could-cause-the-next-great-famine/.

Watenpaugh, Keith David. 2015. *Bread from Stones: The Middle East and the Making of Modern Humanitarianism*. Berkeley, CA: University of California Press.

Watkins, Susan C. and Menken, Jane. 1985. 'Famines in Historical Perspective'. *Population and Development Review* 11: 647–76.

Watts, Michael. 1983. *Silent Violence: Food, Famine and Peasantry in Northern Nigeria*. Berkeley, CA: University of California Press.

WFP. 2016a. 'Breakthrough as WFP Reaches Taiz Enclave Using Voucher Assistance'. 31 July, at: https://www.wfp.org/news/news-release/breakthrough-wfp-reaches-taiz-enclave-using-voucher-assistance.

WFP. 2016b. 'WFP El Nino Response', at http://documents.wfp.org/stellent/groups/public/documents/newsroom/wfp281333.pdf?_ga=1.264027212.1314275398.1478014535.

WFP. 2016c. 'WFP Ethiopia Country Brief', September, at http://documents.wfp.org/stellent/groups/public/documents/ep/wfp273887.pdf?_ga=1.197647471.1314275398.1478014535.

Whiteside, Alan and Waal, Alex de. 2003. '"New Variant Famine": AIDS and Food Crisis in Southern Africa'. *The Lancet* 362: 1234–7.

Wiggins, Steve and Keats, Sharada. 2013. 'Looking Back and Peering Forward: Food Prices and the Food Price Spike of 2007/08'. London: Overseas Development Institute, 28 March.

Wiggins, Steve, Keats, Sharada and Compton, Julia. 2010. 'What Caused the Food Price Spike of 2007/08? Lessons for World Cereals Markets'. London: Overseas Development Institute, Food Prices Project Report.

Wolde Mariam, Mesfin. 1986. *Rural Vulnerability to Famine in Ethiopia, 1958–77*. London: IT Press.

Woodham-Smith, Cecil. 1962. *The Great Hunger: Ireland 1845–1849*. London: Hamish Hamilton.

Woolford, Andrew. 2009. 'Ontological Destruction: Genocide and Aboriginal Peoples in Canada'. *Genocide Studies and Prevention* 4(1): 81–97.

World Bank. 2014. *WDR 2014: Risk and Opportunity: Managing Risk for Development*. Washington, DC: World Development Report.

World Bank. 2016. 'Syria's Economic Outlook: Fall 2016'. Washington, DC: World Bank, at: http://www.worldbank.org/en/country/syria/publication/economic-outlook-fall-2016.

World Health Organization. 2005. 'Health and Mortality Survey among Internally Displaced Persons in Gulu, Kitgum and Pader Districts, Northern Uganda'. Kampala: WHO and Republic of Uganda, Ministry of Health, July.

World Peace Foundation. 2016. 'Mass Famine', at: http://fletcher.tufts.edu/World-Peace-Foundation/Program/Research/Mass-Atrocities-Research-Program/Mass-Famine.

World Peace Foundation. Forthcoming. 'Soviet Union: German Prisoners of War Following World War II'. Project on Mass Atrocity Endings.

Wright, Tim. 2000. 'Distant Thunder: The Regional Economies of Southwest China and the Impact of the Great Depression'. *Modern Asian Studies* 34(3): 697–738.

Xiaoyang, Tang. 2014. 'The Impact of Asian Investment on Africa's Textile Industries'. Tsinghua: Carnegie-Tsinghua Center for Global Policy, August.

Yemen Times. 2015. 'The Province of Saada Labeled as a "Military Target"', 9 May, at: http://www.yementimes.com/en/1875/news/5082/The-Province-of-Saada-labeled-as-a-%E2%80%9C-Military-Target%E2%80%9D.htm.

You, Gene Jiing-Yun and Ringler, Claudia. 2010. 'Hydro-Economic Modeling of Climate Change Impacts in Ethiopia'. Washington, DC: IFPRI Discussion Paper, at: https://www.ifpri.org/publication/hydro-economic-modeling-climate-change-impacts-ethiopia.

Young, Arthur. 1792. *Travels during the Years 1787, 1788 and 1789: Undertaken More Particularly with a View of Ascertaining the Cultivation, Wealth, Resources and National Prosperity of the Kingdom of France*, Vol. 1, 2nd edn. London: Royal Exchange.

Young, Arthur. 1794. *The Example of France, A Warning to Britain*, 4th edn. London: Royal Exchange.

Young, Helen and Jaspars, Susanne. 2009. 'Review of Nutrition and Mortality Indicators for the Integrated Food Security Phase Classification (IPC): Reference Levels and Decision-making'. New York: United Nations Standing Committee on Nutrition, Task Force on Assessment, Monitoring and Evaluation.

Yourish, Karen, Lai, K. K. Rebecca and Watkins, Derek. 2015. 'Death in Syria'. *New York Times*, 14 September, at: http://www.nytimes.com/interactive/2015/09/14/world/middleeast/syria-war-deaths.html.

Index